Practice *Planners*

Arthur E. Jongsma, Jr., Series Editor

Helping therapists help their clients...

Over 250,000 Practice*Planners*™ sold . . .

Practice*Planners*™   Order Form

Treatment Planners cover all the necessary elements for developing formal treatment plans, including detailed problem definitions, long-term goals, short-term objectives, therapeutic interventions, and DSM-IV diagnoses.

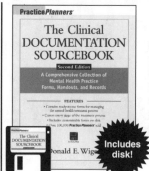

Documentation Sourcebooks provide all the forms and records you need to meet the documentation requirements of the managed care era. All of the documents are also provided on disk so they can be easily customized.

The Complete Adult Psychotherapy Treatment Planner, Second Edition
0-471-31924-4 / $39.95

The Child Psychotherapy Treatment Planner, Second Edition
0-471-34764-7 / $39.95

The Adolescent Psychotherapy Treatment Planner, Second Edition
0-471-34766-3 / $39.95

The Chemical Dependence Treatment Planner
0-471-23795-7 / $39.95

The Continuum of Care Treatment Planner
0-471-19568-5 / $39.95

The Couples Psychotherapy Treatment Planner
0-471-24711-1 / $39.95

The Employee Assistance (EAP) Treatment Planner
0-471-24709-X / $39.95

The Pastoral Counseling Treatment Planner
0-471-25416-9 / $39.95

The Older Adult Psychotherapy Treatment Planner
0-471-29574-4 / $39.95

The Behavioral Medicine Treatment Planner
0-471-31923-6 / $39.95

The Gay and Lesbian Psychotherapy Treatment Planner
0-471-35080-X / $39.95

The Clinical Documentation Sourcebook, Second Edition
0-471-32692-5 / $49.95

The Psychotherapy Documentation Primer
0-471-28990-6 / $45.00

The Couple and Family Clinical Documentation Sourcebook
0-471-25234-4 / $49.95

The Clinical Child Documentation Sourcebook
0-471-29111-0 / $49.95

The Chemical Dependence Treatment Documentation Sourcebook
0-471-31285-1 / $49.95

The Forensic Documentation Sourcebook
0-471-25459-2 / $85.00

The Continuum of Care Clinical Documentation Sourcebook
0-471-34581-4 / $75.00

NEW AND FORTHCOMING

The Group Therapy Treatment Planner
0-471-37449-0 / $39.95

The Family Therapy Treatment Planner
0-471-34768-X / $39.95

The Severe and Persistent Mental Illness Treatment Planner
0-471-35945-9 / $39.95

The Mental Retardation and Developmental Disability Treatment Planner
0-471-38253-1 / $39.95

The Social Work and Human Services Treatment Planner
0-471-37741-4 / $39.95 (12/00)

The Neuropsychological Treatment Planner
0-471-35178-4 / $39.95 (3/01)

Name_____

Affiliation_____

Address_____

City/State/Zip_____

Phone/Fax_____

E-mail_____

www.wiley.com/practiceplanners

To order, call 1-800-753-0655
(Please refer to promo #1-4019 when ordering.)
Or send this page with payment* to:
John Wiley & Sons, Inc., Attn: J. Knott
605 Third Avenue, New York, NY 10158-0012

❏ Check enclosed   ❏ Visa   ❏ MasterCard   ❏ American Express

Card #_____

Expiration Date_____

Signature_____
*Please add your local sales tax to all orders.

Practice Management Tools for Busy Mental Health Professionals

Homework Planners feature dozens of behaviorally based, ready-to-use assignments that are designed for use between sessions, as well as a disk (Microsoft Word) containing all of the assignments—allowing you to customize them to suit your unique client needs.

Brief Therapy Homework Planner
0-471-24611-5 / $49.95

Brief Couples Therapy Homework Planner
0-471-29511-6 / $49.95

Brief Child Therapy Homework Planner
0-471-32366-7 / $49.95

Brief Adolescent Therapy Homework Planner
0-471-34465-6 / $49.95

Chemical Dependence Treatment Homework Planner
0-471-32452-3 / $49.95

Brief Employee Assistance Homework Planner
0-471-38088-1 / $49.95

NEW IN THE PRACTICE*PLANNERS*™ SERIES

Progress Notes Planners contain complete prewritten progress notes for each presenting problem in the companion *Treatment Planners.*

The Adult Psychotherapy Progress Notes Planner
0-471-34763-9 / $39.95 (3/01)

The Adolescent Psychotherapy Progress Notes Planner
0-471-38104-7 / $39.95 (10/00)

The Child Psychotherapy Progress Notes Planner
0-471-38102-0 / $39.95 (1/01)

TheraScribe®

The Treatment Planning and Patient Record Management System

TheraScribe®—the latest version of our popular treatment planning, patient record-keeping software. Facilitates intake/assessment reporting, progress monitoring, and outcomes analysis. Supports group treatment and multiprovider treatment teams. Compatible with our full array of **PracticePlanners**™ libraries, including our *Treatment Planner* software versions.

- This bestselling, easy-to-use Windows®-based software allows you to generate fully customized psychotherapy treatment plans that meet the requirements of all major accrediting agencies and most third-party payers.

- In just minutes, this user-friendly program's on-screen help enables you to create customized treatment plans.

- Praised in the *National Psychologist* and *Medical Software Reviews,* this innovative software simplifies and streamlines record-keeping.

- Available for a single user, or in a network version, this comprehensive software package suits the needs of all practices—both large and small.

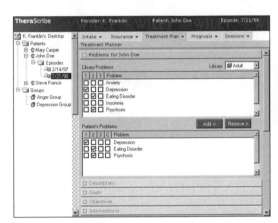

Treatment Planner Upgrade to Thera*Scribe*®

The behavioral definitions, goals, objectives, and interventions from this *Treatment Planner* can be imported into Thera*Scribe*®. For purchase and pricing information, please send in the coupon below or call 1-800-753-0655 or e-mail us at planners@wiley.com.

For more information about **TheraScribe**® or the Upgrade to this *Treatment Planner,* fill in this coupon and mail it to: R. Crucitt, John Wiley & Sons, Inc., 7222 Commerce Center Dr., Ste. 240, Colorado Springs, CO 80919 or e-mail us at planners@wiley.com.

- ❏   Please send me information on **TheraScribe**®
- ❏   Please send me information on the *Treatment Planner* Upgrade to **TheraScribe**®
       Name of *Treatment Planner*_____
- ❏   Please send me information on the network version of **TheraScribe**®

Name_____

Affiliation_____

Address_____

City/State/Zip_____

Phone_____E-mail_____

For a free demo, visit us on the web at: www.wiley.com/therascribe

WILEY

The
Child Psychotherapy
Treatment Planner

The
Child Psychotherapy
Treatment Planner
Second Edition

Arthur E. Jongsma, Jr.

L. Mark Peterson

William P. McInnis

JOHN WILEY & SONS, INC.

New York • Chichester • Weinheim • Brisbane • Singapore • Toronto

ISBN 0-471-34764-7 (book only)
ISBN 0-471-34765-5 (book with disk)

Printed in the United States of America.

10 9 8 7 6 5 4 3 2

CONTENTS

PREFACE

The Child Psychotherapy Treatment Planner is a more focused second edition of *The Child and Adolescent Psychotherapy Treatment Planner* published in 1996 as the second book in Wiley's Practice Planner series. The original book has been extremely well received by the professional community, and now we have limited the focus exclusively to the treatment of children and expanded the list of presenting problems with topics especially relevant to the younger patient. Also, all treatment objectives and therapeutic interventions have been tailored exclusively to children rather than including those for adolescents.

The content chapter taken from the original book has been revised (in terms of organization) and expanded, with the addition of new objectives and interventions especially suited for child treatment. Eight new topics have been added for problems related to Adoption, Anger Management, Attachment Disorder, Blended Family, Disruptive/Attention Seeking, Divorce Reaction, Medical Condition, and Posttraumatic Stress Disorder. Although there is some overlap between this book and the new *Adolescent Psychotherapy Treatment Planner,* nine topics of the child book are completely unique to this work, and all overlapping topics have been revised with a child in mind as the patient.

Since the original *Child and Adolescent Psychotherapy Treatment Planner* was published, we have developed a number of specialized practice planners. The specialized planners are available in electronic version on floppy disk, which allows the information to be imported into *TheraScribe 3.0: The Computerized Assistant to Psychotherapy Treatment Planning* or *TheraScribe 3.5: The Computerized Assistant to Psychotherapy Treatment Planning.* The Practice Planner series also includes several Psychotherapy Homework *Planners* that can be coordinated with the Treatment *Planners* or used independently. Several Documentation *Sourcebooks,* containing useful examples of clinical record-keeping forms and handouts, round out the Practice Planner series. Future plans include the writing of Progress Notes *Planners* coordinated with each of the Treatment *Planners.*

A special effort was taken to coordinate therapeutic interventions in the *Child Psychotherapy Treatment Planner* with homework assignments contained in the *Brief Child Therapy Homework Planner* (Jongsma, Peterson, and McInnis). You will find frequent cross-references to the *Homework* book sprinkled throughout the interventions in this *Planner.*

We would like to recognize those who provided helpful suggestions to use in the development of material in this book. Patricia Edwards, M.A., C.C.C., and Jennifer Phillips, M.Ed., C.C.C.-S.L.P., consulted on speech and language disorders. David Berghuis, M.A., a clinician who works with developmentally disabled clients, offered suggestions regarding objectives and interventions for mentally retarded clients. We are grateful to each of these professionals for their candid and crucial advice.

We would be remiss not to express our indebtedness to Jennifer Byrne, our very capable assistant, who brought order from the chaos of our notes and revisions on the way to completing the final manuscript. Thanks for your patience and dedication, Jen. This project greatly benefited from your thorough organization of endless details and multiple piles of papers. We also continue to be grateful for the editorial leadership and encouragement of Kelly Franklin, the behind-the-scenes genius of the Practice Planner series at John Wiley. And finally, we recognize our wives, Judy, Cherry, and Lynn, as well as the other members of our families, for their patience and support throughout this project.

The
Child Psychotherapy
Treatment Planner

INTRODUCTION

Since the early 1960s, formalized treatment planning has gradually become a vital aspect of the entire health care delivery system, whether it is treatment related to physical health, mental health, child welfare, or substance abuse. What started in the medical sector in the 1960s spread into the mental health sector in the 1970s, as clinics, psychiatric hospitals, and agencies began to seek accreditation from bodies such as the Joint Commission on Accreditation of Healthcare Organizations (JCAHO) to qualify for third-party reimbursements. For most treatment providers to achieve accreditation, they had to begin developing and strengthening their documentation skills in the area of treatment planning. Previously, most mental health and substance abuse treatment providers had, at best, a bare-bones plan that looked similar for most of the individuals they treated. As a result, clients were uncertain about what they were trying to attain in mental health treatment. Goals were vague, objectives were nonexistent, and interventions were applied equally to all clients. Outcome data were not measurable, and neither the treatment provider nor the client knew exactly when treatment was complete. The initial development of rudimentary treatment plans made inroads toward addressing some of these issues.

With the advent of managed care in the 1980s, treatment planning has taken on even more importance. Managed care systems *insist* that clinicians move rapidly from assessment of the problem to the formulation and implementation of the treatment plan. The goal of most managed care companies is to expedite the treatment process by prompting the client and the treatment provider to focus on identifying and changing behavioral problems as quickly as possible. Treatment plans must be *specific* regarding the problems and interventions, *individualized* to meet the client's needs and goals, and *measurable* in terms of setting milestones that can be used to chart the client's progress. Pressure from third-party payers, accrediting agencies, and other outside parties has therefore increased the need for clinicians to produce effective, high-quality treatment plans in a short time frame. However, many mental health providers have little experience in treatment plan development. Our purpose in writing this book is to clarify, simplify, and accelerate the treatment planning process.

TREATMENT PLAN UTILITY

Detailed written treatment plans can benefit not only the client, therapist, treatment team, insurance community, and treatment agency, but also the overall psychotherapy profession. The client is served by a written plan because it stipulates the issues that are the focus of the treatment process. It is very easy for both provider and client to lose sight of the issues that brought the client into therapy. The treatment plan is a guide that structures the focus of the therapeutic contract. Because issues can change as therapy progresses, the treatment plan must be viewed as a dynamic document that can and must be updated to reflect any major change of problem, definition, goal, objective, or intervention.

Clients and therapists benefit from the treatment plan because it forces them to think about therapy outcomes. Behaviorally stated, measurable objectives clearly focus the treatment endeavor. Clients no longer wonder what the therapy is trying to accomplish. Clear objectives also allow the client to channel effort into specific changes that will lead to the long-term goal of problem resolution. Therapy is no longer a vague contract that simply calls for talking honestly and openly about emotions and cognitions until the client feels better. Both client and therapist are concentrating on explicitly stated objectives using specific interventions.

Providers are aided by treatment plans because they are forced to think analytically and critically about therapeutic interventions that are best suited to help the client attain objectives. Therapists were traditionally trained to "follow the client," but now a formalized plan guides the treatment process. The therapist must give advance attention to the technique, approach, assignment, or cathartic target that will form the basis for interventions.

Clinicians benefit from clear documentation of treatment because it provides a measure of added protection from possible client litigation. Malpractice suits are increasing in frequency, and insurance premiums are soaring. The first line of defense against allegations is a complete clinical record detailing the treatment process. A written, individualized, formal treatment plan that is the guideline for the therapeutic process, that has been reviewed and signed by the client, and that is coupled with problem-oriented progress notes is a powerful defense against exaggerated or false claims.

A well-crafted treatment plan that clearly stipulates presenting problems and intervention strategies facilitates the treatment process carried out by team members in inpatient, residential, or intensive out-patient settings. Good communication between team members about which approach is being implemented and who is responsible for which intervention is critical. Team meetings to discuss client treatment used to be the only source of interaction between providers; often, therapeutic conclusions or assignments were not recorded. Now, a thorough treatment plan stipulates in writing the details of objectives, the various interventions (pharmacologic, milieu, group therapy, didactic, recreational, individual therapy, etc.) to be used, and who will implement those interventions.

Every treatment agency or institution is constantly looking for ways to increase the quality and uniformity of documentation in the clinical record. A standardized, written treatment plan with problem definitions, goals, objectives, and interventions in every client's file enhances that uniformity of documentation and eases the task of record reviewers inside and outside the agency. Outside reviewers, such as JCAHO, insist on documentation that clearly outlines assessment, treatment, progress, and discharge status.

The demand for accountability from third-party payers and health maintenance organizations (HMOs) is partially satisfied by a written treatment plan and complete progress notes. More and more managed care systems are demanding a structured therapeutic contract that has measurable objectives and explicit interventions. Clinicians cannot avoid this move toward being accountable to those outside the treatment process.

The psychotherapy profession stands to benefit from the use of more precise, measurable objectives to evaluate success in mental health treatment. With the advent of detailed treatment plans, outcome data can be more easily collected for interventions that are effective in achieving specific goals.

HOW TO DEVELOP A TREATMENT PLAN

The process of developing a treatment plan involves logical steps that build on each other, much like constructing a house. The foundation of any effective treatment plan is the data gathered in a thorough biopsychosocial assessment. As the client presents him- or herself for treatment, the clinician must sensitively listen to and understand the client's struggles in terms of family-of-origin issues, current stressors, emotional status, social network, physical health, coping skills, interpersonal conflicts, self-esteem, and so on. Assessment data may be gathered from a social history, physical exam, clinical interview, psychological testing, or contact with a client's significant others. The integration of the data by the clinician or the multidisciplinary treatment team members is critical for understanding the client, as is an awareness of the basis of the client's struggle. We have identified six specific steps for developing an effective treatment plan based on the assessment data.

Step One: Problem Selection

Although the client may discuss a variety of issues during the assessment, the clinician must ferret out the most significant problems on which to focus the treatment process. Usually, a *primary* problem will surface, and *secondary* problems may also be evident. Some *other* problems may have to be set aside as not urgent enough to require simultaneous treatment. An effective treatment plan can deal with only a few selected problems or treatment will lose its direction. This *Planner* offers 30 problems from which to select those that most accurately represent your client's presenting issues.

As the problems to be selected become clear to the clinician or the treatment team, it is important to include opinions from the client regarding his or her prioritization of issues for which help is being sought. A client's motivation to participate in and cooperate with the treatment process depends, to some extent, on the degree to which treatment addresses his or her greatest needs.

Step Two: Problem Definition

Each individual client presents with unique nuances that reveal how a problem behaviorally impacts his or her life. Therefore, each problem selected for treatment focus requires a specific definition about how it is evidenced in the particular client. The symptom pattern should be associated with diagnostic criteria and codes such as those found in the *Diagnostic and Statistical Manual* or the *International Classification of Diseases*. The *Planner,* following the pattern established by DSM-IV, offers such behaviorally specific definition statements to choose from or to serve as a model for your own personally crafted statements. You will find several behavior symptoms or syndromes listed that may characterize one of the 30 presenting problems.

Step Three: Goal Development

The next step in treatment plan development is that of setting broad goals for the resolution of the target problem. These statements need not be crafted in measurable terms, but can be global, long-term goals that indicate a desired positive outcome to the treatment procedures. The *Planner* suggests several possible goal statements for each problem, but one statement is all that is required in a treatment plan.

Step Four: Objective Construction

In contrast to long-term goals, objectives must be stated in behaviorally measurable language. It must be clear when the client has achieved the established objectives; therefore, vague, subjective objectives are not acceptable. Review agencies (e.g., JCAHO), HMOs, and managed care organizations insist that psychological treatment outcome be measurable. The objectives presented in this *Planner* are designed to meet this demand for accountability. Numerous alternatives are presented to allow construction of a variety of treatment plan possibilities for the same presenting problem. The clinician must exercise professional judgment about which objectives are most appropriate for a given client.

Each objective should be developed as a step toward attaining the broad treatment goal. In essence, objectives can be thought of as a series of steps that, when completed, will result in the achievement of the long-term goal. There should be at least two objectives for each problem, but the clinician may construct as many as are necessary for goal achievement. Target attainment dates may be listed for each objective. New objectives should be added to the plan as the individual's treatment progresses. When all the necessary objectives have been achieved, the client should have resolved the target problem successfully.

Step Five: Intervention Creation

Interventions are the actions of the clinician designed to help the client complete the objectives. There should be at least one intervention for every objective. If the client does not accomplish the objective after the initial intervention, new interventions should be added to the plan. Interventions should be selected on the basis of the client's needs and the treatment provider's full therapeutic repertoire. This *Planner* contains interventions from a broad range of therapeutic approaches, including cognitive, dynamic, behavioral, pharmacologic, family-oriented, and solution-focused brief therapy. Other interventions may be written by the provider to reflect his or her own training and experience. The addition of new problems, definitions, goals, objectives, and interventions to those found in the *Planner* is encouraged, because doing so adds to the database for future reference and use.

Some suggested interventions listed in the *Planner* refer to specific books that can be assigned to the client for adjunctive bibliotherapy. Appendix A contains a full bibliographic reference list of these materials. The books are arranged under each problem for which they are appropriate as assigned reading for clients. When a book is used as part of an intervention plan, it should be reviewed with the client after it is read to enhance the application of the content of the book to the specific client's circumstances. For further information about self-help books, mental health professionals may wish to consult *The Authoritative Guide to Self-Help Books* (1994) by Santrock, Minnett, and Campbell (available from The Guilford Press, New York).

Assigning an intervention to a specific provider is most relevant if the client is being treated by a team in an inpatient, residential, or intensive outpatient setting. Within these settings, personnel other than the primary clinician may be responsible for implementing a specific intervention. Review agencies require that the responsible provider's name be stipulated for every intervention.

Step Six: Diagnosis Determination

The determination of an appropriate diagnosis is based on an evaluation of the client's complete clinical presentation. The clinician must compare the behavioral, cognitive, emotional, and interpersonal symptoms that the client presents to the criteria for diagnosis of a mental illness condition as described in DSM-IV. The issue of differential diagnosis is admittedly a difficult one that research has shown to have rather low interrater reliability. Psychologists have also been trained to think more in terms of maladaptive behavior than in terms of disease labels. In spite of these factors, diagnosis is a reality that exists in the world of mental health care, and it is a necessity for third-party reimbursement. (However, recently, managed care agencies are more interested in behavioral indices that are exhibited by the client than in the actual diagnosis.) The clinician's thorough knowledge of DSM-IV criteria and a complete understanding of the client assessment data will contribute to the most reliable, valid diagnosis. An accurate assessment of behavioral indicators will also contribute to more effective treatment planning.

HOW TO USE THIS PLANNER

Our experience has taught us that learning the skills of effective treatment plan writing can be a tedious and difficult process for many clinicians. It is stressful to try to develop this expertise when under the pressure of increased client loads and short time frames placed on clinicians today by managed care systems. The documentation demands can be overwhelming when we must move quickly from assessment to treatment plan to progress notes. In the process, we must be very specific about how and when objectives can be achieved and how progress is exhibited in each client. *The Child Psychotherapy Treatment Planner* was developed as a tool to aid clinicians in writing a treatment plan in a rapid manner that is clear, specific, and highly individualized according to the following progression:

1. Choose one presenting problem (Step One) you have identified through your assessment process. Locate the corresponding page number for that problem in the *Planner*'s table of contents.
2. Select two or three of the listed behavioral definitions (Step Two) and record them in the appropriate section on your treatment plan form. Feel free to add your own defining statement if you determine that your client's behavioral manifestation of the identified problem is not listed. (Note that while our design for treatment planning is vertical, it will work equally well on plan forms formatted horizontally.)
3. Select a single long-term goal (Step Three) and again write the selection, exactly as it is written in the *Planner* or in some appropriately modified form, in the corresponding area of your own form.
4. Review the listed objectives for this problem and select the ones that you judge to be clinically indicated for your client (Step Four). Remember, it is recommended that you select at least two objectives for each problem. Add a target date or the number of sessions allocated for the attainment of each objective.
5. Choose relevant interventions (Step Five). The *Planner* offers suggested interventions related to each objective in parentheses following the objective statement. But do not limit yourself to those interventions. The entire list is eclectic and may offer options that are more tailored to your theoretical approach or preferred way of working with clients. Also, just as with definitions, goals, and objectives, there is space for you to enter your own interventions into the *Planner*. This allows you to refer to these entries when you create a plan around this problem in the future. You will have to assign responsibility to a specific person for implementation of each intervention if the treatment is being carried out by a multidisciplinary team.
6. At the end of each chapter is a list of DSM-IV diagnoses commonly associated with a client who has this problem. These diagnoses are meant to be suggestions for clinical consideration.

Select a diagnosis listed or assign a more appropriate choice from the DSM-IV (Step Six).

Note: To accommodate those practitioners who tend to plan treatment in terms of diagnostic labels rather than presenting problems, Appendix B lists all of the DSM-IV diagnoses that have been presented in the *Planner* as suggestions for consideration. Each diagnosis is followed by the presenting problem associated with that diagnosis. Providers may look up the presenting problems for a selected diagnosis to review definitions, goals, objectives, and interventions that may be appropriate for their clients with that diagnosis.

Congratulations! You should now have a complete, individualized treatment plan that is ready for immediate implementation and presentation to the client. It should resemble the format of the sample plan that follows.

A FINAL NOTE

One important aspect of effective treatment planning is that each plan should be tailored to the individual client's problems and needs. Treatment plans should not be mass-produced, even if clients have similar problems. The individual's strengths and weaknesses, unique stressors, social network, family circumstances, and symptom patterns *must* be considered in developing a treatment strategy. Drawing on our own years of clinical experience, we have put together a variety of treatment choices. These statements can be combined in thousands of permutations to develop detailed treatment plans. Relying on their own good judgment, clinicians can easily select the statements that are appropriate for the individuals they are treating. In addition, we encourage readers to add their own definitions, goals, objectives, and interventions to the existing samples. It is our hope that *The Child Psychotherapy Treatment Planner* will promote effective, creative treatment planning—a process that will ultimately benefit the client, the clinician, and the mental health community.

SUMMARY

Our experience has taught us that learning the skills of effective treatment plan writing can be a tedious and difficult process for many clinicians. It is stressful to try to develop this expertise when under the pressure of the increased client loads and short time frames placed on clinicians today by managed care systems. The documentation demands can be overwhelming when we must move quickly from assessment to treatment plan to progress notes. In the process, we must be very specific about how and when objectives can be achieved and exhibited in each individual client. This *Planner* was developed as a tool to aid clinicians in writing treatment plans in a rapid manner that is clear, specific, and highly individualized. We have put together a variety of choices to allow for thousands of potential combinations of statements that join to make a completed plan for treatment. Clinicians, with their good judgment, can easily select statements that are appropriate for the individuals they are treating. Each statement can be modified as necessary to more directly apply to a specific individual client. Finally, we believe from our experience that the *Planner* method of treatment plan construction is helpful in that it stimulates creative thoughts by clinicians. New ideas for all components of a treatment plan may come to mind as the *Planner* statements are reviewed. Clinicians can add to the *Planner* by writing in new definitions, goals, objectives, and interventions.

SAMPLE TREATMENT PLAN

Problem: ADHD

Definitions: Short attention span; difficulty sustaining attention on a consistent basis.
Susceptibility to distraction by extraneous stimuli.
Repeated failure to follow through on instructions or complete school assignments or chores in a timely manner.

Goals: Sustain attention and concentration for consistently longer periods of time.
Regularly take medication as prescribed to decrease impulsivity, hyperactivity, and distractibility.
Parents and/or teachers successfully utilize a reward system, contingency contract, or token economy to reinforce positive behaviors and deter negative behaviors.

Objectives	Interventions
1. Complete psychological testing to confirm the diagnosis of ADHD.	1. Arrange for psychological testing to confirm the presence of ADHD in the client.
	2. Give feedback to the client and his/her family regarding psychological testing results.
2. Take prescribed medication as directed by the physician.	1. Arrange for a medication evaluation for the client.
	2. Monitor the client for compliance, side effects, and overall effectiveness of the medication. Consult with the prescribing physician at regular intervals.
3. Parents and teachers reduce extraneous stimuli as much as possible when giving directions to the client.	1. Educate the client's parents and siblings about the symptoms of ADHD.
	2. Teach the client more effective study skills (e.g., clearing away distractions, studying in quiet places, scheduling breaks in studying).

(Continued)

3. Consult with client's teachers to implement strategies to improve school performance (e.g., sitting in front of the class, using a prearranged signal to redirect the client back to task, scheduling breaks between tasks, providing frequent feedback, calling on the client often, arranging for a listening buddy).

4. Parents increase praise and positive verbalizations toward the client.

1. Identify a variety of positive reinforcers or rewards to maintain the client's interest or motivation.

2. Design a reward system and/or contingency contract to reinforce the client's desired positive behaviors and deter impulsive behaviors.

Diagnosis: 314.00   Attention-Deficit/Hyperactivity Disorder, Predominantly Inattentive Type

ACADEMIC UNDERACHIEVEMENT

BEHAVIORAL DEFINITIONS

1. History of overall academic performance that is below the expected level according to the client's measured intelligence or performance on standardized achievement tests.
2. Repeated failure to complete school or homework assignments and/or current assignments on time.
3. Poor organization or study skills that contribute to academic underachievement.
4. Frequent tendency to procrastinate or postpone doing school or homework assignments in favor of playing or engaging in recreational and leisure activities.
5. Family history of members having academic problems, failures, or disinterests.
6. Feelings of depression, insecurity, and low self-esteem that interfere with learning and academic progress.
7. Recurrent pattern of engaging in acting out, disruptive, and negative attention-seeking behaviors when encountering difficulty or frustration in learning.
8. Heightened anxiety that interferes with client's performance during tests or examinations.
9. Excessive or unrealistic pressure placed on client by parents to degree that it negatively affects his/her academic performance.
10. Decline in academic performance that occurs in response to environmental factors or stress (e.g., parents' divorce, death of loved one, relocation, or move).

—. _____
   _____
—. _____
   _____

—.   _____

_____

LONG-TERM GOALS

1. Demonstrate consistent interest, initiative, and motivation in academics and bring performance up to expected level of intellectual or academic functioning.
2. Complete school and homework assignments on a regular and consistent basis.
3. Achieve and maintain healthy balance between accomplishing academic goals and meeting his/her social, emotional, and self-esteem needs.
4. Stabilize moods and build self-esteem so that client is able to cope effectively with the frustrations and stressors associated with academic pursuits and learning.
5. Eliminate the pattern of engaging in acting out, disruptive, or negative attention-seeking behaviors when confronted with difficulty or frustration in learning.
6. Reduce level of anxiety related to taking tests or examinations to a significant degree.
7. Parents establish realistic expectations of the client's learning abilities and implement effective intervention strategies at home to help the client keep up with schoolwork and achieve academic goals.
8. Remove emotional impediments or resolve family conflicts and environmental stressors that will allow for improved academic performance.

—.   _____

_____

—.   _____

_____

—.   _____

_____

SHORT-TERM OBJECTIVES	THERAPEUTIC INTERVENTIONS
1. Complete a psychoeducational evaluation. (1, 3, 4)	1. Arrange for psychoeducational testing to evaluate

2. Complete psychological testing. (2, 3, 4, 46)

3. The client and his/her parents provide psychosocial history information. (1, 2, 3, 4)

4. Cooperate with a hearing, vision, or medical examination. (5, 48)

5. Comply with the recommendations made by the multidisciplinary evaluation team at school regarding educational interventions. (1, 6, 7, 8)

6. Move the client to appropriate classroom setting(s). (1, 6, 9)

7. Parents and teachers implement educational strategies that maximize the child's learning strengths and compensate for learning weaknesses. (7, 8, 9, 18, 19)

8. Participate in outside tutoring to increase knowledge and skills in the area of academic weakness. (8, 9, 10, 15)

9. Cooperate with the recommendations offered by the private learning center. (9, 10, 11, 12, 14)

10. Implement effective study skills to increase the frequency of completion of school assignments and improve academic performance. (10, 11, 12, 13, 33)

11. Develop effective test-taking strategies to decrease anxiety and improve

the presence of a learning disability, and determine whether the client is eligible to receive special education services.

2. Arrange for psychological testing to assess whether possible ADHD or emotional factors are interfering with the client's academic performance.

3. Gather psychosocial history information that includes key developmental milestones and a family history of educational achievements and failures.

4. Provide feedback to the client, his/her family, and school officials regarding psychoeducational and/or psychological evaluation.

5. Refer the client for hearing, vision, or medical examination to rule out possible hearing, visual, or health problems that are interfering with school performance.

6. Attend an Individualized Educational Planning Committee (IEPC) meeting with the parents, teachers, and school officials to determine the client's eligibility for special education services; design educational interventions; and establish educational goals.

7. Consult with the client, parents, and school officials about designing effective learning programs or inter-

test performance.
(12, 14, 22, 23)

12. Parents maintain regular (i.e., daily to weekly) communication with teachers. (16, 17, 18, 19, 20)

13. Use self-monitoring checklists, planners, or calendars to remain organized and help complete school assignments. (11, 12, 13, 32)

14. Complete large projects or long-term assignments consistently and on time. (12, 13, 16, 32)

15. Establish a regular routine that allows time to engage in play, to spend quality time with the family, and to complete homework assignments. (17, 20, 21, 25)

16. Increase praise and positive reinforcement by the parents toward the client in regard to school performance. (18, 19, 20, 21, 37)

17. Parents and teachers identify and utilize a variety of reinforcers to reward client for completion of school and homework assignments. (18, 19, 34, 37)

18. Identify and remove all emotional blocks or learning inhibitions that are within the client and/or the family system. (24, 25, 26, 27, 38)

19. Increase the parents' time spent being involved with the client's homework. (17, 18, 30, 31)

vention strategies that build on the client's strengths and compensate for weaknesses.

8. Recommend that parents seek outside tutoring after school to boost the client's skills in the area of his/her academic weakness (e.g., reading, mathematics, or written expression).

9. Refer the client to a private learning center for extra tutoring in the areas of academic weakness and assistance in improving study and test-taking skills.

10. Teach the client more effective study skills (e.g., remove distractions, study in quiet places, develop outlines, highlight important details, schedule breaks).

11. Encourage the client to use self-monitoring checklists to increase completion of school assignments and improve academic performance.

12. Direct client to use planners or calendars to record school or homework assignments and plan ahead for long-term projects.

13. Utilize "Getting It Done" program in *Brief Child Therapy Homework Planner* (Jongsma, Peterson, and McInnis) to help client complete school and homework assignments on a regular, consistent basis.

20. Parents verbally acknowledge their unrealistic expectations or excessive pressure on the client to perform. (26, 27, 28, 29)

21. Decrease the frequency and intensity of arguments between client and parents over issues related to school performance and homework. (24, 25, 28, 29)

22. Parents verbally recognize that their pattern of overprotectiveness interferes with the client's academic growth and responsibility. (25, 30, 31)

23. Increase the frequency of on-task behavior at school, increasing the completion of school assignments without expressing frustration and the desire to give up. (22, 32, 34, 35)

24. Increase the frequency of positive statements about school experiences and confidence in the ability to succeed academically. (34, 35, 36, 37)

25. Decrease the frequency and severity of acting-out behaviors when encountering frustrations with school assignments. (38, 39, 47)

26. Identify and verbalize how specific, responsible actions lead to improvements in academic performance. (41, 42, 43, 45)

27. Develop a list of resource people within school setting

14. Teach the client more effective test-taking strategies (e.g., study over an extended period of time, review material regularly, read directions twice, recheck work).

15. Consult with teachers and parents about using a "study buddy" or peer tutor to assist client in area of academic weakness and improve study skills.

16. Encourage parents to maintain regular (daily or weekly) communication with teachers to help the client remain organized and keep up with school assignments.

17. Assist the client and his/her parents in developing a routine daily schedule at home that allows the client to achieve a healthy balance of completing school/homework assignments, engaging in independent play, and spending quality time with family and peers.

18. Encourage the parents to give frequent praise and positive reinforcement for the client's effort and accomplishment on academic tasks.

19. Assist the parents in resolving family conflicts that block or inhibit learning and establish new positive family patterns that reinforce the client's academic achievement.

to whom client can turn for support, assistance, or instruction for learning problems. (13, 43, 45)

28. Increase time spent in independent reading. (45, 46, 47)

29. Express feelings about school through artwork and mutual storytelling. (45, 46, 47)

30. Take prescribed medication as directed by the physician. (2, 48)

—. _____
   _____

—. _____
   _____

—. _____
   _____

20. Encourage the parents to demonstrate and/or maintain regular interest and involvement in the client's homework (e.g., parents reading aloud to or alongside the client, using flash cards to improve math skills, rechecking the client's spelling words).

21. Identify a variety of positive reinforcers or rewards to maintain the client's interest and motivation to complete school assignments.

22. Teach the client positive coping mechanisms (e.g., relaxation techniques, positive self-talk, cognitive restructuring) to utilize when encountering anxiety, frustration, or difficulty with schoolwork.

23. Train in relaxation techniques or guided imagery to reduce anxiety before or during the taking of tests.

24. Conduct family sessions that probe the client's family system to identify any emotional blocks or inhibitions to learning.

25. Assist the parents and teachers in the development of systematic rewards for progress and accomplishments (e.g., charts with stars for goal attainment, praise for each success, some material reward for achievement).

26. Conduct family therapy sessions to assess whether the

parents have developed unrealistic expectations or are
placing excessive pressure
on the client to perform.

27. Confront and challenge the
parents about placing excessive pressure on the client.

28. Encourage parents to set
firm, consistent limits and
utilize natural, logical consequences for the client's
noncompliance or refusal to
do homework.

29. Instruct the parents to
avoid unhealthy power
struggles or lengthy arguments over homework each
night.

30. Observe parent-child interactions to assess whether
the parents' overprotectiveness or infantilization of the
client contributes to his/her
academic underachieve-
ment.

31. Assist the parents in developing realistic expectations
of the client's learning potential.

32. Consult with school officials
about ways to improve the
client's on-task behaviors
(e.g., keep the client close to
the teacher, keep the client
close to positive peer role
models, call on the client
often, provide frequent feedback to the client, structure
the material into a series of
small steps).

33. Assign reading of *13 Steps
to Better Grades* (Silver-

man) to improve client's organizational and study
skills; process reading with
therapist.

34. Reinforce the client's successful school experiences
and positive statements
about school.

35. Confront the client's self-
disparaging remarks and
expressed desire to give up
on school assignments.

36. Assign the client the task of
making one positive self-
statement daily about
school and his/her ability,
and have him/her record it
in a journal.

37. Help the client identify
what rewards would in-
crease his/her motivation to
improve academic perfor-
mance, and then implement
the suggestions into the
academic program.

38. Conduct individual play-
therapy sessions to help
client work through and resolve painful emotions, core
conflicts, or stressors that
impede academic perfor-
mance.

39. Help client realize connection between negative or
painful emotions and de-
crease in academic performance.

40. Teach the client positive
coping and self-control
strategies (e.g., cognitive restructuring, positive self-
talk, "stop, look, listen, and

think") to inhibit the impulse to act out or engage in negative attention-seeking behaviors when encountering frustration with schoolwork.

41. Explore periods of time when client completed schoolwork regularly and/or achieved academic success. Identify and encourage client to use similar strategies to improve current academic performance.

42. Examine coping strategies that client has used to solve other problems. Encourage client to use similar coping strategies to overcome problems associated with learning.

43. Identify a list of individuals within the school to whom client can turn for support, assistance, or instruction when he/she encounters difficulty or frustration with learning.

44. Encourage parents to use the "Reading Adventure" program in the *Brief Child Therapy Homework Planner* (Jongsma, Peterson, and McInnis) to increase client's motivation to read. Utilize a reward system to reinforce client for engaging in independent reading.

45. Utilize mutual storytelling techniques whereby therapist and client alternate telling stories through use of puppets, dolls, or stuffed

animals; therapist first models appropriate ways to manage frustration related to learning problems, then client follows by creating a story with similar characters or themes.

46. Have client create a variety of drawings on posterboard or large sheet of paper that reflect how his/her personal and family life would be different if he/she completed homework regularly; process content of drawings with therapist.

47. Instruct client to draw picture of school building, then have client create story that tells what it is like to be a student at that school to assess possible stressors that may interfere with learning and academic progress.

48. Arrange for medication evaluation of the client if it is determined that an emotional problem and/or ADHD are interfering with learning.

___. _____

_____

___. _____

_____

___. _____

_____

DIAGNOSTIC SUGGESTIONS

Axis I:	315.00	Reading Disorder
	315.1	Mathematics Disorder
	315.2	Disorder of Written Expression
	V62.3	Academic Problem
	314.01	Attention-Deficit/Hyperactivity Disorder, Combined Type
	314.00	Attention-Deficit/Hyperactivity Disorder, Predominantly Inattentive Type
	300.4	Dysthymic Disorder
	313.81	Oppositional Defiant Disorder
	312.9	Disruptive Behavior Disorder, NOS
	_____	_____
	_____	_____
Axis II:	317	Mild Mental Retardation
	V62.89	Borderline Intellectual Functioning
	799.9	Diagnosis Deferred
	V71.09	No Diagnosis on Axis II
	_____	_____
	_____	_____

ADOPTION

BEHAVIORAL DEFINITIONS

1. The adoption of an older special-needs child or set of siblings into the family.
2. Relates to significant others in a withdrawing, rejecting way, avoiding eye contact and keeping self at a distance from them.
3. Exhibits a pattern of hoarding or gorging food.
4. Displays numerous aggressive behaviors that are out of proportion for the presenting situations and seem to reflect a need to vent pent-up frustration.
5. Lies and steals often when it is not necessary to do so.
6. Displays an indiscriminate pattern of showing open affection to casual friends and strangers.
7. Parents express frustration with adopted child's development and level of achievement.
8. Parents are anxious and fearful of adopted child's questioning of background ("Where did I come from," "Who do I look like," etc.).

___. _____
_____
___. _____
_____
___. _____
_____

LONG-TERM GOALS

1. Termination of self-defeating, acting-out behaviors and acceptance of self as loved and lovable within an adopted family.

2. Resolution of key adoption issues of loss, abandonment, and rejection.
3. The establishment and maintenance of healthy family connections.
4. Removal of all barriers to enable the establishment of a healthy bond between parents and child(ren).
5. Develop a nurturing relationship with parents.
6. Build and maintain a healthy adoptive family.

—. _____
_____
—. _____
_____
—. _____
_____

SHORT-TERM OBJECTIVES

1. Develop a trusting relationship with therapist that will allow the client, parents, and siblings to openly express their thoughts and feelings. (1)
2. Cooperate with and complete psychosocial assessments. (1, 2)
3. Complete psychological evaluation. (1, 3)
4. Comply with all recommendations of the evaluations or assessments. (4)
5. Parents acknowledge unresolved grief associated with infertility. (5)
6. Family members attend family therapy sessions and report on their perception of the adjustment process. (6)

THERAPEUTIC INTERVENTIONS

1. Actively build the level of trust with client(s) and parents in sessions by consistent eye contact, active listening, unconditional positive regard, and empathic responses to help promote the open expressions of their thoughts and feelings about the adoption.
2. Conduct or refer parents and child(ren) for a psychosocial assessment to assess parents' strength of marriage, parenting style, stress management/coping strengths, and resolution of infertility issue and to assess child's developmental level, attachment capacity, behavior issues, temperament, and strengths.

7. Parents commit to improving communication and affection within the marriage relationship. (7)

8. Attend and actively take part in play-therapy sessions. (8, 9, 10, 11, 12)

9. Reduce acting-out behaviors connected to unresolved rage, loss, and fear of abandonment. (8, 9, 10, 11, 12)

10. Verbalize the connection between anger and/or withdrawal and the underlying feelings of fear, abandonment, and rejection. (8, 9, 13)

11. Identify feelings that are held inside and rarely expressed. (14, 15, 16)

12. Identify and release feelings in socially acceptable, nondestructive ways. (17, 18, 19)

13. Express feelings directly related to being an adopted child. (20, 21)

14. Parents verbalize an increased ability to understand and handle acting-out behaviors. (22, 23, 24, 25)

15. Parents affirm client's identity as based in self, bioparents, and adoptive family. (26, 27)

16. Express and preserve own history and its contribution to identity. (28)

17. Verbalize needs and wishes. (29)

3. Conduct or arrange for psychological evaluation to determine level of behavioral functioning, cognitive style, and intelligence.

4. Summarize assessment data and present findings and recommendations to family.

5. Assess parents' unresolved grief around the issue of their infertility; refer for further conjoint or individual treatment if necessary.

6. Establish a wellness plan whereby family goes at three-month intervals for a checkup with therapist to evaluate how the assimilation and attachment process is proceeding. If all is well, checkups can be annual after the first year.

7. Refer parents to a skills-based marital program such as Prep (e.g., *Fighting For Your Marriage* by Markman, Stanley, and Blumberg) to strengthen marital relationship by improving responsibility, communication, and conflict resolution.

8. Conduct filial therapy (i.e., parent involvement in play-therapy sessions), in which client takes the lead in expressing anger and parent responds empathically to client's feelings (hurt, fear, sadness, helplessness) beneath the anger.

9. Employ psychoanalytic play therapy (e.g., explore and

18. Verbalize a feeling of increased confidence and self-acceptance. (27, 28, 30)

19. Parents verbalize reasonable expectations for client's behavior given client's developmental stage and the process of adjustment to adoption. (31)

20. Parent spends one-on-one time with client in active play. (32)

21. Parents increase the frequency of expressing affection verbally and physically toward client. (33)

22. Parents speak only positively regarding client's bio-parents. (34)

23. Parents feel free to ask questions regarding the details of adoption adjustment. (35)

24. Parents verbalize reasonable discipline and nurturance guidelines. (36, 37, 38)

25. Family members express an acceptance of and trust in each other. (39, 40)

__. _____
     _____

__. _____
     _____

__. _____
     _____

gain understanding of the etiology of unconscious conflicts, fixations, or arrests; interpret resistance transference or core anxieties) to help client work through and resolve issues contributing to the acting-out behaviors.

10. Employ A.C.T. model (Landreth) in play therapy sessions to *acknowledge* feelings, *communicate* limits, and *target* acceptable alternatives to acting-out or aggressive behaviors.

11. Conduct individual play-therapy sessions to provide the opportunity for expression of feelings surrounding past loss, neglect, and/or abandonment.

12. Utilize the *Theraplay* (Jernberg and Booth) attachment-based approach, in which the therapist takes charge by planning and structuring each session. Therapist uses his/her power to entice the client into relationship and to keep the focus of therapy on the relationship, not on intrapsychic conflicts. Also, parents are actively involved and are trained to be cotherapists.

13. Assist the client in making connections between underlying painful emotions of loss, rejection, rage, abandonment, and acting-out and/or aggressive behaviors.

14. Use puppets, dolls, or stuffed toys to tell a story to client about others who have experienced loss, rejection, or abandonment to show how they have resolved these issues. Then ask the client to create a similar story using the puppets, dolls or stuffed toys.

15. Ask client to draw an outline of himself/herself on a sheet of paper, and then instruct him/her to fill the inside with pictures and objects that reflect what he/she has on the inside that fuels the acting-out behaviors.

16. Use expressive art materials such as Play-Doh, clay, or finger paint to create pictures and sculptures that aid the client in expressing and resolving his/her feelings of rage, rejection, and loss.

17. Read with client or have parents read *A Volcano in My Tummy* (Whithouse and Pudney) or *Don't Rant and Rave on Wednesday* (Moser) to help client recognize his/her anger and to present ways to handle angry feelings.

18. Play with client, or have parents play, Talking, Feeling, Doing game (Gardner) or Anger Control game (Berg) to assist client in identifying and expressing feelings and thoughts.

19. Use a feelings chart, felts, or cards to increase client's ability to identify, understand, and express feelings.

20. Ask client to read *How It Feels to Be Adopted* (Krementz), and list two or three items from each age-appropriate vignette that he/she will process with therapist.

21. Assign client to read *I Feel Different* (Stinson) and/or *Adoption Is for Always* (Welvoord-Girrard) to help him/her identify with issues and not feel alone.

22. Affirm often with parents the health of their family while they are working with the disturbed client to avoid triangulation and undermining of parental authority by the client.

23. Refer parents and/or client to an adoption support group.

24. Have parents read *Helping Children Cope with Separation and Loss* (Jenett/Jarratt) and/or *Adoption Wisdom* (Russell) to increase their knowledge and understanding of adoption.

25. Work with parents in conjoint sessions to frame client's acting-out behaviors as "opportunities to reparent the client." Then strategize with them to come up with specific ways to intervene in the problem behaviors.

26. Ask parents to read *The Whole Life Adoption Book* (Schouler) and/or *Making Sense of Adoption* (Melina) to help them gain knowledge and understanding of adoption and to assist client in building a healthy, integrated identity.

27. Educate parents on the importance of affirming the client's entire identity (i.e., self, bioparents, adoptive parents), and show them specific ways to reaffirm the client (e.g., verbally identify talents such as art or music that are similar to those of the biological parents, recognize positive tasks client does that are similar to those of adoptive mom or dad).

28. Assign parents to help client create a "life book" that chronicles the client's life to this point in order to give him/her a visual perspective and knowledge of own history and identity. A form for "Create a Memory Album" can be found in *Brief Child Therapy Homework Planner* (Jongsma, Peterson, and McInnis).

29. Have client complete exercise "Three Wishes Game" from *Brief Child Therapy Homework Planner* (Jongsma, Peterson, and McInnis) to help client express his/her needs and desires.

30. Assign a self-esteem-building exercise from *SEALS & Plus* (Korb-Khara, Azok, and Leutenberg) to help develop self-knowledge, acceptance, and confidence.

31. Process with parents the issue of expectations for client's behavior and adjustment; confront and modify unrealistic expectations and foster realistic expectations considering the client's developmental stage and adjustment to the adoption process.

32. Work with parents to have each spend specific time in daily one-on-one active play with client.

33. Encourage parents to provide large, genuine, daily doses of positive verbal reinforcement and physical affection. Monitor and encourage parents to continue this behavior and to identify positive attachment signs when they appear.

34. Encourage parents to refrain from negative references about bioparents.

35. Conduct sessions with parents to give them opportunities to raise adoption-specific issues of concern to them (e.g., how to handle an open adoption, how much to share with client about bioparents) in order to give them direction and support.

36. Provide parents with education about keeping discipline related to the offense reasonable and always respectful to reduce resentment and rebellion. Recommend *How to Raise Responsible Children* (Glen and Nelson).

37. Ask parents to read *The Seven Habits of Highly Effective Families* (Covey) for suggestions on how to increase their family's health and connections.

38. Have parents spend individual one-on-one time with children who were part of the family prior to the adoption.

39. Refer family to an initiatives weekend (e.g., high and low ropes-course tasks and various group-oriented physical problem-solving activities) to increase trust, cooperation, and connections with each other.

40. In a family session, construct a genogram that includes all family members and shows how everyone is connected to demonstrate client's origins and what he/she has become a part of.

__. _____

_____

__. _____

_____

__. _____

_____

DIAGNOSTIC SUGGESTIONS

Axis I: 309.0   Adjustment Disorder With Depressed Mood
               309.4   Adjustment Disorder With Mixed Disturbance
                          of Emotions and Conduct
               300.4   Dysthymic Disorder
               314.01   Attention Deficit/Hyperactivity Disorder
               309.81   Posttraumatic Stress Disorder
               313.89   Reactive Attachment Disorder of Infancy or
                          Early Childhood

               _____   _____

               _____   _____

Axis II: 799.9   Diagnosis Deferred
               V71.09   No Diagnosis on Axis II

               _____   _____

               _____   _____

ANGER MANAGEMENT

BEHAVIORAL DEFINITIONS

1. Repeated angry outbursts that are out of proportion to the precipitating event.
2. Excessive yelling, swearing, crying, or use of verbally abusive language when efforts to meet desires are frustrated or limits are placed on behavior.
3. Frequent fighting, intimidation of others, and acts of cruelty or violence toward people or animals.
4. Verbal threats of harm to parents, adult authority figures, siblings, or peers.
5. Persistent pattern of destroying property or throwing objects when angry.
6. Consistent failure to accept responsibility for anger-control problems accompanied by repeated pattern of blaming others for poor control of anger.
7. Repeated history of engaging in passive-aggressive behaviors (e.g., forgetting, pretending not to listen, dawdling, procrastinating) to frustrate or annoy other adults or peers.
8. Strained interpersonal relationships with peers due to aggressiveness and anger-control problems.
9. Underlying feelings of depression, anxiety, or insecurity that contribute to angry outbursts and aggressive behaviors.

—. _____
_____

—. _____
_____

—. _____
_____

LONG-TERM GOALS

1. Express anger through appropriate verbalizations and healthy physical outlets on a consistent basis.
2. Significantly reduce the frequency and intensity of temper outbursts.
3. Terminate all destruction of property, physical aggression, and acts of violence or cruelty toward people or animals.
4. Interact consistently with adults and peers in a mutually respectful manner.
5. Markedly reduce frequency of passive-aggressive behaviors by expressing anger and frustration through controlled, respectful, and direct verbalizations.
6. Resolve the core conflicts that contribute to the emergence of anger-control problems.
7. Parents establish and maintain appropriate parent-child boundaries, setting firm, consistent limits when the client reacts in a verbally or physically aggressive or passive-aggressive manner.
8. Demonstrate marked improvement in the ability to listen and respond empathetically to the thoughts, feelings, and needs of other people.

—. _____
   _____

—. _____
   _____

—. _____
   _____

SHORT-TERM OBJECTIVES

1. Complete psychological testing. (1, 3)

2. Complete a psychoeducational evaluation. (2, 3)

3. Cooperate with the mandates of the criminal justice system. (3, 4, 5)

4. Parents establish appropriate boundaries and follow

THERAPEUTIC INTERVENTIONS

1. Arrange for psychological testing to assess whether emotional factors or ADHD are contributing to anger-control problems.

2. Arrange for a psychoeducational evaluation to rule out the presence of a learning disability that may be

through consistently with consequences for anger-control problems. (6, 7, 8, 9)

5. Increase compliance with rules at home and school without protesting or venting strong feelings of anger. (7, 8, 9, 23, 24)

6. Acknowledge instances when anger has not been controlled. (10, 23)

7. Verbalize how feelings of fear, hurt, sadness, or anxiety are connected to anger-control problems. (11, 27, 36)

8. Decrease the frequency and intensity of destructive behaviors and throwing of objects. (12, 14, 19, 20)

9. Reduce the frequency and intensity of angry outbursts and aggressive behaviors. (13, 17, 19, 20, 21)

10. Reduce the frequency of passive-aggressive behaviors. (7, 15, 18, 44)

11. Express anger through controlled, respectful verbalizations and healthy physical outlets. (12, 15, 20, 50, 51)

12. Decrease the frequency of arguments with authority figures. (15, 46, 47, 49)

13. Directly communicate thoughts, feelings, and needs to adults and peers in an assertive, controlled, and mutually respectful manner. (7, 17, 40, 47)

14. Parents agree to and follow through with the implementation of a reward system or

contributing to anger-control problems in the school setting.

3. Provide feedback to the client, his/her parents, school officials, or criminal justice officials regarding psychological and/or psychoeducational testing.

4. Consult with criminal justice officials about the appropriate consequences for the client's destructive and aggressive behaviors (e.g., probation, community service, pay restitution).

5. Encourage the parents not to protect the client from the natural or legal consequences of his/her destructive or aggressive behaviors.

6. Assist the parents in establishing clearly defined rules, boundaries, and consequences for client's angry outbursts and acts of aggression or destruction.

7. Establish clear rules for behavior at home or in school; ask client to repeat the rules to demonstrate an understanding of the expectations so that anger does not escalate when he/she receives consequences for any rule violations.

8. Teach parents effective disciplinary techniques (e.g., time-outs, removal of privileges, response cost) to help manage client's anger-control problems.

contingency contract to reinforce controlled expression of anger. (18, 19, 20)

15. Increase the number of statements that reflect acceptance of responsibility for angry outbursts and aggressive behaviors. (10, 22, 23, 24)

16. Parents increase the frequency of praise and positive reinforcement to the client for showing controlled expression of anger. (16, 18, 19, 20)

17. Decrease the frequency of verbalizations that project the blame for angry outbursts or aggressive behaviors onto other people. (22, 23, 24)

18. Uninvolved or detached parent(s) increase the time spent with client in recreational, school, or work activities around the house. (26, 27, 28, 29)

19. Verbalize an understanding of how angry outbursts or aggressive behaviors are associated with past neglect, abuse, separation, or abandonment. (30, 34, 35)

20. Identify and verbally express feelings associated with past neglect, abuse, separation, or abandonment. (33, 34, 35, 36)

21. Parents verbalize appropriate boundaries for discipline to prevent further occurrences of abuse and

9. Assign parents to read *1-2-3 Magic: Training Your Preschoolers and Preteens to Do What You Want* (Phelan), *Family Rules: Raising Responsible Children* (Kaye), and *Assertive Discipline for Parents* (Canter and Canter); process readings in sessions.

10. Actively build the level of trust with the client through consistent eye contact, active listening, unconditional positive regard, and warm acceptance to help increase his/her ability to identify and express times when angry feelings have not been controlled.

11. Assist the client in making a connection between underlying, painful emotions (e.g., fear, hurt, sadness, anxiety) and angry outbursts or aggressive behaviors.

12. Teach mediational self-control strategies (e.g., relaxation, "stop, look, listen, and think") to help express anger through appropriate verbalizations and healthy physical outlets.

13. Train client to use progressive relaxation or guided imagery techniques to induce calm and decrease the intensity of angry feelings.

14. Identify and confront irrational thoughts that contribute to the emergence of anger-control problems; replace irrational thoughts

ensure the safety of the client and his/her siblings. (25, 30, 31, 32, 33)

22. Increase the frequency of positive interactions with parents, adult authority figures, siblings, and peers. (16, 20, 28, 29)

23. Identify and verbalize unmet emotional needs. (37, 39, 41)

24. Identify and verbalize how poor control of anger negatively affects others. (22, 38, 53, 54)

25. Increase verbalizations of empathy and concern for other people. (40, 52, 53)

26. Parents acknowledge conflict within the marital relationship. (25, 26, 57)

27. Increase participation in extracurricular activities or positive peer group activities. (52, 53, 54)

28. Express feelings of anger through art and music. (42, 43, 44, 45)

29. Increase verbalizations of positive self-statements to help improve anger control. (16, 55, 56)

30. Take medication as prescribed by physician. (1, 58)

—. _____
   _____
—. _____
   _____
—. _____
   _____

with more adaptive ways of thinking to help control anger.

15. Teach client effective communication and assertiveness skills to express anger in a controlled fashion and to meet his/her needs through more constructive actions.

16. Encourage the use of self-monitoring checklists at home or school to develop more effective anger control.

17. Assist the client in identifying successful strategies that have been used on days when he/she controls temper and does not hit sibling(s), peers, or others; process client's responses and reinforce any positive coping mechanisms that he/she uses to manage anger.

18. Encourage the parents to provide frequent praise and positive reinforcement for the client's positive social behaviors and good anger control.

19. Design a reward system and/or contingency contract to reinforce anger control and deter aggressive or destructive behaviors.

20. Design and implement a token economy to increase positive social behaviors and deter destructive or aggressive behaviors.

21. Utilize "Anger Control" exercise in *Brief Child Ther-*

apy Homework Planner
(Jongsma, Peterson, and
McInnis) to reinforce good
control of anger and help
identify core issues that
contribute to emergence of
angry outbursts or aggressive behaviors.

22. Firmly confront client's
destructive and aggressive
behaviors, pointing out
consequences for himself/
herself and others.

23. Confront statements in
which the client blames
others for his/her anger-
control problems and fails
to accept responsibility for
the consequences of his/her
destructive or aggressive
behaviors.

24. Explore and process the factors that contribute to the
pattern of blaming others.

25. Conduct family therapy sessions to explore the dynamics that contribute to the
emergence of anger-control
problems.

26. Assess the family dynamics
by employing the family-
sculpting technique, in
which the client defines the
roles and behaviors of each
family member in a scene of
his/her choosing.

27. Conduct filial therapy (i.e.,
parental involvement in
play sessions) whereby
client takes the lead in expressing anger and parent
responds empathetically to
other feelings (e.g., hurt,

sadness, helplessness) beneath the anger.

28. Hold a family therapy session in which family members are given a task or problem to solve together (e.g., building a craft, producing a drawing); observe family interactions, and process the experience with them afterward.

29. Give a directive to uninvolved or disengaged parent(s) to spend more time with the client in leisure, school, or work activities.

30. Explore family background for a history of physical, sexual, or substance abuse that may contribute to his/her anger-control problems.

31. Insist that parents cease physically abusive or overly punitive methods of discipline.

32. Implement the steps necessary to protect the client or siblings from further abuse (e.g., report abuse to appropriate agencies; remove the client or perpetrator from the home).

33. Encourage and support expression of feelings associated with neglect, abuse, separation, or abandonment.

34. Use the empty-chair technique to assist the client in expressing and working through feelings of anger and hurt about past separation or abandonment.

35. Conduct individual play-therapy sessions to provide the opportunity for expression of feelings surrounding past neglect, abuse, separation, or abandonment.

36. Interpret the feelings expressed in play therapy and relate them to anger and aggressive behaviors.

37. Use child-centered play-therapy approaches to increase mastery of anger control (e.g., provide unconditional positive regard, reflect feelings in nonjudgmental manner, display trust in child's capacity to act responsibly).

38. Employ A.C.T. model (Landreth) in play-therapy sessions to acknowledge feelings, communicate limits, and identify acceptable alternatives to destructive or aggressive behaviors.

39. Employ psychoanalytic play-therapy approach (e.g., explore and gain understanding of the etiology of unconscious conflicts, fixations, or arrests; interpret resistance, transference, or core anxieties) to help client work through and resolve issues contributing to anger control problems.

40. Use puppets, dolls, or stuffed animals to create a story that models appropriate ways to manage anger and resolve conflict; then ask client to create story

with similar characters or themes.

41. Direct client to create stories that can be acted out with puppets, dolls, or stuffed animals to assess unmet needs, family dynamics, or core issues that contribute to anger-control problems.

42. Instruct client to draw a picture of a house, then pretend that he/she lives in the house and describe what it is like to live in that home; process feelings and content of responses to help assess family dynamics.

43. Assign the task of drawing three events or situations that commonly evoke feelings of anger; process thoughts and feelings after drawings are completed.

44. Assign client to draw an outline of human body on large piece of paper or poster board; then instruct client to draw or fill the body with objects, symbols, or pictures indicative of people, actions, or issues that evoke feelings of anger.

45. Instruct client to sing a song or play a musical instrument that reflects feelings of anger; then talk about a time when client felt angry about a particular issue.

46. Assign homework from the therapeutic workbooks *The Angry Monster* (Shore) and

How I Learned to Control My Temper (Shapiro) to help the client develop more effective ways to control anger.

47. Play the therapeutic game The Angry Monster Machine (Shapiro) to help client express his/her anger through more constructive channels.

48. Assign reading of *Sometimes I Like to Fight, But I Don't Do It Much Anymore* (Shapiro) or *The Very Angry Day That Amy Didn't Have* (Shapiro); process the reading with therapist.

49. Assign techniques from *Anger Control Toolkit* (Shapiro, et al.) to help client learn to control anger more effectively.

50. Assign the use of Coping with Anger Target game (Shapiro) at home when strong feelings of anger begin to emerge so that client can remind himself/herself of constructive ways to control anger.

51. Use the Angry Tower technique (Saxe) to help client identify and express feelings of anger: Build tower out of plastic containers; place small item (representing object of anger) on top of tower; then instruct client to throw small fabric ball at tower while verbalizing anger.

52. Encourage participation in extracurricular or positive peer group activities to provide a healthy outlet for anger and to increase self-esteem.

53. Assign the task of showing empathy, kindness, or sensitivity to the needs of others (e.g., assisting sibling with chore, verbalizing compassion for peer's emotional pain).

54. Refer client for group therapy to improve anger control, social judgment, and interpersonal skills.

55. Identify and list the client's positive characteristics to improve self-esteem and frustration tolerance.

56. Assign the client to make one positive self-statement daily and record that in a journal to improve self-esteem and frustration tolerance.

57. Assess the marital dyad for possible conflict and triangulation, in which the focus is deflected away from marital issues and toward client's aggressive behaviors; refer for marital counseling if indicated.

58. Have client evaluated for medication to improve anger control and stabilize moods.

—. _____

_____

—. _____
_____
—. _____
_____

DIAGNOSTIC SUGGESTIONS

Axis I:	313.81	Oppositional Defiant Disorder
	312.34	Intermittent Explosive Disorder
	312.30	Impulse-Control Disorder NOS
	312.8	Conduct Disorder/Childhood-Onset Type
	312.9	Disruptive Behavior Disorder NOS
	314.01	Attention-Deficit Disorder, Predominantly Hyperactive-Impulsive Type
	314.9	Attention-Deficit Hyperactivity Disorder NOS
	V71.02	Child Antisocial Behavior
	V61.20	Parent-Child Relational Problem
	_____	_____
	_____	_____
Axis II:	799.9	Diagnosis Deferred
	V71.09	No Diagnosis on Axis II
	_____	_____
	_____	_____

ANXIETY

BEHAVIORAL DEFINITIONS

1. Excessive anxiety, worry, or fear that markedly exceeds the level for the client's stage of development.
2. High level of motor tension, such as restlessness, tiredness, shakiness, or muscle tension.
3. Autonomic hyperactivity, such as rapid heartbeat, shortness of breath, dizziness, dry mouth, nausea, or diarrhea.
4. Hypervigilance, such as feeling constantly on edge, concentration difficulties, trouble falling or staying asleep, and a general state of irritability.
5. A specific fear that has become generalized to cover a wide area and has reached the point where it significantly interferes with the client's and the family's daily life.
6. Excessive anxiety or worry due to parent's threat of abandonment, overuse of guilt, denial of autonomy and status, friction between parents, or interference with physical activity.

—. _____
   _____
   _____

—. _____
   _____
   _____

—. _____
   _____

LONG-TERM GOALS

1. Reduce the overall frequency and intensity of the anxiety response so that daily functioning is not impaired.

2. Stabilize the anxiety level while increasing the ability to function on a daily basis.
3. Resolve the key issue that is the source of the anxiety or fear.
4. Interact with the world without excessive fear, worry, or anxiety.

—. _____
_____
_____

—. _____
_____
_____

—. _____
_____
_____

SHORT-TERM OBJECTIVES

1. Openly share anxious thoughts and feelings with therapist. (1, 2)
2. Verbally identify specific fears, worries, and anxieties. (1, 2, 3, 4)
3. Verbalize an increased understanding of anxious feelings and their causes. (5, 6, 7, 8)
4. Report a decrease in frequency of experiencing anxiety. (3, 4, 8)
5. Implement positive self-talk to reduce or eliminate the anxiety. (9, 10)
6. Develop and implement appropriate relaxation and cognitive diversion activities to decrease the level of anxiety. (11)
7. Identify areas of conflict that precipitate anxiety. (12, 13, 14, 15, 16)

THERAPEUTIC INTERVENTIONS

1. Actively build the level of trust with the client through consistent eye contact, active listening, unconditional positive regard, and warm acceptance to help increase his/her ability to identify and express anxious feelings.
2. Use a therapeutic game (Talking, Feeling, Doing, available from Creative Therapeutics, or The Ungame available from The Ungame Company) to expand client's awareness of feelings, self, and others.
3. Conduct play-therapy sessions in which the client's anxieties, fears, and worries are explored, expressed, and resolved.
4. Ask client to complete and process the exercise "Finding and Losing Your Anxiety" from *Brief Child*

8. State a connection between anxiety and underlying, previously unexpressed wishes or thoughts. (17)

9. Identify and utilize specific coping strategies for anxiety reduction. (18, 19, 20, 21)

10. Increase participation in daily social and academic activities. (22, 24)

11. Increase physical exercise as a means of reducing anxious feelings. (23)

12. Participate in a camp that focuses on confidence building. (24)

13. Set aside time for overthinking about anxieties. (25)

14. Parents verbalize an understanding of the client's anxieties and fears. (26, 27, 28)

15. Parents verbalize constructive ways to respond to client's anxiety. (29)

16. Participate in family therapy sessions that identify and resolve conflicts between family members. (30, 31)

17. Parents reduce their attempts to control the child. (32, 33)

18. Express confidence and hope that anxiety can be overcome. (34, 35, 36)

__. _____
   _____

__. _____
   _____

__. _____
   _____

Therapy Homework Planner (Jongsma, Peterson, and McInnis).

5. Assess the client's anxiety by using the Squiggle Wiggle game (Winnicott), in which therapist or parent makes a squiggly line and then the client is asked to make a picture out of the squiggle and tell a story about that picture to help reveal to the therapist and parent what is going on internally with the client.

6. Assign client the task of drawing two or three situations that generally bring on anxious feelings.

7. Conduct psychoanalytical play-therapy sessions (e.g., explore and gain understanding of etiology of unconscious conflicts, fixations, or arrests; interpret resistance or core anxieties) to help client work through to resolution the issues that are the source of his/her anxiety.

8. Utilize child-centered play-therapy approaches (e.g., provide unconditional positive regard, reflect feelings in nonjudgmental manner, display trust in child's capacity to work through issues) to increase client's ability to cope with anxious feelings.

9. Explore distorted cognitive messages that mediate the anxiety response.

10. Help the client develop reality-based, positive cognitive messages that will increase self-confidence in coping with fears and anxieties.

11. Train client to use progressive relaxation or guided imagery techniques to induce calm and decrease the intensity and frequency of feelings of anxiety.

12. Use puppets, felts, or sand tray to enact situations that provoke anxiety in the client. Involve the client in creating such scenarios, and model positive cognitive responses to the situations that bring on anxiety.

13. Play the therapeutic game My Home and Places (Flood) with the client to help identify and talk about divorce, peers, alcohol abuse, or other situations that make client anxious.

14. Instruct client to sing a song or play a musical instrument that reflects his/her anxious feelings; then discuss a time when client felt that anxiety.

15. Ask the client to develop a list of key past and present conflicts within the family and with peers. Process this list with the therapist.

16. Assist client in working toward resolution (using problem solving, assertiveness, acceptance, cognitive

restructuring, etc.) of key past and present conflicts.

17. Use an interpretive interview method in which the therapist interviews the client to help express motivation and feelings. Then assist the client in making a connection between fears or anxieties and unexpressed or unacceptable wishes or "bad" thoughts.

18. Use a narrative approach (White) in which the client writes out the story of his/her anxiety or fear and then acts out the story with the therapist to externalize the issues. Then work with the client to reach a resolution or develop an effective way to cope with the anxiety or fear. See "An Anxious Story" from *Brief Child Therapy Homework Planner* (Jongsma, Peterson, and McInnis).

19. Assign client to complete exercises from *My Own Thoughts and Feelings: A Growth & Recovery Workbook for Children* (Deatin). Process each exercise with therapist to increase client's understanding of and ability to cope with and handle anxious feelings.

20. Conduct sessions with a focus on anxiety-producing situations in which techniques of storytelling, drawing pictures, and viewing photographs are used to as-

sist client in talking about and reducing the level of anxiety or fear.

21. Use a mutual storytelling technique (Gardner) in which the client tells a story about a central character who becomes anxious. The therapist then interprets the story for its underlying meaning and retells the client's story while weaving in healthier adaptations to fear or anxiety and resolution of conflicts.

22. Assist client in identifying behavioral anxiety-coping strategies (e.g., increased social involvement, participation in school-related activities); contract for implementations.

23. Assist client in developing a schedule of physical activity that reduces anxiety.

24. Encourage the parents to seek an experiential camp or weekend experience for the client that will focus on the issues of fears, taking risks, and building confidence. Process the experience with the client and his/her parents.

25. Advocate and encourage overthinking (e.g., help client explore and prepare for every conceivable thing that could possibly happen to him/her in facing a new or anxiety-producing situation). Monitor weekly results and redirect as needed.

26. Educate the client's parents to increase their awareness and understanding of which fears and anxieties are normal for various stages of child development.

27. Assign the client's parents to read books related to child development and parenting, such as *Between Parent and Child* (Ginott) or *How to Talk So Kids Will Talk* (Faber and Mazlish).

28. Refer the client's parents to a parenting class or support group.

29. Work with the parents in family sessions to develop their skills in effectively responding to the client's fears and anxieties with calm confidence rather than fearful reactivity (e.g., parents remind client of a time he/she effectively handled a fearful situation or express confidence in client's ability to face the fearful situation).

30. Conduct family session in which the system is probed to determine the level of fear or anxiety that is present or to bring to the surface underlying conflicts.

31. Work in family sessions to resolve conflicts and to increase the family's level of healthy functioning.

32. Use a structural approach in the family session, adjusting roles to encourage the parents to work less on control-

ling children and more on allowing kids to be kids.

33. Conduct family sessions to develop and offer strategic directions designed to increase the physical freedom of the children and to adjust the parental control of the system.

34. Use a metaphor, fairy tale, or parable to get the client's attention, to evoke possibilities or abilities, to intersperse suggestions, and to implant hope of a good outcome. (See *101 Play Therapy Techniques* by Maruasti.)

35. Assist the client in developing internal structures for self-regulation and the ability to tolerate his/her anxiety by evoking the memory of the therapist as a soothing, encouraging, internal object to help when he/she confronts an anxiety-producing situation/issue. (See *The Therapist on the Inside* by Grigoryen.)

36. Prescribe a Prediction Task (Shuzer) for anxiety management. (Client predicts the night before whether the anxiety will bother him/her the next day. Therapist directs client to be a good detective and bring back key elements that contributed to it being a "good" day so therapist then can reinforce or construct a so-

lution to increasing the frequency of good days.)

—. _____
   _____

—. _____
   _____

—. _____
   _____

DIAGNOSTIC SUGGESTIONS

Axis I: 300.02   Generalized Anxiety Disorder
300.00   Anxiety Disorder NOS
309.24   Attention-Deficit/Hyperactivity Disorder,
Combined Type
309.21   Separation Anxiety Disorder

_____   _____

Axis II: 799.9   Diagnosis Deferred
V71.09   No Diagnosis on Axis II

_____   _____

_____   _____

ATTACHMENT DISORDER

BEHAVIORAL DEFINITIONS

1. Brought into family through adoption after coming from an abusive, neglectful biological family.
2. Consistent pattern of failing to initiate or respond to social interactions in an age-appropriate way (e.g., withdrawing and rejecting behavior toward primary caregivers, a general detached manner toward everyone).
3. Pattern of becoming friendly too quickly and/or showing indiscriminate affection to strangers.
4. Three years old or older and has no significant bond with any caregiver.
5. Resists accepting care from others, usually being very insistent he/she does not need help from anyone.
6. Hoarding or gorging food.
7. Aggressive behaviors toward peers, siblings, and caregivers.
8. Frequent lying without remorse.
9. Stealing petty items without a need for them.
10. By age seven, little or no sign of conscience development is evident (e.g., shows no guilt or remorse when confronted with his/her misbehavior).
11. Excessive clinginess to primary caregiver, becoming emotionally distraught when out of caregiver's immediate presence.
12. Has experienced persistent disregard for his/her emotional and/or physical needs.
13. Has been subjected to frequent changes in primary caregiver.

—. _____

_____

—. _____

_____

—. _____
_____

LONG-TERM GOALS

1. Establishment and maintenance of a bond with primary caregivers.
2. Resolution of all barriers to forming healthy connections with others.
3. Capable of forming warm physical and emotional bonds with parents.
4. Has a desire for and initiates connections with others.
5. Keeps appropriate distance from strangers.
6. Tolerates reasonable absence from presence of parent or primary caregiver without panic.

—. _____
_____
_____

—. _____
_____
_____

—. _____
_____

SHORT-TERM OBJECTIVES

1. Openly express thoughts and feelings. (1, 2, 3)
2. Cooperate with and complete all assessments and testing. (4, 5)
3. Comply with all recommendations of assessments and evaluations. (6)
4. Parents commit to improving the communication and affection within the marriage relationship. (7)

THERAPEUTIC INTERVENTIONS

1. Actively build the level of trust with client through consistent eye contact, active listening, unconditional positive regard, and empathic responses to help promote the open expressions of his/her thoughts and feelings.

2. Conduct a celebrity-style interview with client to elicit information (school likes/dislikes, favorite food, music, best birthday, hopes,

5. Parents acknowledge unresolved grief associated with infertility. (8)

6. Parents verbalize reasonable expectations regarding client's attachment progress. (9, 10)

7. Parent(s) make a verbal commitment to take an active role in client's treatment and in developing skills to work with client and his/her issues. (11, 12, 13)

8. Attend and actively take part in play-therapy sessions. (14, 15, 16)

9. Client and parents verbalize an understanding of the dynamics of attachment and trauma. (17, 18)

10. Parents acknowledge their frustrations regarding living with a detached child and state their commitment to keep trying. (19, 20, 38)

11. Share fears attached to new situations. (21)

12. Identify specific positive talents, traits, and accomplishments about self. (22)

13. Verbalize memories of the past that have shaped current identity and emotional reactions. (23)

14. Parents acknowledge client's history and affirm him/her as an individual. (24)

15. Parent(s) spend one-on-one time with client in active play. (25)

wishes, dreams, "if I had a million dollars," etc.) in order to build relationship and help client learn more about himself/herself.

3. Conduct all sessions in a consistent and predictable manner so that all is clear for the client and he/she can start to take a risk and trust therapist.

4. Conduct or refer parents and client for a psychosocial evaluation to assess strength of parents' marriage, parenting style, stress management/coping strengths, and resolution of infertility issue and to assess client's developmental level, attachment capacity, behavior issues, temperament, and strengths.

5. Conduct or arrange for psychological evaluation to determine level of behavioral functioning, cognitive style, and intelligence.

6. Summarize assessment data and present findings and recommendations to family.

7. Refer parents to a skills-based marital program such as Prep (e.g., *Fighting For Your Marriage* by Markman, Stanley, and Blumberg) to strengthen marital relationship by improving personal responsibility, communication, and conflict resolution.

8. Assess parents' unresolved grief around the issue of

16. Parents increase the frequency of expressing affection verbally and physically toward client. (26, 35)

17. Report an increased ability to trust, giving examples of trust. (27, 28)

18. Recognize and express angry feelings without becoming emotionally out of control. (29, 30)

19. Parents demonstrate firm boundaries on client's anger expression. (31, 32, 33)

20. Family engages in social/recreational activities together. (34, 35)

21. Accept physical contact with family members without withdrawal. (35)

22. Parents use respite care to protect self from burnout. (36, 37, 38)

23. Parents respond calmly but firmly to client's detachment behavior. (39, 40)

24. Parents give client choices and allow him/her to make own decisions. (41)

25. Complete a psychotropic medication evaluation and comply with all recommendations. (42)

26. Take medication as prescribed and report all side effects. (43)

27. Report a completion to the process of mourning losses in life. (44, 45)

__. _____

_____

their infertility; refer for further conjoint or individual treatment if necessary.

9. Process with parents the issue of expectations for client's behavior and adjustment; confront and modify unrealistic expectations regarding their child's emotional attachment progress and foster more realistic expectations considering the client's history.

10. Explore with parents the reality that "strong relationships involve love, understanding, trust, time, money, sharing, giving, stimulating, and inspiring; they seldom come automatically, and love may be last thing on the list rather than the first." (See *Anxiously Awaiting Attachment* by Paddock.)

11. Elicit from parents a firm commitment to be an active part of client's treatment by participating in sessions and being cotherapist in the home.

12. Work with parents in conjoint sessions to frame client's acting-out behaviors as "opportunities to reparent the client." Then strategize with them to come up with specific ways to intervene in the problem behaviors.

13. Train and empower the parents as "cotherapists" (e.g., being patient, showing unconditional positive regard,

___. _____
      _____
___. _____
      _____

setting limits firmly but
without hostility, verbalizing love and expectations
clearly, seeking to understand messages of pain and
fear beneath the acting-out
behavior) in the process of
developing the client's capacity to form healthy
bonds/connections.

14. Utilize the *Theraplay* (Jernberg and Booth) attachment-
based approach, in which
the therapist takes charge
by planning and structuring
each session. Therapist
uses his/her power to entice
the client into relationship
and to keep the focus of
therapy on the relationship,
not on intrapsychic con-
flicts. Also, parents are actively involved and are
trained to be cotherapists.

15. Employ A.C.T. model (Landreth) in play-therapy sessions to *acknowledge*
feelings, *communicate* limits, and *target* acceptable alternatives to acting-out or
aggressive behaviors.

16. Conduct filial therapy (i.e.,
parent involvement in play-
therapy sessions), whereby
client takes the lead in expressing anger and parent
responds empathically to
client's feelings (hurt, fear,
sadness, helplessness) beneath the anger.

17. Provide education to parents and client on the nature of attachment and the

overall affect of trauma on children and families.

18. Teach client that his/her detachment is a normal reaction to painful experiences of rejection, disappointment, broken implied and explicit promises, abandonment, and/or abuse; emphasize client's need to separate current family from past abuse.

19. Suggest parents read *The Difficult Child* (Turecki) or *The Challenging Child* (Greenspan) to provide understanding, ideas, and encouragement in continuing to work with their child.

20. Empathize with parents' frustrations regarding living with a detached child; allow them to share their pain and disappointment while reinforcing their commitment to keep trying.

21. Have client complete "Dixie Overcomes Her Fears" from *Brief Child Therapy Homework Planner* (Jongsma, Peterson, and McInnis) to help client share fears and gain self-acceptance.

22. Assign a self-esteem-building exercise from *SEALS & Plus* (Korb-Khara, Azok, and Leutenberg) to help develop self-knowledge, acceptance, and confidence.

23. Assign parents to help client create a "life book"

that chronicles the client's life to this point in order to give a visual perspective and knowledge of his/her history and identity. A form for "Create a Memory Album" can be found in *Brief Child Therapy Homework Planner* (Jongsma, Peterson, and McInnis).

24. Educate parents on the importance of affirming the client's entire identity (i.e., self, bioparents, adoptive parents), and show them specific ways to reaffirm him/her.

25. Work with parents to have each spend specific time in daily one-on-one active play with client.

26. Encourage parents to provide large, genuine, daily doses of positive verbal reinforcement and physical affection. Monitor and encourage parents to continue this behavior and to identify positive attachment signs when they appear.

27. Have client attend an initiative or adventure-based summer camp to build his/her self-esteem, trust in self and others, conflict-resolution skills, and relationship skills.

28. Conduct a family session in which parents, client, and therapist take part in a trust walk. (One person is blindfolded and led around by a guide through a num-

ber of tasks. Then roles are reversed and process is repeated.) The object is to increase client's awareness of his/her trust issues and to expand his/her sense of trust. Process and repeat at intervals over course of treatment as a way to measure client's progress in building trust.

29. Train client in meditation and focused breathing as self-calming techniques to use when tension, anger, or frustration is building.

30. Read and process with client *Don't Rant and Rave on Wednesday* (Moser) to assist him/her in finding ways to handle angry feelings in a controlled, effective way.

31. Support and encourage parents to maintain firm control, anticipate and stop manipulative behaviors, avoid power struggles, and stick with behavior management techniques.

32. Help parents design preventive safety measures (i.e., supervision and environmental controls) if client's behavior becomes dangerous or frightening.

33. Direct parents to give constant feedback, structure, and repeated emphasis of expectations to client in order to reassure him/her that parents are firmly in control and that they will

not allow client's intense feelings to get out of hand.

34. Encourage parents to engage client and family in many "cohesive shared experiences" (James), such as attending church, singing together at home, attending sports events, building and work projects, and helping others.

35. Assign family the homework exercise of 10 minutes of physical touching twice daily for two weeks (see James in *Handbook for Treatment of Attachment-Trauma Problems in Children*) to decrease client's barriers to others. (This can take the form of snuggling with parent while watching television, feet or shoulder massage, being held in a rocking chair, or physical recreation games.) Process the experience with therapist at the end of two weeks.

36. Assist parents in developing a list of potential respite care providers.

37. Encourage and monitor parents' use of respite care on a scheduled basis to avoid burnout and to keep their energy level high, as well as to build trust with client through the natural process of leaving and returning.

38. Meet with parents conjointly on a regular basis to allow them to vent their concerns and frustrations in dealing

day in and day out with client. Also, provide parents with specific suggestions to handle difficult situations when they feel stuck.

39. Educate parents to understand the psychological meaning and purpose for the client's detachment, and train them to implement appropriate interventions to deal day to day with the behavior in a therapeutic way (e.g., calmly reflecting on client's feelings, ignoring negative behavior as much as is reasonably possible, rewarding any approximation of prosocial behavior, and practicing unconditional positive regard).

40. Monitor parents' implementation of interventions for detachment behavior and evaluate the effectiveness of their interventions. Assist in making adjustments to interventions so that client's intense feelings do not get out of hand.

41. Ask parents to give the client as many choices as is reasonable and possible to impart a sense of control and empowerment to him/her.

42. Arrange for client to have a psychiatric evaluation for medication.

43. Monitor client for compliance, side effects, and overall effectiveness of the medications.

44. Play The Good Mourning Game (Bisenius and Norris) to introduce the idea of loss and the process of mourning to client.

45. Assist, guide, and support the client in working through each stage of the grief process. (See Grief/ Loss Unresolved in this *Planner.*)

__. _____

_____

__. _____

_____

__. _____

_____

DIAGNOSTIC SUGGESTIONS

Axis I:	313.89	Reactive Attachment Disorder of Infancy and Early Childhood
	314.9	Attention Deficit/Hyperactivity Disorder NOS
	296.3x	Major Depressive Disorder, Recurrent
	300.4	Dysthymic Disorder
	309.4	Adjustment Disorder With Mixed Disturbance of Emotions and Conduct
	309.81	Posttraumatic Stress Disorder
	300.3	Obsessive-Compulsive Disorder
	313.81	Oppositional Defiant Disorder
	_____	_____
	_____	_____
Axis II:	799.9	Diagnosis Deferred
	V71.09	No Diagnosis on Axis II
	_____	_____
	_____	_____

ATTENTION-DEFICIT/HYPERACTIVITY DISORDER (ADHD)

BEHAVIORAL DEFINITIONS

1. Short attention span; difficulty sustaining attention on a consistent basis.
2. Susceptibility to distraction by extraneous stimuli.
3. Gives impression that he/she is not listening well.
4. Repeated failure to follow through on instructions or complete school assignments or chores in a timely manner.
5. Poor organizational skills as demonstrated by forgetfulness, inattention to details, and losing things necessary for tasks.
6. Hyperactivity as evidenced by a high energy level, restlessness, difficulty sitting still, or loud or excessive talking.
7. Impulsivity as evidenced by difficulty awaiting turn in group situations, blurting out answers to questions before the questions have been completed, and frequent intrusions into others' personal business.
8. Frequent disruptive, aggressive, or negative attention-seeking behaviors.
9. Tendency to engage in careless or potentially dangerous activities.
10. Difficulty accepting responsibility for actions, projecting blame for problems onto others, and failing to learn from experience.
11. Low self-esteem and poor social skills.

—. _____
_____

—. _____
_____

—. _____
_____

LONG-TERM GOALS

1. Sustain attention and concentration for consistently longer periods of time.
2. Increase the frequency of on-task behaviors.
3. Demonstrate marked improvement in impulse control.
4. Regularly take medication as prescribed to decrease impulsivity, hyperactivity, and distractibility.
5. Parents and/or teachers successfully utilize a reward system, contingency contract, or token economy to reinforce positive behaviors and deter negative behaviors.
6. Parents set firm, consistent limits and maintain appropriate parent-child boundaries.
7. Improve self-esteem.
8. Develop positive social skills to help maintain lasting peer friendships.

—. _____

_____

—. _____

_____

—. _____

_____

SHORT-TERM OBJECTIVES

1. Complete psychological testing to confirm the diagnosis of ADHD. (1, 3)

2. Complete psychological testing to rule out emotional factors or learning disabilities as the basis for maladaptive behaviors. (2, 3)

3. Take prescribed medication as directed by the physician. (4, 5)

4. Increase frequency of completion of school assign-

THERAPEUTIC INTERVENTIONS

1. Arrange for psychological testing to confirm the presence of ADHD in the client.

2. Arrange for psychological testing to rule out emotional factors or learning disabilities as the basis for the client's maladaptive behavior.

3. Give feedback to the client and his/her family regarding psychological testing results.

4. Arrange for a medication evaluation for the client.

ments, chores, and household responsibilities.
(7, 8, 9, 11, 50)

5. Parents develop and utilize an organized system to keep track of school assignments, chores, and household responsibilities.
(7, 8, 12)

6. Establish a routine schedule to help complete homework, chores, and household responsibilities.
(10, 13, 14, 19, 21)

7. Parents and teachers reduce extraneous stimuli as much as possible when giving directions to the client.
(6, 10, 11, 16)

8. The parents maintain communication with the school to increase the client's compliance with completion of school assignments. (9, 15)

9. Teachers utilize a *listening buddy* who sits next to the client in the classroom to quietly repeat instructions as needed. (10, 11)

10. Teachers schedule breaks between intensive instructional periods and alternate complex activities with less stressful activities to sustain the client's interest and attention. (10, 11)

11. Postpone recreational activities (e.g., playing basketball or video games with friends) until after completing homework or chores.
(17, 19, 20, 21)

5. Monitor the client for compliance, side effects, and overall effectiveness of the medication. Consult with the prescribing physician at regular intervals.

6. Educate the client's parents and siblings about the symptoms of ADHD.

7. Assist the parents in developing and implementing an organizational system to increase the client's on-task behaviors and completion of school assignments, chores, or household responsibilities (e.g., using calendars, charts, notebooks, and class syllabi).

8. Assist the parents in developing a routine schedule to increase the client's compliance with school, chores, or household responsibilities.

9. Encourage the parents and teachers to maintain regular communication about the client's academic, behavioral, emotional, and social progress.

10. Teach the client more effective study skills (e.g., clearing away distractions, studying in quiet places, scheduling breaks in studying).

11. Consult with client's teachers to implement strategies to improve school performance (e.g., sitting in front row during class, using a prearranged signal to redirect the client back to task,

12. Teachers reinforce client's on-task behaviors, completion of school assignments, and good impulse control. (18, 22, 24)

13. Decrease motor activity as evidenced by the ability to sit still for longer periods of time. (5, 22, 38, 51)

14. Parents set firm limits and use natural, logical consequences to deter the client's impulsive behaviors. (19, 20, 23, 25)

15. Parents identify and use a variety of effective reinforcers to increase positive behaviors. (18, 22, 23, 24)

16. Parents increase praise and positive verbalizations toward the client. (18, 22, 36, 37, 42)

17. Client and his/her parents comply with the implementation of a reward system, contingency contract, or token economy. (22, 23, 24, 25)

18. Reduce the frequency and severity of temper outbursts, acting out, and aggressive behaviors. (17, 26, 28, 29, 49)

19. Express anger through respectful verbalizations and healthy physical outlets. (17, 27, 49, 51)

20. Increase verbalizations of acceptance of responsibility for misbehavior. (30, 31, 32)

21. Identify and verbalize how annoying or impulsive be-

scheduling breaks from tasks, providing frequent feedback, calling on the client often, arranging for a listening buddy).

12. Assign the parents to read *The ADD Hyperactivity Handbook for Schools* (Parker) to improve the client's school performance and behavior; process the reading with therapist.

13. Teach the client more effective test-taking strategies (e.g., reviewing material regularly, reading directions twice, rechecking work).

14. Assign the client to read *13 Steps to Better Grades* (Silverman) to improve organizational and study skills.

15. Encourage parents and teachers to employ "Getting It Done" program in *Brief Child Therapy Homework Planner* (Jongsma, Peterson, and McInnis) to help client complete school and homework assignments. Utilize school contract and reward system to reinforce completion of assignments.

16. Instruct the parents on how to give proper directions (e.g., gain the client's attention, make one request at a time, clear away distractions, repeat instructions, and obtain frequent feedback from the client).

17. Teach the client mediational and self-control strategies (e.g., "stop, look,

haviors negatively impact others. (17, 31, 32, 45, 46)

22. Identify and implement effective problem-solving strategies. (26, 27, 34, 35)

23. Identify stressors or painful emotions that trigger increase in hyperactivity and impulsivity. (33, 34, 35)

24. Increase frequency of positive interactions with parents. (22, 25, 36, 37)

25. Recognize appropriate and inappropriate ways to elicit attention from family members, authority figures, or peers. (30, 31, 40, 43, 46)

26. Increase frequency of socially appropriate behaviors with siblings and peers. (39, 40, 41, 43, 45)

27. Decrease the frequency of arguments and physical fights with siblings. (27, 28, 39, 40, 44)

28. Increase the frequency of positive self-statements. (36, 43, 47)

29. Increase participation in extracurricular activities or positive peer group activities. (40, 41, 43)

30. Increase verbalizations of empathy and concern for other people. (32, 34, 44, 45, 48)

31. Express feelings through artwork, mutual story-telling, or therapeutic games. (45, 47, 48)

listen, and think") to delay gratification and inhibit impulses.

18. Identify a variety of positive reinforcers or rewards to maintain the client's interest or motivation.

19. Conduct family therapy sessions to assist the parents in establishing clearly identified rules and boundaries.

20. Establish clear rules for the client at home and school; ask him/her to repeat the rules to demonstrate an understanding of the expectations.

21. Assist parents in increasing structure to help the client learn to delay gratification for longer-term goals (e.g., completing homework or chores before playing basketball).

22. Design a reward system and/or contingency contract to reinforce the client's desired positive behaviors and deter impulsive behaviors.

23. Encourage the parents to use natural, logical consequences for the client's disruptive and negative attention-seeking behaviors.

24. Design and implement a token economy to improve the client's academic performance, social skills, and impulse control.

25. Assign the client's parents to read *Effective Discipline for Children 2–12* (Phelan),

32. Increase brain-wave control, which results in improved attention span and decreased impulsivity and hyperactivity. (51, 52, 53)

__. _____
   _____
__. _____
   _____
__. _____
   _____

Your Hyperactive Child (Ingersoll), or *Taking Charge of ADHD* (Burkley); process the reading with the therapist.

26. Teach the client effective problem-solving skills (e.g., identifying the problem, brainstorming alternative solutions, selecting an option, implementing a course of action, and evaluating).

27. Use *Let's Work It Out: A Conflict Resolution Tool Kit* (Shore, available from Childswork/Childsplay, LLC) in session to teach client effective problem-solving skills.

28. Assign reading of *The Very Angry Day That Amy Didn't Have* (Shapiro) or *Sometimes I Like to Fight, but I Don't Do It Much Anymore* (Shapiro) to teach client effective ways to control anger.

29. Utilize the therapeutic game Stop, Relax & Think (Shapiro, available from Childswork/Childsplay, LLC) to assist the client in developing self-control.

30. Teach effective communication and assertiveness skills to express feelings in a controlled fashion and meet his/her needs through more constructive actions.

31. Firmly confront client's impulsive behaviors, pointing out consequences for himself/herself and others.

32. Confront statements in which client blames others for his/her annoying or impulsive behaviors and fails to accept responsibility for his/her actions.

33. Help client make a connection between unpleasant or painful emotions and increased impulsive or disruptive behaviors.

34. Explore and identify stressful events or factors that contribute to an increase in impulsivity, hyperactivity, and distractibility. Help client and parents develop positive coping strategies (e.g., "stop, look, listen, and think," relaxation techniques, and positive self-talk) to manage stress more effectively.

35. Assess periods of time when client demonstrated good impulse control and engaged in fewer disruptive behaviors; process client's responses and reinforce positive coping mechanisms that he/she used to deter impulsive or disruptive behaviors.

36. Instruct parent(s) to observe and record three to five positive behaviors by client in between therapy sessions. Reinforce positive behaviors and encourage client to continue to exhibit these behaviors.

37. Encourage parent(s) to spend 15 to 20 minutes

daily of one-on-one time with client to create closer parent-child bond. Allow client to take lead in selecting activity or task.

38. Assign the client to read *Putting on the Brakes* (Quinn and Stern) or *Sometimes I Drive My Mom Crazy, but I Know She's Crazy About Me* (Shapiro); process the reading with the therapist.

39. Identify and reinforce positive behaviors to assist the client in establishing and maintaining friendships.

40. Encourage the client to participate in extracurricular or positive peer group activities to improve his/her social skills.

41. Arrange for the client to attend group therapy to build social skills.

42. Encourage the client's parents to participate in an ADHD support group.

43. Give homework assignment where client identifies 5 to 10 strengths or interests; review list in following session and encourage client to utilize strengths or interests to establish friendships.

44. Assign the task of showing empathy, kindness, or sensitivity to the needs of others (e.g., allowing sibling or peer to take first turn in video game, helping with school fund-raiser).

45. Utilize the therapeutic game The Helping, Sharing, and Caring Game (Gardner) to help develop positive social skills.

46. Utilize "Social Skills Exercise" in *Brief Child Therapy Homework Planner* (Jongsma, Peterson, and McInnis) to teach client self-monitoring techniques to improve social skills.

47. Instruct client to create drawing(s) reflecting the positive and negative aspects of his/her high energy level; process content of drawing(s) with therapist.

48. Use puppets, dolls, or stuffed animals to create a story that models positive ways to utilize energy and gain attention from peers; then ask client to create story with similar characters or themes.

49. Use the Angry Tower technique (Saxe) to help client express anger in a controlled, nonharmful manner. Build tower out of plastic containers or blocks; place small object on top of tower (representing object of anger); instruct client to throw small fabric ball at tower while verbalizing feelings of anger.

50. Encourage the client to use self-monitoring checklists to improve attention, academic performance, and social skills.

51. Use brain-wave biofeedback techniques to improve the client's attention span, impulse control, and ability to relax.

52. Encourage the client to transfer the biofeedback training skills of relaxation and cognitive focusing to everyday situations (e.g., classroom and home).

53. Use Heartbeat Audiotapes (Lamb, available from Childswork/Childsplay, LLC) that play background music at 60 beats per minute to help calm client and improve concentration while studying or learning new material.

—. _____
   _____

—. _____
   _____

—. _____
   _____

DIAGNOSTIC SUGGESTIONS

Axis I:	314.01	Attention-Deficit/Hyperactivity Disorder, Combined Type
	314.00	Attention-Deficit/Hyperactivity Disorder, Predominantly Inattentive Type
	314.01	Attention-Deficit/Hyperactivity Disorder, Predominantly Hyperactive-Impulsive Type
	314.9	Attention-Deficit/Hyperactivity Disorder NOS
	312.8	Conduct Disorder/Childhood-Onset Type
	313.81	Oppositional Defiant Disorder

	312.9	Disruptive Behavior Disorder NOS
	296.xx	Bipolar I Disorder
	_____	_____
	_____	_____
Axis II:	799.9	Diagnosis Deferred
	V71.09	No Diagnosis on Axis II
	_____	_____
	_____	_____

AUTISM/PERVASIVE DEVELOPMENTAL DISORDER

BEHAVIORAL DEFINITIONS

1. Pervasive lack of interest in or responsiveness to other people.
2. Chronic failure to develop social relationships appropriate to the development level.
3. Lack of spontaneity and emotional or social reciprocity.
4. Significant delays in or total lack of spoken-language development.
5. Impairment in sustaining or initiating conversation.
6. Oddities in speech and language as manifested by echolalia, pronominal reversal, or metaphorical language.
7. Inflexible adherence to repetition of nonfunctional rituals or stereotyped motor mannerisms.
8. Persistent preoccupation with objects, parts of objects, or restricted areas of interest.
9. Marked impairment or extreme variability in intellectual and cognitive functioning.
10. Extreme resistance or overreaction to minor changes in routines or environment.
11. Emotional construction or blunted affect.
12. Recurrent pattern of self-abusive behaviors (e.g., head banging, biting, or burning himself/herself.

__. _____

   _____

__. _____

   _____

__. _____

   _____

LONG-TERM GOALS

1. Develop basic language skills and the ability to simply communicate with others.
2. Establish and maintain a basic emotional bond with primary attachment figures.
3. Achieve the educational, behavioral, and social goals identified on the Individualized Educational Plan (IEP).
4. Family members develop acceptance of the client's overall capabilities and place realistic expectations on his/her behavior.
5. Engage in reciprocal and cooperative interactions with others on a regular basis.
6. Stabilize mood and tolerate changes in routine or environment.
7. Eliminate all self-abusive behaviors.
8. Attain and maintain the highest realistic level of independent functioning.

—. _____
   _____
—. _____
   _____
—. _____
   _____

SHORT-TERM OBJECTIVES

1. Complete an intellectual and cognitive evaluation. (1, 4)
2. Complete a speech/language evaluation. (2, 4)
3. Complete a neurological evaluation and/or neuropsychological testing. (3, 4)
4. Participate in a psychiatric evaluation regarding the need for psychotropic medication. (4, 5)
5. Comply fully with the recommendations offered by

THERAPEUTIC INTERVENTIONS

1. Arrange for an intellectual and cognitive assessment to gain greater insights into the client's strengths and weaknesses.
2. Refer the client for speech/language evaluation.
3. Arrange for neurological evaluation or neuropsychological testing of the client to rule out organic factors.
4. Consult with specialists who performed evaluation and then provide feedback

the assessment(s) and Individualized Educational Planning Committee (IEPC). (6, 7)

6. Comply with the move to an appropriate classroom setting. (6, 7)

7. Comply with the move to an appropriate alternative residential setting. (8)

8. Attend speech and language therapy sessions. (9)

9. Increase the frequency of appropriate spontaneous verbalizations toward the therapist. (9, 10, 11)

10. Increase frequency of communication or interactions with others. (9, 13)

11. Decrease the oddities or peculiarities in speech and language. (9, 11, 12, 13, 14)

12. Decrease the frequency and severity of temper outbursts and erratic shifts in mood. (14, 15, 16, 39)

13. Decrease the frequency and severity of self-abusive or aggressive behaviors. (14, 17, 18, 39)

14. Parents actively participate in treatment of client's speech and behavior. (4, 7, 13, 15, 18, 26)

15. Participate in play or work activity with the parents, peers, or sibling(s) for 20 minutes each day. (19, 20, 21)

to the client's parents regarding all evaluation and assessment findings.

5. Arrange for psychiatric evaluation of the client.

6. Attend an IEPC review to establish the client's eligibility for special education services, to update and revise educational interventions, and to establish new behavioral and educational goals.

7. Consult with the parents, teachers, and other appropriate school officials about designing effective learning programs, classroom assignments, or interventions that build on the client's strengths and compensate for weaknesses.

8. Consult with parents, school officials, and mental health professionals about the need to place the client in an alternative residential setting (e.g., foster care, group home, or residential program).

9. Refer the client to speech/language pathologist to improve his/her speech and language abilities.

10. Actively build a level of trust with the client through consistent eye contact, frequent attention and interest, unconditional positive regard, and warm acceptance to facilitate increased communication.

16. Parents express reasonable expectations for client's future. (22)

17. Parents utilize respite care to reduce stress related to being caregiver. (23)

18. Parents participate in a support group. (24, 25)

19. Demonstrate essential self-care and independent living skills. (26, 27, 28, 29, 34)

20. Parents report feeling a closer bond with the client. (30, 31, 32)

21. Channel strengths or areas of interest into a positive, constructive activity. (33)

22. Identify and express basic emotions. (34, 35, 36)

23. Increase frequency of social contacts with peers. (37, 38, 39)

24. Complete vision, hearing, or medical examination. (40, 41)

__. _____
   _____

__. _____
   _____

__. _____
   _____

11. Employ frequent use of praise and positive reinforcement to increase the client's initiation of verbalizations as well as acknowledgment and responsiveness to others' verbalizations.

12. In conjunction with speech therapist, design and implement a response-shaping program using positive reinforcement principles to facilitate the client's language development.

13. Provide the parents with encouragement, support, and reinforcement or modeling methods to foster the client's language development.

14. Teach the parents behavioral management techniques (e.g., time-out, response cost, overcorrection, removal of privileges) to decrease the client's idiosyncratic speech, excessive self-stimulation, temper outbursts, and self-abusive behaviors.

15. Design a token economy for use in the home, classroom, or residential program to improve the client's social skills, anger management, impulse control, and speech/language abilities.

16. Develop a reward system or contingency contract to improve the client's social skills and anger control.

17. Use aversive therapy techniques to stop or limit the

client's self-abusive or self-stimulating behaviors.

18. Counsel the parents to develop interventions to manage the client's self-abusive behaviors, including positive reinforcement, response cost, and, if necessary, physical restraint.

19. Encourage family members to regularly include the client in structured work or play activities for 20 minutes each day.

20. Assign the client and his/her parents a task (e.g., swimming, riding a bike) that will help build trust and mutual dependence.

21. Encourage detached parent(s) to increase their involvement in the client's daily life, leisure activities, or schoolwork.

22. Educate the client's parents and family members about the maturation process in individuals with autism or pervasive developmental disorders and the challenges that this process presents.

23. Refer parents to, and encourage them to use, respite care on a periodic basis.

24. Refer the client's parents to a support group.

25. Direct parents to join the Autism Society of America to expand their social network, to gain additional

knowledge of the disorder, and to give them support and encouragement.

26. Counsel the parents about teaching the client essential self-care skills (e.g., combing hair, bathing, brushing teeth).

27. Monitor and provide frequent feedback to the client regarding progress toward developing self-care skills.

28. Use operant conditioning principles and response-shaping techniques to help client develop self-help skills (e.g., dressing self, making bed, fixing sandwich) and improving personal hygiene.

29. Encourage parents to use "Activities of Daily Living Program" in *Brief Child Therapy Homework Planner* (Jongsma, Peterson, and McInnis) to improve client's personal hygiene and self-help skills.

30. Instruct parents to sing songs (e.g., nursery rhymes, lullabies, popular hits, songs related to client's interests) with client to help establish closer parent-child bond and increase verbalizations in home environment.

31. To facilitate closer parent-child bond, use filial play-therapy approaches (i.e., parental involvement in session) with higher-functioning client to increase parents' awareness

of client's thoughts, feelings, and needs.

32. Conduct family therapy sessions to provide parents and siblings with the opportunity to share and work through their feelings pertaining to client's autism or pervasive developmental disorder.

33. Redirect the client's preoccupation with a single object or restricted area of interest to turn it into a productive activity (e.g., learning to tune instruments or using interest with numbers to learn how to budget allowance money).

34. Instruct parents to observe positive and/or adaptive behaviors by client in between therapy sessions. Encourage parents to praise and reward these behaviors.

35. Utilize art therapy (e.g., drawing, painting, sculpting) with higher-functioning client to help him/her express basic needs or emotions and facilitate closer relationship with parents, caretakers, or therapist.

36. Use Feelings Poster (available from Childswork/ Childsplay, LLC) to help higher-functioning client identify and express basic emotions.

37. Consult with parents and teachers about increasing frequency of client's social contacts with peers (work-

ing with student aide in class, attending Sunday school, participating in Special Olympics).

38. Refer the client to a summer camp program to foster social contacts.

39. Employ applied behavior analysis in home, school, or residential setting to alter maladaptive behaviors. First, define and operationalize target behaviors. Next, select antecedents and consequences for specific behaviors. Then observe and record client's response to reinforcement interventions. Finally, analyze data to assess treatment effectiveness.

40. Refer client in early childhood years for vision and/or hearing examination to rule out vision or hearing problems that may be interfering with his/her social and speech/language development.

41. Refer client for medical examination to rule out health problems that may be interfering with speech/language development.

__. _____

_____

__. _____

_____

__. _____

_____

DIAGNOSTIC SUGGESTIONS

Axis I:

299.00	Autistic Disorder
299.80	Pervasive Developmental Disorder NOS
299.80	Rett's Disorder
299.10	Childhood Disintegrative Disorder
299.80	Asperger's Disorder
313.89	Reactive Attachment Disorder of Infancy or Early Childhood
307.3	Stereotypic Movement Disorder
295.xx	Schizophrenia
_____	_____

Axis II:

317	Mild Mental Retardation
319	Mental Retardation, Severity Unspecified
799.9	Diagnosis Deferred
V71.09	No Diagnosis on Axis II
_____	_____
_____	_____

BLENDED FAMILY

BEHAVIORAL DEFINITIONS

1. Children from a previous union of respective parents are united into a single family unit resulting in interpersonal conflict, anger, and frustration.
2. Resistance and defiance on part of child toward new stepparent.
3. Open conflict between siblings from different parents now residing in the same family system.
4. Defiance, either overt or covert in nature, from one or several siblings toward the stepparent.
5. Verbal threats to the biological parent that client will go live with other parent, report abuse, and so on.
6. Interference from ex-spouse in the daily life of the new system.
7. Anxiety and concern by both new partners regarding bringing their two families together.
8. No clear lines of communication or responsibilities assigned within the blended family, making for confusion, frustration, and unhappiness.
9. Internal conflicts regarding loyalty to the noncustodial parent results in distance from the stepparent.

__. _____
_____

__. _____
_____

__. _____
_____

LONG-TERM GOALS

1. Achieve a reasonable level of family connectedness and harmony whereby members support, help, and are concerned for each other.
2. Become an integrated blended family system that is functional and bonded to each other.
3. Attain a level of peaceful coexistence whereby daily issues can be negotiated without becoming ongoing unresolved conflicts.
4. Accept stepparent and/or stepsiblings and treat them with respect, kindness, and cordiality.
5. Establish a new family identity in which each member feels he/she belongs and is valued.
6. Accept the new blended family system as not inferior to the nuclear family, just different.
7. Establish a strong bond between the couple as a parenting team that is free from triangulation and able to stabilize the family.

—. _____

_____

—. _____

_____

—. _____

_____

SHORT-TERM OBJECTIVES

1. Each family member openly share thoughts and feelings regarding the blended family. (1)
2. Attend and freely participate in play-therapy sessions with therapist. (2, 3, 4, 5)
3. Attend and actively take part in family or sibling group sessions. (2, 6, 7, 9)
4. Family members verbalize realistic expectations and

THERAPEUTIC INTERVENTIONS

1. Within family therapy sessions, actively build the level of trust with each family member through consistent eye contact, active listening, unconditional positive regard, and acceptance to allow each to identify and express openly his/her thoughts and feelings regarding the blended family.
2. In a family session, use a set of markers and large sheet of drawing paper for

rejection of myths regarding stepfamilies. (7, 8, 9)

5. Identify losses/changes in each of their lives. (6, 10, 11)

6. Family members demonstrate increased skills in recognizing and expressing feelings. (12, 13, 14, 15, 16)

7. Family members verbalize expanded knowledge of stepfamilies. (10, 17, 18, 19)

8. Family members demonstrate increased negotiating skills. (20, 21)

9. Family members report a reduced level of tension between all members. (20, 22, 23, 24)

10. Family members report increased trust of each other. (25, 26, 43)

11. Each parent take primary role of disciplining own children. (27)

12. Parents attend a stepparenting didactic group to increase parenting skills. (28)

13. Family members attend weekly family meetings in the home to express feelings. (29)

14. Parents create and institute new family rituals. (30, 31, 32)

15. Parents identify and eliminate triangulation within the system. (17, 33, 34)

16. Parents report a strengthening of marital bond. (35, 36, 37)

the following exercise: Therapist begins a drawing by making a scribble line on the paper, then has each family member add to the line using a colored marker of his/her choice. When drawing is complete, family can be given the choice to either each interpret the drawing or to develop a mutual story based on the drawing (see Lowe in *101 Favorite Play Therapy Techniques*).

3. Use child-centered playtherapy approaches (e.g., providing unconditional positive regard, reflecting feelings in nonjudgmental manner, displaying trust in child's capacity to resolve issues) to assist client in adjusting to changes, grieving losses, and cooperating with new stepfamily.

4. Conduct individual playtherapy sessions to provide the client the opportunity to express feelings about losses and changes in his/her life.

5. Seize opportunities in play therapy (especially when client is playing with groups of animals, army figures, dollhouse, puppets, etc.), as well as in sibling and family sessions, to emphasize the need for everyone within the family to respect and cooperate with each other.

17. Family members report an increased sense of loyalty and connectedness. (38, 39, 40, 41)

18. Parents spend one-on-one time with each child. (42)

19. Report a development of bonding between each member. (3, 21, 41, 42, 43)

—. _____
_____

—. _____
_____

—. _____
_____

6. Conduct family, sibling, and marital sessions to address the issues of loss, conflict negotiation, parenting, stepfamily psychoeducation, joining, rituals, and relationship building.

7. In a family session, ask each member to list their expectations for the new family. Members will share and process their lists with the whole family and therapist.

8. Remind family members that "instant love" of new family members is a myth. It is unrealistic to expect children to immediately like (much less to love) the partner who is serving in the new-parent role.

9. Help family members accept the position that siblings from different biological families need not like or love one another, but that they should be mutually respectful and kind.

10. Instruct family to read *Changing Families: An Interactive Guide for Kids and Grownups* (Fassler, Lash, and Ives) to help them identify the changes and give them ways to adjust and thrive.

11. Assign sibling members in session to complete a list of losses and changes each has experienced over the last year and then for all years. Give empathic confirmation while they share

the list in session and help them see the similarities of their experiences to those of siblings.

12. Conduct the following exercise in a sibling session: Place several phone books and/or Sunday papers in center of room and instruct clients to tear the paper into small pieces and throw the shredded paper into the air. The only two rules are that the paper must be thrown *up,* not at anyone, and that the participants must clean up afterward. Process experience around releasing energy and emotion. Give positive feedback for follow-through and cooperation in cleaning up (see Daves in *101 Favorite Play Therapy Techniques*).

13. Have family or siblings play The Ungame (available from The Ungame Company) or Talking, Feeling, Doing game (available from Childswork/Childsplay, LLC) to promote each family member's awareness of self and his/her feelings.

14. Educate the family on identifying, labeling, and expressing feelings appropriately.

15. Use a feelings chart, feelings felt board, or feelings cards to help the client and/or family members learn to identify and express their feelings.

16. In a family session, help the family practice identifying and expressing feelings by doing a feelings exercise (e.g., "I feel sad when _____," "I feel excited when _____"). Therapist should affirm and acknowledge each member as they share during the exercise.

17. Have parents or teens read all or part of *Stepfamily Realities* (Newman) or *Stepfamilies Stepping Ahead* (Stepfamily Association of America) to expand their knowledge of stepfamilies and their development.

18. Refer parents to the Stepfamily Association of America (1-800-735-0329 to obtain additional information and resources on stepfamilies.

19. Assign parents to read *How to Win as a Stepfamily* (Visher and Visher), and process key concepts they gathered from the reading.

20. Train family members in building negotiating skills (e.g., identifying problems, brainstorming solutions, evaluating pros and cons, compromising, agreeing on a solution, making an implementation plan) and have them practice these skills on issues that present in family sessions.

21. Assign siblings to complete the exercise "Negotiating a Peace Treaty" from *Brief*

Child Therapy Homework Planner (Jongsma, Peterson, and McInnis) to specify their conflicts and suggest solutions.

22. Inject humor whenever appropriate in family or sibling sessions to decrease tensions/conflict and to model balance and perspective. Give positive feedback to members who create appropriate humor.

23. Hold a family sibling session in which each child completes and shares results of the exercise "Cloning the Perfect Sibling" from *Brief Child Therapy Homework Planner* (Jongsma, Peterson, and McInnis) to focus on developing an appreciation of each sibling's differences/uniqueness.

24. In a brief, solution-focused intervention, reframe or normalize the conflictual situation to show clients that it's a stage the family needs to get through. Identify next stage as the coming-together stage, and talk about when they might be ready to move there and how they could begin (see O'Hanlon and Beadle in *A Guide to Possibility Land*).

25. Read and process with the family the story of *Stone Soup* (Brown), focusing on the issues of risk, mistrust, and cooperation.

26. In a family session, read Dr. Seuss's *The Sneetches* to show members the folly of top-dog–underdog one-upmanship, and insider-outsider attitudes.

27. Encourage each parent to take the primary role in disciplining his/her own children, and have each refrain from all negative references to ex-spouses.

28. Refer parents to a parenting group for stepparents.

29. Assist parents in implementing a once-a-week family meeting in which issues can be raised and resolved and members encouraged to share their thoughts, complaints, and compliments.

30. Work with parents to create and implement daily rituals (e.g., mealtimes, bedtime stories, household chores, time alone with parents, and times together) in order to give structure and connection to the system.

31. Conduct a family session in which rituals from both former families are examined. Then work with family to retain the rituals that are appropriate and will work in the new system and combine them with new rituals.

32. Give the family the assignment to create birthday rituals for the new blended unit.

33. Educate parents on patterns of interactions within families, focusing on the pattern of triangulation and its dysfunctional aspects.

34. Create with parents a genogram that denotes the family's pattern of interaction, giving special attention to triangular interactions. Assist parents in identifying their triangles and in designing ways to break, dissolve, or end them.

35. Refer couple to skills-based marital therapy based on strengthening avenues of responsibilities, communication, and conflict resolution (see Prep, *Fighting For Your Marriage* by Markman, Stanley, and Blumberg).

36. Work with dyad in conjoint sessions to deal with issues of having time away alone, privacy, and individual space; develop specific ways for these things to regularly occur.

37. Hold conjoint session(s) with couple to process the issue of showing affection toward each other. Help the couple develop appropriate boundaries and ways of showing affection that do not give rise to unnecessary anger in their children.

38. Conduct family sessions in which a genogram is developed for the entire new fam-

ily system to show how everyone is interconnected.

39. Refer family to an initiatives camp weekend to increase cooperation, conflict resolution, and sense of trust. Process the experiences with family in next family session.

40. In a family session, assign the family to design on poster board a coat of arms for the family that reflects where they came from and where they are now. Process this experience when completed and have family display it in their home.

41. Complete and process with siblings a cost-benefit analysis (see Burns in *Ten Days to Self-Esteem*) to evaluate the pluses and minuses of becoming a family or resisting the process. Use positive outcome to move beyond resistance to begin the process of joining.

42. Work with parents to build into each of their schedules one-on-one time with each child and stepchild in order to give them undivided attention and to build/maintain relationships.

43. Emphasize and model in family, sibling, and couple sessions the need for the family to build their new relationships slowly, allowing everyone time and space to adjust and develop

a level of trust with each
other.

—. _____

_____

—. _____

_____

—. _____

_____

DIAGNOSTIC SUGGESTIONS

Axis I: 309.0   Adjustment Disorder With Depressed Mood
309.3   Adjustment Disorder With Disturbance of
Conduct
309.24 Adjustment Disorder With Anxiety
309.81 Posttraumatic Stress Disorder
300.4   Dysthymic Disorder
V62.81 Relational Problem NOS

_____   _____

_____   _____

Axis II: 799.9   Diagnosis Deferred
V71.09 No Diagnosis on Axis II

_____   _____

_____   _____

CONDUCT DISORDER/DELINQUENCY

BEHAVIORAL DEFINITIONS

1. Persistent refusal to comply with rules or expectations in the home, school, or community.
2. Excessive fighting, intimidation of others, cruelty or violence toward people or animals, and destruction of property.
3. History of stealing at home, at school, or in the community.
4. School adjustment characterized by disrespectful attitude toward authority figures, frequent disruptive behaviors, and detentions or suspensions for misbehavior.
5. Repeated conflict with authority figures at home, at school, or in the community.
6. Impulsivity as manifested by poor judgment, taking inappropriate risks, and failing to stop and think about consequences of actions.
7. Numerous attempts to deceive others through lying, conning, or manipulating.
8. Consistent failure to accept responsibility for misbehavior accompanied by a pattern of blaming others.
9. Little or no remorse for misbehavior.
10. Lack of sensitivity to the thoughts, feelings, and needs of other people.

—. _____
_____
—. _____
_____
—. _____
_____

LONG-TERM GOALS

1. Demonstrate increased honesty, compliance with rules, sensitivity to the feelings and rights of others, control over impulses, and acceptance of responsibility for his/her behavior.
2. Comply with rules and expectations in the home, school, and community on a consistent basis.
3. Eliminate all illegal and antisocial behaviors.
4. Terminate all acts of violence or cruelty toward people or animals and the destruction of property.
5. Express anger in a controlled, respectful manner on a consistent basis.
6. Demonstrate marked improvement in impulse control.
7. Resolve the core conflicts that contribute to the emergence of conduct problems.
8. Parents establish and maintain appropriate parent-child boundaries, setting firm, consistent limits when the client acts out in an aggressive or rebellious manner.
9. Demonstrate empathy, concern, and sensitivity for the thoughts, feelings, and needs of others on a regular basis.

__. _____

_____

_____

__. _____

_____

_____

__. _____

_____

SHORT-TERM OBJECTIVES

1. Complete psychological testing. (1, 3)
2. Complete a psychoeducational evaluation. (2, 3)
3. Cooperate with the recommendations resulting from the psychological assessments and the requirements mandated by the

THERAPEUTIC INTERVENTIONS

1. Arrange for psychological testing of the client to assess whether emotional factors or ADHD are contributing to his/her impulsivity and acting-out behaviors.
2. Arrange for a psychoeducational evaluation of the client to rule out the pres-

criminal justice system. (3, 4, 5, 6)

4. Move to an appropriate alternative setting to manage aggressive and rebellious behaviors. (4, 5, 6)

5. Recognize and verbalize how feelings are connected to misbehavior. (8, 9, 47, 49)

6. Increase the number of statements that reflect the acceptance of responsibility for misbehavior. (10, 11, 12, 49)

7. Decrease the frequency of verbalizations that project the blame for the problems onto other people. (10, 11, 12)

8. Express anger through appropriate verbalization and healthy physical outlets. (13, 14, 15, 16, 17)

9. Reduce the frequency and severity of aggressive, destructive, and antisocial behaviors. (7, 10, 21, 22)

10. Increase compliance with rules at home and school. (7, 19, 21, 22, 24)

11. Decrease frequency of lying, conning, and manipulating others. (10, 11, 21, 38)

12. Postpone recreational activity (e.g., playing basketball with friends) until after completing homework or chores. (14, 19, 20)

13. Parents establish appropriate boundaries, develop clear rules, and follow

ence of a learning disability that may be contributing to the impulsivity and acting-out behaviors in the school setting.

3. Provide feedback to the client, his/her parents, school officials, or criminal justice officials regarding psychological and/or psychoeducational assessments.

4. Consult with criminal justice officials about the appropriate consequences for the client's antisocial behaviors (e.g., paying restitution, performing community service, serving probation).

5. Consult with parents, school officials, and criminal justice officials about the need to place the client in an alternative setting (e.g., foster home, group home, or residential program).

6. Encourage and challenge the parents not to protect the client from the legal consequences of his/her antisocial behaviors.

7. Assist the client's parents in establishing clearly defined rules, boundaries, and consequences for misbehavior.

8. Actively build the level of trust with the client through consistent eye contact, active listening, unconditional positive regard, and warm acceptance to help increase his/her ability to identify and express feelings.

through consistently with consequences for misbehavior. (7, 19, 20, 24)

14. Client and parents agree to and follow through with the implementation of a reward system, contingency contract, or token economy. (18, 21, 22, 23)

15. Parents increase the frequency of praise and positive reinforcement to the client. (20, 21, 22, 40)

16. Increase the time spent with the uninvolved or detached parent(s) in leisure, school, or household activities. (25, 26, 27, 28)

17. Parents verbalize appropriate boundaries for discipline to prevent further occurrences of abuse and to ensure the safety of the client and his/her siblings. (25, 29, 30, 31)

18. Verbalize an understanding of how current acting-out and aggressive behaviors are associated with past neglect, abuse, separation, or abandonment. (29, 32, 33, 34, 35)

19. Identify and verbally express feelings associated with past neglect, abuse, separation, or abandonment. (32, 33, 34, 35)

20. Increase participation in extracurricular activities or positive peer group activities. (36, 39, 40, 41)

9. Assist the client in making a connection between feelings and reactive behaviors.

10. Firmly confront the client's antisocial behavior and attitude, pointing out consequences for himself/herself and others.

11. Confront statements in which the client blames others for his/her misbehaviors and fails to accept responsibility for his/her actions.

12. Explore and process the factors that contribute to the client's pattern of blaming others (harsh punishment experiences, family pattern of blaming others, etc.).

13. Teach mediational and self-control strategies (e.g., relaxation, "stop, look, listen, and think") to help express anger in a controlled, respectful manner.

14. Encourage the client to use self-monitoring checklists at home or school to develop more effective anger and impulse control.

15. Utilize the therapeutic workbook *The Angry Monster* (Shore) to help the client develop more effective anger and impulse control.

16. Assign reading of *The Very Angry Day That Amy Didn't Have* (Shapiro) and *Sometimes I Like to Fight, but I Don't Do It Much Anymore*

21. Identify how acting-out behaviors negatively affect others. (10, 36, 41, 49)

22. Increase verbalizations of empathy and concern for other people. (37, 39, 41)

23. Identify and list resources or coping strategies to help control anger and deter impulsive behaviors. (39, 40, 42, 43)

24. Express feelings in individual play-therapy sessions or therapeutic games. (33, 44, 45, 46, 47)

25. Express feelings through artwork and mutual story-telling. (48, 49, 50, 51)

26. Parents acknowledge marital conflict and agree to seek treatment. (52)

27. Parent(s) acknowledge a substance abuse problem and agree to seek treatment. (53)

28. Comply with a physician evaluation and take medication as prescribed. (1, 54, 55)

__·__ _____
_____

__·__ _____
_____

__·__ _____
_____

(Shapiro) to teach effective ways to manage anger.

17. Teach effective communication and assertiveness skills to express feelings in a controlled fashion and to meet his/her needs through more constructive actions.

18. Use "Anger Control" exercise in *Brief Child Therapy Homework Planner* (Jongsma, Peterson, and McInnis) to reinforce good control of anger and help client identify core issues that contribute to emergence of angry outbursts or aggressive behaviors.

19. Assist the parents in increasing structure to help the client learn to delay gratification for longer-term goals (e.g., completing homework or chores before playing basketball).

20. Establish clear rules for the client at home or school; ask him/her to repeat the rules to demonstrate an understanding of the expectations.

21. Design a reward system and/or contingency contract for the client to reinforce identified positive behaviors and deter impulsive behaviors.

22. Design and implement a token economy to increase the client's positive social behaviors and deter impulsive, acting-out behaviors.

23. Encourage the parents to provide frequent praise and positive reinforcement for the client's positive social behaviors and good impulse control.

24. Assign the client's parents to read *1-2-3 Magic: Training Your Preschoolers and Preteens to Do What You Want* (Phelan), *Family Rules: Raising Responsible Children* (Kaye), and *Assertive Discipline for Parents* (Canter and Canter).

25. Conduct family therapy sessions to explore the dynamics that contribute to the emergence of the client's behavioral problems.

26. Use the family-sculpting technique, in which the client defines the roles and behaviors of each family member in a scene of his/her choosing, to assess the family dynamics.

27. Conduct a family therapy session in which the client's family members are given a task or problem to solve together (e.g., building a craft); observe family interactions and process the experience with them afterward.

28. Give a directive to uninvolved or disengaged parent(s) to spend more time with the client in leisure, school, or household activities.

29. Explore the client's family background for a history of neglect and physical or sexual abuse that may contribute to his/her behavioral problems.

30. Confront the client's parents to cease physically abusive or overly punitive methods of discipline.

31. Implement the steps necessary to protect the client or siblings from further abuse (e.g., report abuse to the appropriate agencies; remove the client or perpetrator from the home).

32. Encourage and support the client in expressing feelings associated with neglect, abuse, separation, or abandonment.

33. Conduct individual play-therapy sessions to provide the client an opportunity to express feelings surrounding past neglect, abuse, separation, or abandonment.

34. Assign client the task of writing a letter to an absent parent or use the empty-chair technique to assist the client in expressing and working through feelings of anger and sadness about past abandonment.

35. Assign the client to read "The Lesson of Salmon Rock . . . Fighting Leads to Loneliness" in *Brief Child Therapy Homework Planner* (Jongsma, Peterson, and McInnis) to help him/her

express feelings connected with past separations, losses, or abandonment and recognize negative consequences of aggressive behaviors.

36. Arrange for the client to participate in group therapy to improve his/her social judgment and interpersonal skills.

37. Use *Let's Work It Out: A Conflict Resolution Tool Kit* (Shore) to teach client more effective ways to resolve conflict with peers.

38. Teach client the value of honesty as a basis for building trust and mutual respect in all relationships.

39. Encourage the client to participate in extracurricular or positive peer group activities to provide a healthy outlet for anger, to improve social skills, and to increase self-esteem.

40. Refer the client to the Big Brothers/Big Sisters organization to provide a positive role model.

41. Assign the client the task of showing empathy, kindness, or sensitivity to the needs of others (e.g., reading a bedtime story to sibling, washing dishes for parent when ill).

42. Instruct parents to observe positive behaviors by client in between therapy sessions; reinforce positive be-

haviors and encourage client to continue to demonstrate these behaviors.

43. Explore periods of time during which client demonstrated good impulse control and behaved responsibly; process responses and reinforce positive coping strategies used to exercise self-control and deter impulsive behaviors.

44. Using child-centered play-therapy principles (e.g., demonstrating genuine interest and unconditional positive regard, reflecting feelings, expressing trust in client's capacity to act responsibly), help client assume greater responsibility for his/her actions.

45. Employ psychoanalytic play-therapy approaches (e.g., allow child to take lead; explore the etiology of unconscious conflicts, fixations, or developmental arrests; interpret resistance, transference, and core anxieties) to help client work through and resolve issues contributing to emergence of behavioral problems.

46. Use the Angry Tower technique (Saxe) to help client identify and express feelings of anger: Build tower out of plastic containers; place small item (representing object of anger) on top of tower; instruct client to throw small fabric ball at

tower while verbalizing anger.

47. Utilize the therapeutic game Talking, Feeling, Doing, available from Creative Therapeutics, to increase the client's awareness of his/her thoughts feelings.

48. Use puppets, dolls, or stuffed animals to create a story that models appropriate ways to control anger and resolve conflict; then ask client to create story with similar characters or themes.

49. Tell client to draw pictures reflecting how acting-out behaviors affect self and/or others; process content of drawings and reinforce expressions of empathy and concern for others.

50. Assign client to draw an outline of human body on large piece of paper or poster board; then instruct client to draw or fill in the body with objects, symbols, or pictures that reflect things or issues that evoke feelings of anger.

51. Assign the task of drawing three events or situations that commonly evoke feelings of anger, hurt, or sadness; process thoughts and feelings after drawings are completed.

52. Assess the marital dyad for possible conflict and triangulation that shifts the focus

from marriage issues to the client's acting-out behaviors.

53. Evaluate parent(s) for presence of substance-abuse problem and refer for appropriate treatment if needed.

54. Arrange for a medication evaluation of the client to improve his/her impulse control and stabilize moods.

55. Monitor client for medication compliance, side effects, and effectiveness.

___. _____
      _____

___. _____
      _____

___. _____
      _____

DIAGNOSTIC SUGGESTIONS

Axis I:	312.8	Conduct Disorder/Childhood-Onset Type
	313.81	Oppositional Defiant Disorder
	312.9	Disruptive Behavior Disorder NOS
	314.01	Attention-Deficit/Hyperactivity Disorder, Predominantly Hyperactive-Impulsive Type
	314.9	Attention-Deficit/Hyperactivity Disorder NOS
	312.34	Intermittent Explosive Disorder
	V71.02	Child Antisocial Behavior
	V61.20	Parent-Child Relational Problem
	_____	_____
	_____	_____
Axis II:	799.9	Diagnosis Deferred
	V71.09	No Diagnosis on Axis II
	_____	_____
	_____	_____

DEPRESSION

BEHAVIORAL DEFINITIONS

1. Sad or flat affect.
2. Preoccupation with the subject of death.
3. Suicidal thoughts and/or actions.
4. Moody irritability.
5. Isolation from family and/or peers.
6. Deterioration of academic performance.
7. Lack of interest in previously enjoyed activities.
8. Refusal to communicate openly.
9. Use of street drugs to elevate mood.
10. Low energy.
11. Little or no eye contact and frequent verbalizations of low self-esteem.
12. Reduced appetite.
13. Increased sleep.
14. Poor concentration and indecision.
15. Feelings of hopelessness, worthlessness, or inappropriate guilt.
16. Unresolved grief issues.
17. Mood-related hallucinations or delusions.

—. _____
   _____

—. _____
   _____

—. _____
   _____

LONG-TERM GOALS

1. Acknowledge the depression verbally and resolve its causes, leading to normalization of the emotional state.
2. Elevate the mood and show evidence of the usual energy, activities, and socialization level.
3. Reduce irritability and increase normal social interaction with family and friends.
4. Show a renewed typical interest in academic achievement, social involvement, and eating patterns, as well as occasional expressions of joy and zest for life.

—. _____
    _____
—. _____
    _____
—. _____
    _____

SHORT-TERM OBJECTIVES

1. Complete psychological testing to evaluate the depth of the depression. (1, 2)
2. State the connection between rebellion, self-destruction, or withdrawal and the underlying depression. (3, 4, 5, 6)
3. Verbally acknowledge unhappiness with life. (5, 7, 15, 16, 25)
4. Specify what is missing from life to cause the unhappiness. (7, 9, 15, 16, 41)
5. Specify what in the past or present life contributes to sadness. (7, 10, 11, 15, 16)

THERAPEUTIC INTERVENTIONS

1. Arrange for the administration of psychological testing to facilitate a more complete assessment of the depth of the client's depression.
2. Give feedback to the client (and his/her family) regarding psychological testing results.
3. Assess the client's level of self-understanding about self-defeating behaviors linked to the depression.
4. Interpret the client's acting-out behaviors as a reflection of the depression.
5. Confront the client's acting-out behaviors as avoidance

6. Express emotional needs to significant others. (8, 12, 13, 14)

7. Express feelings of sadness, hurt, and anger in play-therapy setting. (15, 16, 17, 18)

8. Identify negative self-talk that precipitates feelings of hopelessness, helplessness, and depression. (19)

9. Implement positive self-talk to strengthen feelings of self-acceptance, self-confidence, and hope. (20)

10. Stop the verbalized interest in the subject of death. (4, 5, 21, 22)

11. Terminate suicidal behaviors and/or verbalizations of the desire to die. (21, 22, 23)

12. Initiate and respond actively to social communication with family and peers. (13, 14, 24, 25)

13. Cooperate with an evaluation of the necessity for psychotropic medications. (26, 27)

14. Take prescribed medications as directed by the physician. (26, 27, 28)

15. Improve academic performance as evidenced by better grades and positive teacher reports. (29, 30)

16. Eat nutritional meals regularly without strong urging from others. (31)

of the real conflict involving unmet emotional needs.

6. Ask client to complete the homework assignment "Surface Behavior/Inner Feelings" in *Brief Child Therapy Homework Planner* (Jongsma, Peterson, and McInnis); process the responses to this homework to show the connection between angry, irritable behaviors and feelings of hurt and sadness.

7. Reinforce the client's open expression of underlying feelings of anger, hurt, and disappointment.

8. Explore the client's fears regarding abandonment or the loss of love from others.

9. Ask the client to discuss what is missing from his/her life that contributes to the unhappiness.

10. Probe present aspects of the client's life that contribute to the sadness.

11. Explore the emotional pain from the client's past that contributes to the feelings of hopelessness and low self-esteem.

12. Hold a family therapy session to facilitate the expression of conflict with family members.

13. Support the client's expression of emotional needs to family members and significant others.

17. Adjust sleep hours to those typical of the developmental stage. (27, 32)

18. Verbalize a feeling of being loved and accepted by family and friends. (7, 33, 34)

19. Describe an interest and participation in social and recreational activities. (33, 35, 36)

20. Reduce anger and irritability as evidenced by friendly, pleasant interactions with family and friends. (4, 5, 12, 13, 37)

21. Express negative feelings through artistic modalities. (38, 39, 40)

22. Draw pictures that aid in verbalizing factors that contribute to depression. (41)

23. Verbalize the connection between acting-out behavior and underlying feelings of emotional pain. (40)

24. Verbalize the life changes that would result in a reduction of sadness and an increase in hope. (41)

__. _____
   _____

__. _____
   _____

__. _____
   _____

14. Teach parents to encourage, support, and tolerate the client's respectful expression of his/her thoughts and feelings.

15. Arrange for a play-therapy setting that allows the client to express feelings toward himself/herself and others.

16. Interpret the feelings expressed in play therapy as those of the client toward real life.

17. Use child-centered play-therapy approach (e.g., demonstrate genuine interest, provide unconditional positive regard, reflect feelings, profess trust in client's inner direction) to promote insight into depression and mobilize inner resources to build self-esteem and a sense of hope for the future.

18. Using psychoanalytic play therapy (e.g., allowing client to take the lead; exploring etiology of unconscious conflicts, fixations, or developmental arrests; interpreting resistance, transference, and core depression), assist client in overcoming hopelessness, low self-esteem, and depression.

19. Assist in identifying the cognitive messages that the client gives to himself/herself that reinforce helplessness and hopelessness.

20. Teach and reinforce positive cognitive messages that fa-

cilitate the growth of the
client's self-confidence and
self-acceptance.

21. Monitor the potential for
self-harm and refer the
client to a protective setting
if necessary.

22. Reinforce statements of
hope for the future and desire to live.

23. Contract with the client for
no self-harm.

24. Encourage the client's participation in social/recre-
ational activities that
enrich life.

25. Use therapeutic feelings
games (e.g., Talking, Feeling, Doing) to assist the
client in being more verbal.

26. Assess the client's need for
psychotropic medications.

27. Arrange for a prescription
of antidepressant medica-
tions for the client.

28. Monitor medication effectiveness and side effects.

29. Challenge and encourage
the client's academic effort.

30. Arrange for a tutor to increase the client's sense of
academic mastery.

31. Monitor and encourage the
client's food consumption.

32. Monitor the client's sleep
patterns and the restfulness
of sleep.

33. Encourage and reinforce
parents to give warm, positive, affirming expression of
love to client.

34. Assist parents in establishing a routine of positive, structured activity with client (e.g., playing table games, playing at a park, watching client's favorite video together).

35. Explore with client pleasurable interests and activities that could be pursued; assign participation, and process the experience.

36. Urge the client to formulate a plan that leads to taking action to meet his/her social and emotional needs.

37. Reinforce pleasant social interaction between client and friends and/or family members.

38. Use art therapy (drawing, coloring, painting, collage, sculpture, etc.) to help client express depressive feelings; use artistic products as springboard for further elaboration of emotions and their causes.

39. Ask client to draw pictures of experiences that contribute to feelings of sadness and hurt; process these feelings.

40. Ask client to produce a kinetic family drawing to help assess factors contributing to depression.

41. Assign client the homework of writing three ways he/she would like to change the world to bring increased feelings of joy, peace, and

security (see "Three Ways to Change the World" in *Brief Child Therapy Homework Planner* by Jongsma, Peterson, and McInnis).

___. _____
    _____

___. _____
    _____

___. _____
    _____

DIAGNOSTIC SUGGESTIONS

Axis I:	300.4	Dysthymic Disorder
	296.2x	Major Depressive Disorder, Single Episode
	296.3x	Major Depressive Disorder, Recurrent
	296.89	Bipolar II Disorder
	296.0x	Bipolar I Disorder
	301.13	Cyclothymic Disorder
	309.0	Adjustment Disorder With Depressed Mood
	310.1	Personality Change Due to (Axis III Disorder)
	V62.82	Bereavement
	_____	_____
Axis II:	799.9	Diagnosis Deferred
	V71.09	No Diagnosis on Axis II
	_____	_____
	_____	_____

DISRUPTIVE/ATTENTION SEEKING

BEHAVIORAL DEFINITIONS

1. Repeated attempts to draw attention to self through silly behaviors, immature or regressive actions, loud talking, and making inappropriate noises or gestures.
2. Frequent disruptions in classroom by interrupting teacher and/or interfering with classmate's attention and concentration by talking excessively, blurting out remarks, speaking without permission, and laughing or making noises at inappropriate times.
3. Strained sibling and peer relationships due to annoying or antagonistic behaviors (e.g., teasing, mocking, name-calling, or picking on others).
4. Recurrent pattern of creating conflict with siblings or peers by failing to follow agreed-upon rules in play or game activities, refusing to share or cooperate, and demanding that others do things his/her way.
5. Obstinate refusal to comply with reasonable requests by authority figures in home or school settings.
6. Argumentativeness as manifested by unwillingness to back down or bend during an argument with family members, peers, or adult authority figures.
7. Lack of sensitivity to or awareness of how attention-seeking behaviors impact other people.
8. Poor social skills as manifested by lack of awareness of important social cues and/or failure to follow expected social norms.
9. Numerous complaints by siblings or peers of inappropriate touching or contact and intrusions into personal space.

—. _____

_____

—. _____

_____

—. _____

_____

LONG-TERM GOALS

1. Terminate disruptive attention-seeking behaviors and increase co-operative, prosocial interactions.
2. Gain attention, approval, and acceptance from other people through appropriate verbalizations and positive social behaviors.
3. Demonstrate marked improvement in impulse control as manifested by a significant reduction in the frequency of disruptive, antagonistic, annoying, or negative attention-seeking behaviors.
4. Establish and maintain positive sibling relationships and lasting peer friendships.
5. Comply with rules and expectations in home and school settings on a regular basis.
6. Parents set firm, consistent limits on client's disruptive or negative attention-seeking behaviors and maintain appropriate parent-child boundaries.
7. Resolve core conflicts that contribute to the emergence of disruptive, antagonistic, annoying, or negative attention-seeking behaviors.
8. Improve social skills as evidenced by consistently being alert to important social cues and following expected rules of engagement in play, classroom, extracurricular, or social activities.
9. Display empathy, concern, and respect for others' thoughts, feelings, and needs on a regular basis.

—. _____

_____

—. _____

_____

—. _____

_____

SHORT-TERM OBJECTIVES	THERAPEUTIC INTERVENTIONS
1. Complete psychological testing. (1, 3)	1. Arrange for psychological testing of client to assess whether emotional factors

2. Complete a psychoeducational evaluation. (2, 3)

3. Reduce the frequency and severity of disruptive or negative attention-seeking behaviors at home and/or school. (4, 5, 6, 7, 9)

4. Decrease the frequency and severity of antagonistic or annoying behaviors toward siblings and peers. (5, 6, 12, 13)

5. Increase compliance with rules at home and school. (6, 7, 8, 10, 11)

6. Parents establish appropriate boundaries, develop clear rules, and follow through consistently with consequences for the client's disruptive or annoying behaviors. (5, 6, 7, 8)

7. Parent(s) implement a reward system or contingency contract to reduce client's disruptive behavior and increase prosocial behaviors. (9, 10, 11)

8. Parents increase the frequency of praise and positive reinforcement to client. (9, 10, 11, 20)

9. Express anger through controlled, respectful verbalizations and healthy physical outlets. (12, 13, 14, 16, 44)

10. Increase frequency of socially appropriate behaviors with siblings and peers. (10, 11, 16, 21, 36, 44)

11. Increase frequency of on-task behaviors in classroom

or ADHD are contributing to his/her disruptive, antagonistic, annoying, or negative attention-seeking behaviors.

2. Arrange for a psychoeducational evaluation of client to rule out the presence of a learning disability that may be contributing to the disruptive and negative attention-seeking behaviors in the school setting.

3. Provide feedback to client's parents or school officials regarding psychological and/or psychoeducational testing.

4. Actively build the level of trust with client through consistent eye contact, active listening, unconditional positive regard, and warm acceptance to help increase his/her ability to acknowledge and identify his/her disruptive behaviors.

5. Consult with parents, teachers, and school officials to design and implement interventions (e.g., sitting in front row during class, providing frequent feedback, calling on client often, utilizing teacher's aide to assist with learning problems) to deter client's impulsivity, improve academic performance, and increase positive behaviors in classroom.

6. Assist parents in establishing clearly defined bound-

and completion of school or homework assignments. (5, 8, 10, 13)

12. Postpone recreational activities (e.g., playing basketball or video games with friends) until after completing homework or chores. (7, 8, 13)

13. Recognize and verbalize how unpleasant or negative emotions are connected to disruptive, antagonistic, or negative attention-seeking behaviors. (4, 15, 24)

14. Increase the number of statements that reflect the acceptance of responsibility for annoying or disruptive behaviors. (17, 18, 19)

15. Decrease the frequency of verbalizations that project the blame for disruptive behaviors onto other people. (17, 18, 19)

16. Identify appropriate and inappropriate ways to elicit attention from family members, authority figures, or peers. (16, 21, 22, 23)

17. Uninvolved or detached parent(s) increase time spent with the client in leisure, school, or work activities. (25, 26, 27)

18. Verbalize an understanding of how current disruptive and annoying behaviors are associated with past neglect, abuse, separation, or abandonment. (28, 30, 31, 32, 38)

aries and consequences for disruptive, antagonistic, annoying, and negative attention-seeking behaviors.

7. Establish clear rules for the client in home or school; ask him/her to repeat the rules to demonstrate an understanding of the expectations.

8. Consult with parents about increasing structure in home to help client delay gratification for longer-term goals (e.g., completing homework or chores before playing video games or socializing with peers).

9. Encourage parents to provide frequent praise and positive reinforcement for client's positive social behaviors and good impulse control.

10. Design a reward system and/or contingency contract for client to reinforce identified positive behaviors, completion of school and homework assignments, and reduce frequency of disruptive and negative attention-seeking behaviors.

11. Design and implement a token economy to increase the client's positive social behaviors and deter disruptive and negative attention-seeking behaviors.

12. Teach mediational and self-control strategies (e.g., relaxation, "stop, look, listen, and think") to help client delay impulse to act out and

19. Parents verbalize appropriate boundaries for discipline to prevent further occurrences of abuse and to ensure the safety of the client and his/her siblings. (28, 29, 30)

20. Identify and verbally express feelings associated with past neglect, abuse, separation, or abandonment. (28, 30, 31, 32)

21. Increase participation in extracurricular activities or positive peer group activities. (33, 34, 35, 37)

22. Identify and verbalize how annoying and disruptive behaviors negatively impact others. (34, 35, 36, 37)

23. Increase verbalizations of empathy and concern for other people. (34, 35, 37)

24. Express feelings in therapeutic games or individual play-therapy sessions. (36, 37, 38, 39)

25. Express feelings through art therapy and mutual storytelling. (40, 41, 42, 43)

26. Parents increase communication, intimacy, and consistency. (25, 46)

27. Parents acknowledge marital conflict that may contribute to client's disruptive behavior. (45, 46)

28. Take medication as prescribed by the physician. (1, 47)

engage in negative attention-seeking behaviors.

13. Encourage the client to use self-monitoring checklists at home or school to improve impulse control and social skills.

14. Use "Stop, Think, and Act" exercise in *Brief Child Therapy Homework Planner* (Jongsma, Peterson, and McInnis) to help client develop an awareness of how disruptive behaviors lead to negative consequences for self and others.

15. Help client to make a connection between unpleasant or negative emotions and annoying or disruptive behaviors.

16. Teach effective communication and assertiveness skills to help client meet his/her needs for attention and approval through appropriate verbalizations and positive social behaviors.

17. Firmly confront client's annoying and disruptive behaviors, pointing out consequences for himself/herself and others.

18. Confront statements in which client blames others for his/her annoying or disruptive behaviors and fails to accept responsibility for his/her actions.

19. Explore and process the factors that contribute to pat-

—. _____
     _____
—. _____
     _____
—. _____
     _____

tern of blaming others for behavioral problems.

20. Instruct parents and teacher to observe and record positive behaviors by client in between therapy sessions; reinforce and encourage client to continue to engage in the positive behaviors.

21. Assess periods of time during which client displays positive social behaviors. Reinforce any strengths or resources used to gain approval and acceptance from peers.

22. Introduce idea that client can change pattern of engaging in disruptive or negative attention-seeking behaviors by asking the following question: "What will you be doing when you stop getting into trouble?" Process client's responses and help him/her develop action plan to accomplish goals or desired behavior changes.

23. Prescribe symptom by directing client to engage in annoying or disruptive behaviors for a specific length of time or at a set time each day to help disrupt established patterns of negative behaviors. Intervention seeks to diffuse power of gaining negative attention through the annoying or disruptive behaviors.

24. Explore possible stressors or frustrations (e.g., lengthy separation from parent,

learning problems, failure experiences) that might cause negative behaviors to reappear in the future. Help client and family members identify how to manage stressors or frustrations.

25. Conduct family therapy sessions to explore the dynamics that contribute to the emergence of client's disruptive and negative attention-seeking behaviors.

26. Conduct filial play-therapy sessions (i.e., parental involvement in session) to help improve quality of parent-child relationship and increase parents' awareness of the factors contributing to client's disruptive or annoying behaviors.

27. Give a directive to uninvolved or disengaged parent(s) to spend more time with client in leisure, school, or household activities.

28. Explore the client's family background for a history of physical, sexual, or substance abuse, which may contribute to his/her disruptive behaviors.

29. Implement steps necessary to protect client or siblings from further abuse (e.g., report abuse to appropriate agencies; remove client or perpetrator from the home).

30. Encourage and support the client in expressing feelings associated with neglect,

abuse, separation, or abandonment.

31. Use child-centered play-
therapy approaches (e.g.,
provide unconditional positive regard, offer nonjudgmental reflection of
feelings, display trust in
child's capacity to act responsibly) to help the client
express and work through
feelings surrounding past
neglect, abuse, separation,
or abandonment.

32. Use the empty-chair technique to assist the client in
expressing and working
through feelings of anger
and sadness about past neglect, abuse, separation, or
abandonment.

33. Encourage the client to participate in extracurricular
or positive peer group activities to provide a healthy
outlet for anger, improve social skills, and increase self-
esteem.

34. Assign the task of showing
empathy, kindness, or sensitivity to the needs of
others (e.g., reading a bedtime story to a sibling, helping a classmate with
reading or math problems).

35. Refer for group therapy to
improve social judgment
and interpersonal skills.

36. Use You & Me: A Game of
Social Skills (Shapiro) to
help the client develop positive social skills.

37. Utilize The Helping, Sharing, and Caring Game

(Gardner) to promote greater expression of empathy and concern for other people.

38. Interpret the feelings expressed in individual play-therapy sessions and relate them to the client's negative attention-seeking behaviors.

39. Employ psychoanalytic play-therapy principles (e.g., explore and gain understanding of the etiology of unconscious conflicts, fixations, or arrests; interpret resistance, transference, or core anxieties) to help the client work through and resolve issues contributing to disruptive behaviors.

40. Use puppets, dolls, or stuffed animals to create a story that models appropriate ways to gain approval and acceptance from peers; then ask the client to create story with similar characters or themes.

41. Direct the client to create stories that can be acted out with puppets, dolls, or stuffed animals to assess unmet needs, family dynamics, or core issues that contribute to emergence of disruptive or negative attention-seeking behaviors.

42. Instruct the client to draw a picture of a house, then pretend that he/she lives in the house and describe what it

is like to live in the home; process feelings and content of responses to help assess family dynamics.

43. Use the Color-Your-Life technique (O'Connor) to improve client's ability to identify and verbalize feelings instead of acting them out: Ask client to match colors to different emotions (e.g., red—anger, blue—sad, black—very sad, yellow—happy) and then fill up blank page with colors that reflect his/her feelings about different life events.

44. Assign the reading of *How I Learned to Think Things Through* (Shapiro) to improve client's impulse control and ability to stop and think about possible consequences of negative social behaviors.

45. Assign the client's parents to read *1-2-3 Magic: Training Your Preschoolers and Preteens to Do What You Want* (Phelan), *Family Rules* (Kaye), and *Assertive Discipline for Parents* (Canter and Canter).

46. Assess the marital dyad for possible conflict and triangulation that shifts the focus from marital issues to the client's disruptive behaviors. Refer couple for counseling if marital discord exists.

47. Arrange for medication evaluation to improve impulse control and stabilize moods.

__. _____
   _____

__. _____
   _____

__. _____
   _____

DIAGNOSTIC SUGGESTIONS

Axis I:	312.9	Disruptive Behavior Disorder, NOS
	314.01	Attention-Deficit/Hyperactivity Disorder, Predominantly Hyperactive-Impulsive Type
	314.01	Attention-Deficit/Hyperactivity Disorder, Combined Type
	312.8	Conduct Disorder/Childhood-Onset Type
	313.81	Oppositional Defiant Disorder
	309.3	Adjustment Disorder With Disturbance of Conduct
	309.4	Adjustment Disorder With Mixed Disturbance of Emotions and Conduct
	V71.02	Child Antisocial Behavior
	V61.20	Parent-Child Relational Problem
	_____	_____
	_____	_____
Axis II:	799.9	Diagnosis Deferred
	V71.09	No Diagnosis on Axis II
	_____	_____
	_____	_____

DIVORCE REACTION

BEHAVIORAL DEFINITIONS

1. Infrequent contact or loss of contact with a parental figure due to separation or divorce.
2. Loss of contact with positive support network due to geographic move.
3. Intense emotional reaction (e.g., crying, begging, pleading, temper outbursts) around separation of parental figures and/or when making the transfer from one parent's home to another.
4. Persistent fears and worries about being abandoned or separated from parent(s).
5. Feelings of guilt accompanied by unreasonable belief regarding behaving in some manner to cause parent's divorce and/or failing to prevent divorce from occurring.
6. Strong feelings of grief and sadness combined with feelings of low self-worth, lack of confidence, social withdrawal, and loss of interest in activities that normally bring pleasure.
7. Marked increase in frequency and severity of acting-out, oppositional, and aggressive behaviors since the onset of parents' marital problems, separation, or divorce.
8. Significant decline in school performance and lack of interest or motivation in school-related activities.
9. Appearance of regressive behaviors (e.g., thumb sucking, baby talk, rocking, bed-wetting).
10. Pseudomaturity as manifested by denying or suppressing painful emotions about divorce and often assuming parental roles or responsibilities.
11. Numerous psychosomatic complaints in response to anticipated separations, stress, or frustration.

—. _____
_____

—. _____
  _____
—. _____
  _____

LONG-TERM GOALS

1. Accept parents' separation or divorce with consequent understanding and control of feelings and behavior.
2. Alleviate fears of abandonment and establish loving, secure relationship with parent(s).
3. Eliminate feelings of guilt and statements that reflect self-blame for parents' divorce.
4. Elevate and stabilize mood.
5. Parents establish and maintain consistent visitation arrangement that meets client's emotional needs.
6. Parents establish and maintain appropriate parent-child boundaries in discipline and assignment of responsibilities.
7. Parents consistently demonstrate mutual respect for one another, especially in front of the children.
8. Create a strong, supportive social network outside of the immediate family to offset loss of nurturance or support from within family.

—. _____
  _____
—. _____
  _____
—. _____
  _____

SHORT-TERM OBJECTIVES

1. Identify and express feelings related to parents' separation or divorce. (1, 2, 3, 6, 7, 8)

THERAPEUTIC INTERVENTIONS

1. Actively build the level of trust with client through consistent eye contact, active listening, unconditional positive regard, and warm

2. Tell story of parents' separation or divorce. (2, 4, 5, 8)

3. Describe how parents' separation or divorce has impacted his/her personal and family life. (4, 5, 6, 7, 8)

4. Express thoughts and feelings within the family system regarding parental separation or divorce. (2, 9, 10, 13)

5. Parents demonstrate understanding and empathy for how divorce has impacted client's life. (9, 10, 13, 17, 43)

6. Recognize and affirm self as not being responsible for parents' separation or divorce. (11, 12, 13, 14)

7. Parents verbalize an acceptance of responsibility for dissolution of the marriage. (13, 14)

8. Recognize and verbally acknowledge that parents will not be reuniting in the future and that he/she cannot bring parents back together. (3, 12)

9. Identify positive and negative aspects of parents' separation or divorce. (2, 5, 15, 48)

10. Identify and verbalize unmet needs to parent(s). (10, 17, 18, 34)

11. Reduce the frequency and severity of angry, depressed, and anxious moods. (2, 16, 19, 44, 56)

12. Decrease the frequency and intensity of emotional out-

acceptance to improve his/her ability to identify and express feelings connected to parents' separation or divorce.

2. Explore, encourage, and support the client in verbally expressing and clarifying his/her feelings associated with the separation or divorce.

3. Read *Dinosaurs Divorce: A Guide for Changing Families* (Brown and Brown) or *Divorce Workbook: A Guide for Kids and Families* (Ives, Fassler, and Lash) to assist client in expressing his/her feelings about divorce and changes in family system.

4. Create photo album by first instructing client to gather a diverse collection of photographs covering many aspects of his/her life; then place pictures in photo album during session while allowing client to verbalize his/her feelings about changes in family system.

5. Develop a time line whereby client records significant developments that have positively or negatively impacted his/her personal and family life, both before and after divorce. Allow client to verbalize feelings about divorce and subsequent changes in family system.

6. Use Color-Your-Life technique (O'Connor) to im-

bursts around periods of separation or transfer from one parent's home to another. (18, 19, 21, 22)

13. Parents verbally recognize how their guilt and failure to follow through with limits contributes to client's acting-out or aggressive behaviors. (23, 24)

14. Express feelings of anger about parents' separation or divorce through controlled, respectful verbalizations and healthy physical outlets. (19, 20, 21, 22)

15. Reduce the frequency and severity of acting-out, oppositional, and aggressive behaviors. (21, 22, 23, 25, 26)

16. Parents establish appropriate boundaries and follow through with consequences for acting-out and oppositional or aggressive behaviors. (23, 24, 25, 26)

17. Complete school and homework assignments on a regular basis. (27, 28, 30)

18. Decrease the frequency of somatic complaints. (2, 16, 29)

19. Parents assign appropriate amount of household responsibilities or tasks to client and siblings. (30, 31, 35, 36)

20. Noncustodial parent verbally recognizes pattern of overindulgence and begins to set limits on money spending and/or time spent

prove client's ability to identify and verbalize feelings: Ask client to match colors with different emotions (e.g., red—anger, purple—rage, yellow—happy, blue—sad, black—very sad) and then instruct client to fill a blank page with colors that reflect his/her feelings about parents' separation or divorce.

7. Use "Feelings and Faces" exercise from *Brief Child Therapy Homework Planner* (Jongsma, Peterson, and McInnis): Client first draws pictures of different emotions on blank faces and then shares time when he/she experienced those emotions about parents' separation or divorce.

8. Use empty-chair technique to help client express mixed emotions he/she feels toward both parents about separation or divorce.

9. Hold family therapy sessions to allow client and siblings to express feelings about separation or divorce in presence of parent(s).

10. Encourage parents to provide opportunities (e.g., family meetings) at home to allow client and siblings to express feelings about separation/divorce and subsequent changes in family system.

11. Explore the factors contributing to client's feelings

in leisure or recreational activities. (31, 32, 33)

21. Noncustodial parent begins to assign household responsibilities and/or require client to complete homework during visits. (28, 29, 31, 32, 33)

22. Reduce frequency of regressive, immature, and irresponsible behaviors. (32, 33, 34)

23. Identify age-appropriate ways to meet needs for attention, affection, and acceptance. (32, 33, 34)

24. Parents cease making unnecessary, hostile, or overly critical remarks about other parent in presence of children. (37, 38)

25. Parents recognize and agree to cease the pattern of soliciting information and/or sending messages to other parent through the children. (38, 39)

26. Disengaged or uninvolved parent follows through with recommendations to spend greater quality time with client. (40, 41, 42, 43)

27. Identify and express thoughts and feelings connected with neglect, abuse, or abandonment. (8, 40, 44, 45)

28. Identify and express feelings about parents' separation or divorce, neglect, abuse, or abandonment in individual play-therapy ses-

of guilt and self-blame about parents' separation/divorce.

12. Assist client in realizing that his/her negative behaviors did not cause parent's divorce to occur and that he/she does not have the power or control to bring parents back together.

13. Conduct family therapy sessions where parent(s) affirm client and siblings as not being responsible for separation or divorce.

14. Challenge and confront statements by parents that place blame or responsibility for separation or divorce on the children.

15. Give homework assignment in which client lists both positive and negative aspects of parents divorce; process list in next session and allow client to express different emotions.

16. Empower the client by reinforcing his/her ability to cope with divorce and make healthy adjustments.

17. Give parents directive of spending 10 to 15 minutes of one-on-one time with client and siblings on a regular or daily basis.

18. Consult with client and parents about establishing routine or ritual (e.g., snuggling and reading books together, playing board games, watching favorite video) to

sions or playing of therapeutic games.
(43, 44, 45, 50, 51)

29. Identify and express feelings through mutual storytelling and artwork.
(46, 47, 48, 49)

30. Express feelings of anger, sadness, and loneliness related to move and change in school setting. (2, 10, 46, 48)

31. Increase participation in positive peer group and extracurricular or school-related activities. (52, 53)

32. Increase contacts with adults and build a support network outside the family. (54)

33. Complete psychological testing to assess for significant affective or anxiety disorder. (47, 55)

34. Take prescribed medication as directed by the physician. (56, 57)

—. _____
  _____

—. _____
  _____

—. _____
  _____

help decrease his/her emotional distress around periods of separation or transfer from one parent's home to another.

19. Assist client in making a connection between underlying painful emotions about divorce and angry outbursts or aggressive behaviors.

20. Use "Surface Behavior/ Inner Feelings" exercise in *Brief Child Therapy Homework Planner* (Jongsma, Peterson, and McInnis) to help client recognize how an increase in acting-out behaviors is connected to emotional pain surrounding parents' divorce.

21. Identify appropriate and inappropriate ways to express anger about parents' separation or divorce.

22. Use the Angry Tower technique (Saxe) to help client identify and express feelings of anger about divorce: Build tower out of plastic containers; place small object (representing anger) on top of tower; instruct client to throw small fabric ball at tower while verbalizing feelings of anger connected to divorce.

23. Encourage and challenge parents not to allow guilt feelings about divorce to interfere with the need to impose consequences for acting-out or oppositional behaviors.

24. Assist parents in establishing clearly defined rules, boundaries, and consequences for acting-out, oppositional, or aggressive behaviors.

25. Assign parents to read *1-2-3 Magic: Training Your Preschoolers and Preteens to Do What You Want* (Phelan) to help manage client's increased acting-out, oppositional, and aggressive behaviors; process the reading with therapist.

26. Design a reward system and/or contingency contract with client to reinforce good anger control and deter acting-out, oppositional, or aggressive behaviors.

27. Assist parent(s) in establishing new routine to help client complete school or homework assignments.

28. Design and implement a reward system and/or contingency contract to reinforce completion of school and homework assignments or good academic performance.

29. Refocus the client's discussion from physical complaints to emotional conflicts and the expression of feelings.

30. Hold family therapy sessions to establish effective parent-child boundaries, identify appropriate rules, and discuss roles and division of responsibilities for all family members.

31. Give directive to noncustodial parent to assign a chore or have client complete school or homework assignment during visit.

32. Encourage noncustodial parent to set limits on client's misbehavior and refrain from overindulging client during visits.

33. Teach how enmeshed or overly protective parent(s) reinforce the client's regressive, immature, or irresponsible behaviors by failing to set necessary limits.

34. Have client and parents identify age-appropriate ways for client to meet needs for attention, affection, acceptance; process list and encourage client to engage in age-appropriate behaviors.

35. Challenge parent(s) to assert appropriate parental authority and take active steps to prevent overly responsible child from assuming too many parental or household responsibilities.

36. Instruct parent(s) to schedule or allow time for overly responsible child to engage in positive peer group or extracurricular activities.

37. Challenge and confront parent(s) to cease making unnecessary hostile or overly critical remarks about the other parent in the presence of client.

38. Counsel parent(s) about not placing client in the middle by soliciting information about the other parent or sending messages through the client to the other parent about adult matters.

39. Challenge and confront client about playing one parent against the other to meet needs, obtain material goods, or avoid responsibility.

40. Use individual therapy sessions to help client express feelings about infrequent contact with noncustodial parent, abandonment, or abuse.

41. Hold individual and/or family therapy session to challenge and encourage noncustodial parent to maintain regular visitation and involvement in client's life.

42. Give directive to the disengaged or distant parent to spend more time or perform specific task with client (e.g., going on outing to zoo, assisting client with homework, working on a project around the home).

43. Use family theraplay principles (e.g., active involvement by parent in session, with parent responding empathically to client's feelings or needs) to strengthen or facilitate closer parent-child relationship.

44. Use psychoanalytic play-therapy approaches (e.g., with child taking lead, explore the etiology of unconscious conflicts, fixations, or developmental arrests; interpret resistance, transference, and core anxieties) to help client work through and resolve issues connected to parent's separation or divorce.

45. Use child-centered play-therapy approaches (e.g., display genuine interest, provide unconditional positive regard, and offer nonjudgmental reflection of feelings) to help client express and work through feelings associated with separation, divorce, abuse, or abandonment.

46. Use mutual storytelling technique whereby therapist and client alternate telling stories through the use of puppets, dolls, or stuffed animals: Therapist first models appropriate ways to express emotions related to separation or divorce; then client follows by creating a story with similar characters or themes.

47. Have client draw a variety of pictures reflecting his/her feelings about parent's divorce or how divorce has impacted his/her life; place pictures in a notebook that is given to client at end of therapy as a keepsake.

48. Instruct client to draw pictures of both mother's and father's homes and then have him/her share what it is like to live in or visit each home to assess quality of relationship with each parent.

49. Tell client to draw outline of body on large piece of paper or poster board; then have client fill in outline with symbols or objects that reflect his/her feelings about divorce.

50. Play therapeutic game My Two Homes (Shapiro) to help client express feelings and learn effective coping strategies to adjust to divorce.

51. Instruct client and parent to read *All About Divorce* (Fields) at home; have parent read book while client acts out feelings and concerns about divorce with dolls or shares feelings in written assignment.

52. Encourage client to participate in school, extracurricular, or positive peer group activities to offset loss of time spent with parent(s).

53. Refer client to a Children of Divorce group to assist client in expressing feelings and help him/her understand that he/she is not alone in going through divorce process.

54. Identify a list of adult individuals (school counselor,

neighbor, uncle or aunt, Big Brother or Big Sister, member of clergy, etc.) outside of family to whom client can turn for support, guidance, and nurturance to help cope with divorce, family move, or change in schools.

55. Arrange for psychological testing to rule out the presence of an affective or anxiety disorder.

56. Refer client for medication evaluation to help stabilize moods and improve anger control.

57. Monitor medication compliance, effectiveness, and side effects.

__. _____
    _____

__. _____
    _____

__. _____
    _____

DIAGNOSTIC SUGGESTIONS

Axis I:	309.0	Adjustment Disorder With Depressed Mood
	309.24	Adjustment Disorder With Anxiety
	309.28	Adjustment Disorder With Mixed Anxiety and Depressed Mood
	309.3	Adjustment Disorder With Disturbance of Conduct
	309.4	Adjustment Disorder With Mixed Disturbance of Emotions and Conduct
	300.4	Dysthymic Disorder
	300.02	Generalized Anxiety Disorder
	309.21	Separation Anxiety Disorder

	313.81	Oppositional Defiant Disorder
	300.81	Undifferentiated Somatoform Disorder
	_____	_____
	_____	_____
Axis II:	799.9	Diagnosis Deferred
	V71.09	No Diagnosis on Axis II
	_____	_____
	_____	_____

ENURESIS/ENCOPRESIS

BEHAVIORAL DEFINITIONS

1. Repeated pattern of voluntary or involuntary voiding of urine into bed or clothes during the day or at night after age 5, when continence is expected.
2. Repeated passage of feces, whether voluntary or involuntary, in inappropriate places (e.g., clothing or floor) after age 5, when continence is expected.
3. Feelings of shame associated with enuresis or encopresis that cause the avoidance of situations (e.g., overnight visits with friends) that might lead to further embarrassment.
4. Social ridicule, isolation, or ostracism by peers because of enuresis or encopresis.
5. Frequent attempts to hide feces or soiled clothing because of shame or fear of further ridicule, criticism, or punishment.
6. Excessive anger, rejection, or punishment by the parent(s) or caretaker(s) centered around toilet-training practices, which contributes to low self-esteem.
7. Strong feelings of fear or hostility, which are channeled into acts of enuresis and encopresis.
8. Poor impulse control, which contributes to lack of responsibility with toilet-training practices.
9. Deliberate smearing of feces.

—. _____

_____

—. _____

_____

—. _____
    _____

LONG-TERM GOALS

1. Eliminate all diurnal and/or nocturnal episodes of enuresis.
2. Terminate all episodes of encopresis, whether voluntary or involuntary.
3. Resolve the underlying core conflicts contributing to the emergence of enuresis or encopresis.
4. Parents eliminate rigid and coercive toilet-training practices.
5. Family eradicates the hostile-dependent behavior cycle: Soiling or wetting angers the parents; the parents respond in an overly critical or hostile manner; the client "punishes" the parents for their anger by soiling or wetting.
6. Cease all incidents of smearing of feces.
7. Increase self-esteem.

—. _____
    _____

—. _____
    _____

—. _____
    _____

SHORT-TERM OBJECTIVES

1. Comply with the physician's orders for medical tests and medications. (1, 2, 3)
2. Take prescribed medication as directed by the physician. (2, 3)
3. Complete psychological testing. (4, 29, 38)
4. Parents consistently comply with the use of bell-and-pad

THERAPEUTIC INTERVENTIONS

1. Refer the client for a medical examination to rule out organic or physical causes of the enuresis or encopresis.
2. Arrange for a medication evaluation of the client.
3. Monitor the client for medication compliance, side effects, and effectiveness. Consult with the prescrib-

conditioning procedures to treat nocturnal enuresis. (5, 6, 8, 9, 10)

5. Reduce the frequency of enuretic behavior. (5, 6, 7, 8, 9)

6. Reduce the frequency of encopretic behavior. (6, 12, 13, 14)

7. Increase the client's role in implementing the toilet-training practices and interventions. (11, 12, 14, 15, 19)

8. Verbalize how anxiety or fears associated with toilet-training practices are unrealistic or irrational. (16, 17)

9. Identify the negative social consequences that may occur from peers if enuresis or encopresis continues. (11, 13, 15, 18)

10. Parent(s) verbally recognize how rigid toilet-training practices or hostile, critical remarks contribute to the client's enuresis or encopresis. (20, 21, 22, 23, 24)

11. Decrease the frequency and severity of hostile, critical remarks by the parents regarding the client's toilet training. (21, 22, 23, 24)

12. Increase the parents' empathetic responses to the client's thoughts, feelings, and needs. (22, 23, 41)

13. Increase the disengaged parent's involvement in toilet-training practices. (26)

14. Strengthen the relationship with the disengaged parent

ing physician at regular intervals.

4. Conduct psychological testing to rule out the presence of ADHD, impulse-control disorder, or serious underlying emotional problems; provide feedback on the testing to the client and his/her parents.

5. Train the client and his/her parents to treat enuresis by using bell-and-pad conditioning procedures in which a urine-sensitive pad causes an alarm to sound when involuntary wetting occurs.

6. Design and counsel the parents on the use of positive reinforcement procedures to increase the client's bladder or bowel control.

7. Teach the client and his/her parents effective urine-retention training techniques that increase the client's awareness of the sensation or need to urinate.

8. Train the client's parents or caretakers in the use of staggered-awakening procedures, using a variable-interval schedule, to control nocturnal enuresis.

9. Design and implement dry-bed techniques, training the parents and the client in response inhibition, positive reinforcement, rapid awakening, gradual increase of fluid intake, self-correction of accidents, and decreased

as demonstrated by in-
creased time spent with the
client. (27, 28)

15. Understand and verbally
recognize the secondary
gain that results from
enuresis or encopresis.
(24, 25, 39, 40)

16. Identify and express feelings associated with past
separation, loss, trauma, or
rejection experiences and
how they are connected to
current enuresis/encopresis.
(29, 30, 31, 32)

17. Decrease the frequency of
self-descriptive statements
that reflect feelings of low
self-esteem, shame, or embarrassment. (34, 35, 36)

18. Increase the frequency of
positive self-descriptive
statements that reflect improved self-esteem.
(33, 34, 35, 36)

19. Appropriately express
anger verbally and physi-
cally rather than channel-
ing anger through enuresis,
encopresis, or smearing of
feces. (37)

20. Express feelings through
artwork and mutual story-
telling. (33, 38)

—. _____

   _____

—. _____

   _____

—. _____

   _____

critical comments about
toilet-training behavior.

10. Employ overlearning
method (e.g., require client
to drink specific amount of
fluid shortly before bedtime)
along with use of bell-and-
pad conditioning procedures
in latter stages of treatment
to help prevent relapse of
nocturnal enuresis.

11. Use "Dry Bed Training Program" in *Brief Child Therapy Homework Planner*
(Jongsma, Peterson, and
McInnis) to help client assume greater responsibility
in managing nocturnal
enuresis.

12. Train the client and his/her
parents how to implement a
systematic operant condi-
tioning program that com-
bines positive reinforcement
techniques with the use of
glycerine suppositories and
enemas if the client does
not defecate voluntarily
each day.

13. Use "Bowel Control Training Program" in *Brief Child
Therapy Homework Planner*
(Jongsma, Peterson, and
McInnis) to help client assume greater responsibility
in developing bowel control
and recognize negative consequences that result from
encopretic incidents.

14. Encourage and challenge
the client to assume active
responsibility for achieving
mastery of bladder and/or

bowel control (e.g., keeping a record of wet and dry days, setting an alarm clock for voiding times, cleaning soiled underwear or linens).

15. Challenge and confront the client's and/or parent's lack of motivation or compliance in following through with recommended therapeutic interventions.

16. Explore client's irrational cognitive messages that produce fear or anxiety associated with toilet training.

17. Assist the client in realizing how anxiety or fears associated with toilet training are irrational or unrealistic.

18. Identify and discuss negative social consequences the client may experience from peers in order to increase his/her motivation to master bladder/bowel control.

19. Inquire into what client does differently on days when he/she demonstrates good bladder/bowel control and does not have any enuretic or encopretic incidents; process client's responses and reinforce any effective strategies that are used to gain bladder/bowel control.

20. Counsel the client's parents on effective, nonabusive toilet-training practices.

21. Conduct family therapy sessions to assess the dynamics that contribute to the emer-

gence or reinforcement of the client's enuresis, encopresis, or smearing of feces.

22. Explore parent-child interactions to asses whether the parents' toilet-training practices are excessively rigid or whether the parents make frequent hostile, critical remarks about the client.

23. Confront and challenge the parent(s) about making overly critical or hostile remarks that contribute to the client's low self-esteem, shame and embarrassment, and anger.

24. Assess parent-child interactions for the presence of a hostile-dependent cycle whereby the client's wetting or soiling angers the parents, the parents respond in an overly critical or hostile manner, the client seeks to "punish" the parents for their strong display of anger, and so on.

25. Assist the client and his/her parents in developing insight into the secondary gain (parental attention, avoidance of separation from parents, physician, or counselor attention, etc.) received from enuresis or encopresis.

26. Assign the disengaged parent the responsibility of overseeing or teaching the client effective toilet-training practices (e.g., keeping a record of wet and

dry days, gently awakening the client for bladder voiding, reminding or teaching the client how to clean soiled underwear or linens).

27. Give a directive to the disengaged parent to spend quality time with the client (e.g., working on homework together, going to the park, or engaging in a sporting activity).

28. Encourage client and parents to engage in "free play" during family play-therapy sessions to assess the quality of the parent-child relationships and gain an understanding of the family dynamics that contribute to the development of enuresis or encopresis.

29. Determine whether the client's enuresis, encopresis, or smearing of feces is associated with past separation, loss, traumatization, or rejection experiences.

30. Explore, encourage, and support the client in verbally expressing and clarifying feelings associated with past separation, loss, trauma, or rejection experiences.

31. Use child-centered play-therapy principles (e.g., provide unconditional positive regard; reflect feelings in nonjudgmental manner; demonstrate trust in client's capacity to act responsibly) to help client express and

work through feelings associated with past separation, loss, trauma, or rejection experiences and move toward assuming greater responsibility with toilet-training practices.

32. Employ psychoanalytic play-therapy approaches (e.g., explore and gain understanding of the etiology of unconscious conflicts, fixations, or arrests; interpret resistance, transference, or core anxieties) to help client work through and resolve issues contributing to bladder/bowel-control problems.

33. Use mutual storytelling technique whereby the therapist and client alternate telling stories through use of puppets, dolls, or stuffed animals; therapist models appropriate ways for client to gain control and/or attention from others.

34. Teach the client effective communication and assertiveness skills to improve his/her ability to express thoughts and feelings through appropriate verbalizations.

35. Identify and list the client's positive characteristics to help decrease feelings of shame and embarrassment; reinforce the client's positive self-statements.

36. Assign the client to make one positive self-statement

daily and record that in a journal.

37. Teach the client appropriate physical outlets that allow the expression of anger in a constructive manner rather than through inappropriate wetting or soiling.

38. Instruct client to draw picture that reflects how enuretic or encopretic incidents affect self-esteem.

39. Use a strategic family therapy approach in which the therapist does not talk about enuresis or encopresis but discusses what might surface if this problem were resolved (i.e., camouflaged problems may be revealed).

40. Utilize Ericksonian therapy intervention of prescribing the symptom, whereby client is instructed to pick out a specific night of the week where he/she will deliberately wet the bed; paradoxical intervention allows client to control enuresis by making the unconscious behavior a conscious maneuver.

41. Direct parents to use *Once Upon a Time Potty Book and Doll Set* (available from Childswork/Childsplay, LLC) to increase preschool child's motivation to develop bladder/bowel control.

—. _____

_____

___.   _____
       _____
___.   _____
       _____

DIAGNOSTIC SUGGESTIONS

Axis I: 307.6   Enuresis (Not Due to a General Medical
                         Condition)
               787.6   Encopresis, With Constipation and Overflow
                         Incontinence
               307.7   Encopresis, Without Constipation and
                         Overflow Incontinence
               300.4   Dysthymic Disorder
               296.xx   Major Depressive Disorder
               299.80   Pervasive Developmental Disorder NOS
               309.81   Posttraumatic Stress Disorder
               313.81   Oppositional Defiant Disorder
               314.01   Attention-Deficit/Hyperactivity Disorder,
                         Combined Type

               _____   _____

               _____   _____

Axis II: 799.9   Diagnosis Deferred
               V71.09   No Diagnosis on Axis II

               _____   _____

               _____   _____

FIRE SETTING

BEHAVIORAL DEFINITIONS

1. Has set one or more fires in the last six months.
2. Has been regularly observed playing with fire, fireworks, or combustible substances.
3. Is around fire wherever it occurs.
4. Consistently has matches, lighters, candles, and so forth in his/her possession.
5. Has an easily discernable fascination and/or preoccupation with fire.
6. Does not experience tension or sexual arousal prior to fire-setting behavior or gratification or relief when witnessing the fire.

—. _____
   _____
   _____

—. _____
   _____
   _____

—. _____
   _____

LONG-TERM GOALS

1. Secure the safety of the client, the family, and the community.
2. Terminate the fascination and preoccupation with fire.
3. Redirect or rechannel fascination with fire into constructive arenas.
4. Establish the existence of a psychotic process or major affective disorder and procure placement in an appropriate treatment program if indicated.

—. _____
   _____

___. _____
  _____
  _____

___. _____
  _____

SHORT-TERM OBJECTIVES

1. Parents consistently guide and supervise the client's behavior. (1, 2, 6, 9)

2. Report a decrease in the impulse to set fires. (3)

3. Identify the constructive and the destructive aspects of fire. (4)

4. Interview a firefighter and/or nurse about the dangers of fire. (5)

5. Demonstrate steps necessary to prevent destruction from fire. (8, 9)

6. Parents to monitor client for possessing articles connected with fire (matches, lighters, etc.). (1, 2, 8)

7. Demonstrate steps necessary to prevent destruction from fire. (8, 9)

8. Increase the frequency of positive interactions and connectness between family members. (10, 11, 12, 15)

9. Client and family demonstrate the ability to identify, express, and tolerate unpleasant feelings. (11, 12, 13)

10. Parents and caregivers identify and implement

THERAPEUTIC INTERVENTIONS

1. Meet with parents and work with them to expand their ability to consistently structure and supervise the client's behavior.

2. Monitor parents' efforts to structure, set limits on, and supervise client, giving support, encouragement, and redirection as appropriate.

3. Assist client and parents in developing ways to increase client's impulse control through use of positive reinforcement at times of apparent control.

4. Assign and work with client and parents to create two collages, one that emphasizes fire's positive aspects and one that focuses on fire's destructive aspects. Discuss with the client as the collage is presented.

5. Construct with client and parents a list of questions for client to ask a firefighter or a nurse in a local burn unit. Then help arrange an interview with one of these individuals. Afterward, process the experience and information gathered.

ways of satisfying client's unmet emotional needs. (14)

11. Describe instances of chaos and/or violence within the family. (15)

12. Increase positive time spent with father or another significant male figure in his/her life. (4, 16, 17)

13. Cooperate in a psychiatric evaluation for psychotropic medication. (18)

14. Verbalize feelings of rejection and anger. (19)

15. Identify instances of physical or sexual abuse. (20)

16. Cooperate in an evaluation for ADHD. (21)

17. Comply with all recommendations of the psychiatric or ADHD evaluation. (22, 23)

__. _____
    _____
__. _____
    _____
__. _____
    _____

6. Assign family an operant-based intervention in which parent allows client to strike matches under supervision, noting need for caution. A sum of money will be placed next to the pack and client will receive a predetermined sum as well as warm praise for each match left unstruck. Monitor intervention and give redirection and feedback as needed.

7. Assign an intervention of stimulus satiation in which client is given a box of matches with parent(s) instructing client how to safely strike. Allow client to strike as many as he/she would like. Monitor intervention and redirect as needed.

8. Assist and coach parents in implementing one of the three steps given in the exercise "Fireproofing Your Home and Family" from *Brief Child Therapy Homework Planner* (Jongsma, Peterson, and McInnis). Process the assignment in the next family session.

9. Ask father (or male father figure) to teach client how to safely build a fire. Father to emphasize need for strict control of and respect for the power of fire. Therapist will provide materials for fire in session (matches, sticks, coffee can). Therapist will monitor and process the assignment.

10. Use a family-system approach to address fire-setting behavior; require the entire family to attend an agreed-on number of sessions during which the family's roles, ways of communicating, and conflicts will be explored and confronted.

11. Assign each family member to complete the exercise "When a Fire Has No Fuel" from *Brief Child Therapy Homework Planner* (Jongsma, Peterson, and McInnis). Process the assignment in the next family session.

12. Assist the family members in learning to identify, express, and tolerate their own feelings and those of other family members.

13. Gently probe client's emotions in order to help client become better able to identify and express his/her feelings.

14. Assess client's unmet needs for attention, nurturance, and affirmation. Assist all caregivers (parents, siblings, teachers, baby-sitters, and extended family) in identifying actions (e.g., loud talk, acts of showing off, making up stories) that they can engage in to help satisfy client's emotional needs.

15. Assess the degree of chaos and/or violence in family leading to client's desire for

power and control over his/her environment. Encourage more structure, predictability, and respect within family.

16. Ask father to identify three things he could do to relate more to client. Then assign him to implement two of the three and monitor the results.

17. Work with mother or other caregiving person to obtain a Big Brother or Big Sister for client.

18. Assess whether fire setting is associated with a psychotic process or major affective disorder that may need psychotropic medication treatment. Refer for evaluation if necessary.

19. Probe client's feelings of hurt and anger over relationship rejection with peers and/or family. Interpret fire setting as an expression of rage.

20. Assess whether fire setting is associated with sexual and/or physical abuse.

21. Assess for the presence of ADHD.

22. Assist the family in following through with the recommendations from the psychiatric or ADHD evaluations.

23. Assist family in placing client in a residential treatment program for intense treatment of serious psychi-

atric disturbance if indicated.

—. _____

_____

—. _____

_____

—. _____

_____

DIAGNOSTIC SUGGESTIONS

Axis I: 312.8 Conduct Disorder
314.9 Attention-Deficit/Hyperactivity Disorder NOS
309.3 Adjustment Disorder With Disturbance of
Conduct
309.4 Adjustment Disorder With Mixed Disturbance
of Emotions and Conduct
312.30 Impulse-Control Disorder NOS
298.9 Psychotic Disorder NOS
296.xx Major Depressive Disorder

_____ _____

_____ _____

Axis II: 799.9 Diagnosis Deferred
V71.09 No Diagnosis on Axis II

_____ _____

_____ _____

GENDER IDENTITY DISORDER

BEHAVIORAL DEFINITIONS

1. Repeatedly states the desire to be, or feels he/she is, the opposite sex.
2. Preference for dressing in clothes typically worn by the other sex.
3. Prefers the roles of the opposite sex in make-believe play or fantasies.
4. Insists on participating in games and pastimes that are typical of the other sex.
5. Prefers playmates of the opposite sex.
6. Frequently passes as the opposite sex.
7. Insists that he/she was born the wrong sex.
8. Verbalizes a disgust with or rejection of his/her sexual anatomy.

—. _____
_____

—. _____
_____

—. _____
_____

LONG-TERM GOALS

1. Terminate the confusion regarding sexual identity and accept own gender and sexual anatomy.
2. Stop dressing as and playing like the opposite sex.
3. Accept the genitalia as a normal part of the body and terminate the repulsion of or desire to change it.
4. Establish and maintain lasting (i.e., six months or longer), same-sex peer friendship.

—. _____
   _____
   _____

—. _____
   _____
   _____

—. _____
   _____

SHORT-TERM OBJECTIVES

1. Openly express feelings regarding sexual identity and identify the causes for rejection of gender identity. (1, 2, 3)

2. Identify negative, distorted cognitive messages regarding gender identity. (4)

3. Replace negative self-talk regarding gender with positive thoughts. (5, 6)

4. Reduce the frequency of critical and repulsive statements made regarding sexual anatomy. (5, 6, 7)

5. Identify positive aspects of own sexual role. (5, 6, 7, 8, 9)

6. Express comfort with or even pride in sexual identity. (8, 9)

7. Parents explore their subtle and direct messages to the client that reinforce gender identity confusion. (10, 11)

8. Demonstrate increased self-esteem as evidenced by positive statements made

THERAPEUTIC INTERVENTIONS

1. Actively build the level of trust with the client through consistent eye contact, active listening, unconditional positive regard, and warm acceptance to help him/her increase the ability to identify and express feelings.

2. Explore the client's reasons for attraction to an opposite-sex identity.

3. Use play-therapy techniques to explore the client's sexual attitudes and causes for the rejection of gender identity.

4. Use cognitive therapy techniques to identify negative messages the client gives to himself/herself about sexual identity.

5. Assist client in identifying positive, realistic self-talk that can replace negative cognitions regarding gender identity.

6. Confront and reframe the client's self-disparaging comments about gender identity and sexual anatomy.

about talents, traits, and appearance. (9, 12)

9. Identify any negative feelings for same-sex parent and the reasons for these feelings. (13)

10. Same-sex parent (or parent substitute) and client agree to increase time spent together in activities. (14, 15, 16)

11. Verbalize the desire to be with the same-sex parent or other significant adult in quiet and active times. (14, 15, 16, 17)

12. Opposite-sex parent encourage and reinforce gender-appropriate dress, play, and peer-group identification as well as a stronger relationship between the client and the same-sex parent. (10, 16, 17, 18)

13. Increase time spent in socialization with same-sex peers. (18, 19, 20)

14. Dress consistently in clothes typical of same-sex peers without objection. (18, 20, 21)

15. List some positive role models for own sexual identity and tell why they are respected. (7, 22, 23)

16. Disclose any physical or sexual abuse. (1, 2, 3, 24)

—· _____

_____

7. Assist the client in identifying positive aspects of his/her own sexual identity.

8. Assign a mirror exercise in which the client talks positively to himself/herself regarding sexual identity.

9. Reinforce the client's positive self-descriptive statements.

10. Hold family therapy sessions to explore the dynamics that may reinforce the client's gender confusion.

11. Meet with the parents to explore their attitudes and behaviors that may contribute to the client's sexual identity confusion.

12. Assist the client in developing a list of his/her positive traits, talents, and physical characteristics.

13. Explore for any feelings of hurt, anger, or distrust of same-sex parent or parent substitute and the causes for these negative feelings.

14. Assign the same-sex parent to increase time and contact with the client in play and work activities while urging the opposite-sex parent to support the client in appropriate gender identification.

15. Assign the homework "One on One" in *Brief Child Therapy Homework Planner* (Jongsma, Peterson, and McInnis) to structure client's time spent with same-sex adult.

___. _____
    _____
    _____
___. _____
    _____

16. Help the client obtain the volunteer services of a same-sex Big Brother or Big Sister.

17. Conduct family therapy sessions in which client can explore and express his/her feelings toward same-sex parent; work toward resolution of any negativity in these feelings.

18. Encourage the parents in positively reinforcing appropriate gender identity, dress, and social behavior in the client.

19. Assign the client to initiate social (play) activities with same-sex peers.

20. Monitor and give positive feedback when the client's dress, socialization, and peer identity are appropriate.

21. Review whether client's desire to cross-dress is related to times of high stress in the family or occurs when client is feeling ignored.

22. Assign the client to list some positive, same-sex role models and process reasons for respecting these individuals.

23. Assign the homework "I Want to Be Like . . ." in *Brief Child Therapy Homework Planner* (Jongsma, Peterson, and McInnis) to structure role-model identification.

24. Explore the possibility that the client was physically or sexually abused. (See Physical/Emotional Abuse Victim

and Sexual Abuse Victim
sections in this *Planner.*)

—.   _____

      _____

—.   _____

      _____

—.   _____

      _____

DIAGNOSTIC SUGGESTIONS

Axis I: 302.6   Gender Identity Disorder in Children
           302.6   Gender Identity Disorder NOS

          _____   _____

Axis II: 799.9   Diagnosis Deferred
          V71.09   No Diagnosis on Axis II

          _____   _____

          _____   _____

GRIEF/LOSS UNRESOLVED

BEHAVIORAL DEFINITIONS

1. Loss of contact with a parent figure due to the parent's death.
2. Loss of contact with a parent figure due to termination of parental rights.
3. Loss of contact with a parent figure due to the parent's incarceration.
4. Loss of contact with a positive support network due to a geographic move.
5. Loss of meaningful contact with a parent figure due the parent's emotional abandonment.
6. Strong emotional response exhibited when the loss is mentioned.
7. Lack of appetite, nightmares, restlessness, inability to concentrate, irritability, tearfulness, or social withdrawal that began subsequent to a loss.
8. Marked drop in school grades, increase in angry outbursts, hyperactivity, or clinginess when separating from parents.
9. Feelings of guilt associated with the unreasonable belief in having done something to cause the loss or not having prevented it.
10. Avoidance of talking at length or in any depth about the loss.

___. _____

   _____

___. _____

   _____

___. _____

   _____

LONG-TERM GOALS

1. Begin a healthy grieving process around the loss.
2. Complete the process of letting go of the lost significant other.
3. Work through the grieving and letting-go process and reach the point of emotionally reinvesting in life with joy.
4. Successfully grieve the loss within a supportive emotional environment.
5. Resolve the loss and begin reinvesting in relationships with others and in age-appropriate activities.
6. Resolve feelings of guilt, depression, or anger associated with loss and return to adaptive level of functioning.

—. _____

_____

_____

—. _____

_____

_____

—. _____

_____

SHORT-TERM OBJECTIVES

1. Tell the story of the loss. (1, 2, 3, 4, 5, 6)
2. Develop a trusting relationship with the therapist as evidenced by the open communication of feelings and thoughts associated with the loss. (1, 7, 8, 15)
3. Attend and freely participate in art- and play-therapy sessions. (9, 10, 11, 12)
4. Identify feelings connected with the loss. (13, 14, 15, 43)
5. Verbalize and experience feelings connected with the loss. (13, 14, 15, 16)

THERAPEUTIC INTERVENTIONS

1. Actively build level of trust with the client through consistent eye contact, active listening, unconditional positive regard, and warm acceptance while asking him/her to identify and express feelings associated with the loss.
2. Ask the client to write a letter to the lost person describing his/her feelings and read this letter to the therapist.
3. Ask the client to tell the story of the loss through drawing pictures of his/her experience.

6. Attend a grief support group. (17)

7. Verbalize questions about the loss and work to obtain answers for each. (18, 19)

8. Verbalize an increase in understanding the process of grieving and letting go. (8, 20, 21, 22)

9. Decrease the expression of feelings of guilt and blame for the loss. (23, 24, 25, 26)

10. Identify positive things about the deceased loved one and/or the lost relationship and how these things may be remembered. (27, 28, 43)

11. Verbalize and resolve feelings of anger or guilt focused on himself/herself, on God, or on the decreased loved one that block the grief process. (26, 29, 30, 31)

12. Say good-bye to lost loved one. (32)

13. Visit the grave of deceased loved one to say good-bye. (33)

14. Parents verbalize an increase in their understanding of the grief process. (8, 34, 35)

15. Parents increase their verbal openness about the loss. (35, 36, 37)

16. Participate in memorial services, funeral services, or other grieving rituals. (38)

17. Parents identify ways to encourage and support the

4. Use a mutual storytelling technique (Gardner) in which the client tells his/her story. The therapist interprets the story for its underlying meaning and then tells a story using the same characters in a similar setting, but weaves into the story a healthy way to adapt to and resolve the loss.

5. Use a before-and-after drawing technique (*The Before and After Drawing Technique* by Cangelasi) to help guide the client in telling the story, through drawings, of how he/she was before and after the loss; work through the connected feelings.

6. Suggest that the client act out or tell about the loss by using puppets or felt figures on a board.

7. Read with the client *Where Is Daddy?* (Gogg) or *Emma Says Goodbye* (Nystrom) or a similar story about loss, and afterward discuss the story.

8. Educate the client and his/her parents about the stages of the grieving process and teach parents how to answer any of the client's questions.

9. Using child-centered play-therapy approaches (e.g., providing unconditional positive regard, reflecting feelings in nonjudgmental manner, displaying trust in

client in the grieving process. (34, 35, 38)

18. Parents who are losing custody verbally say good-bye
to the client. (35, 39, 40)

19. Attend and participate in a
formal session to say good-
bye to the parents whose
parental rights are being
terminated. (39, 40)

20. Verbalize positive memories
of the past and hopeful
statements about the fu-
ture. (41, 42, 43)

—. _____
_____
—. _____
_____
—. _____
_____

child's capacity to act responsibility), assist client in
working through his/her
loss.

10. Conduct individual play-
therapy sessions with the
client to provide the environment for expressing and
working through feelings
connected to his/her loss.

11. Use various art-therapy
techniques with Play-Doh,
clay, finger paints, and/or
markers to creatively ex-
press feelings connected to
client's loss. Have client
give an explanation of
his/her creation.

12. Conduct a play-therapy session around the use of "Art
or Verbal Metaphor for
Children Experiencing
Loss" (see Short in *101 Favorite Play Therapy Tech-
niques*) in which the client
is asked to talk about what
his/her life was like prior to
and after the loss using stories and drawings. Mirror,
acknowledge, and validate
client's feelings.

13. Assist the client in identifying his/her feelings by using
the Five Faces technique
(see *Helping Children Cope
with Separation and Loss*
by Jewett).

14. Play either the Goodbye
Game (available from
Childswork/Childsplay,
LLC) or The Good Mourn-
ing Game (Bisenius and

Norris) with client to assist him/her in exploring grief.

15. Assist the client in identifying, labeling, and expressing feelings connected with the loss.

16. Assign the client to keep a daily grief journal of drawings representing thoughts and feelings associated with the loss; review the journal in therapy sessions.

17. Refer client to a grief support group for children.

18. Expand client's understanding of death by reading to him/her *Lifetimes* (Mellonie and Ingpen), and discuss all questions that arise from the reading.

19. Assist the client in developing a list of questions about a specific loss; then try to direct him/her to resources (books, member of clergy, parent, counselor, etc.) for possible answers for each question.

20. Use *The Empty Place: A Child's Guide Through Grief* (Temes) to work client through his/her grief process.

21. Read to client *Don't Despair on Thursday* (Moser) and process the various suggestions given to handle the feelings connected to his/her grief.

22. Assign the client to interview a member of the clergy about death and to inter-

view an adult who has experienced and successfully worked through the death of a loved one.

23. Explore the client's thoughts and feelings of guilt and blame surrounding the loss, replacing irrational thoughts with realistic thoughts.

24. Use a Despart Fable (see *Helping Children Cope with Separation and Loss* by Jewett) or similar variation to help the client communicate blame for the loss (e.g., the therapist states, "A child says softly to himself, 'Oh, I did wrong.' What do you suppose the child believes he/she did wrong?").

25. Help the client lift the self-imposed curse he/she believes to be the cause for the loss by asking the person who is perceived as having imposed the curse to take it back or by using a pretend phone conversation in which the client apologizes for the behavior that he/she believes is the cause for the curse.

26. Suggest an absolution ritual ("confess" to a clergy person, apologize to an empty chair for deceased, etc.) for the client to implement to relieve the guilt or blame for the loss. Monitor the results and adjust as necessary.

27. Ask the client to list positive things about the de-

ceased and how he/she plans to remember each. Then process the list.

28. Ask the client to bring to a session pictures or mementos connected with the loss and to talk about them with the therapist.

29. Encourage and support the client in sessions to look angry, then to act angry, and finally to verbalize the anger.

30. Work with the client using behavioral techniques such as kneading clay, kicking a paper bag stuffed with newsprint, or using foam bats to hit objects without damage in order to release repressed feelings of anger; explore the targets and causes for anger.

31. Have the client complete an exercise related to an apology or forgiveness (e.g., writing a letter asking for forgiveness from deceased, using empty-chair technique to apologize) and process it with the therapist.

32. Assign client to write a good-bye letter to a significant other or to make a good-bye drawing and then process the letter or drawing with the therapist. See "Grief Letter" in *Brief Child Therapy Homework Planner* (Jongsma, Peterson, and McInnis).

33. Assign the client to visit the grave of the loved one with

an adult to communicate feelings and say good-bye, perhaps by leaving a letter or drawing; process the experience.

34. Teach parents specific ways to provide comfort, consolation, love, companionship, and support to the client in grief (e.g., bringing up the loss occasionally for discussion, encouraging the client to talk freely of the loss, suggesting photographs of the loved one be displayed, spending one-on-one time with client in quiet activities that may foster sharing of feelings, spending time with client in diversion activities).

35. Assign the client's parents to read *Learning to Say Good-bye* (LeShan) or *Helping Children Cope with Separation and Loss* (Jewett) to help them become familiar with the grieving process.

36. Conduct family sessions in which each member of the client's family talks about his/her experience related to the loss.

37. Refer the client's parents to a grief/loss support group.

38. Encourage the parents to allow the client to participate in the rituals and customs of grieving if the client is willing to be involved.

39. Conduct a session with the parents who are losing cus-

tody of the client to prepare them to say good-bye to the client in a healthy, affirming way.

40. Facilitate a good-bye session with the client and the parents who are losing custody to give the client permission to move on with his/her life. If parents who are losing custody or current parents are not available, ask them to write a letter that can be read at the session, or conduct a role play in which the client says good-bye to each parent.

41. Assist the client in making a record of his/her life in a book format to help visualize the past, present, and future life. When it is completed, have the client keep a copy and give another to the current parents.

42. Assign client to complete the exercise "Create a Memory Album" from *Brief Child Therapy Homework Planner* (Jongsma, Peterson, and McInnis) to help client preserve memories of lost loved one.

43. Assign client to read "Petey's Journey Through Sadness" in *Brief Child Therapy Homework Planner* (Jongsma, Peterson, and McInnis) to help client express positive memories of a lost loved one.

__. _____
   _____
__. _____
   _____
__. _____
   _____

DIAGNOSTIC SUGGESTIONS

Axis I: 296.2x   Major Depressive Disorder, Single Episode
              296.3x   Major Depressive Disorder, Recurrent
              V62.82   Bereavement
              309.0   Adjustment Disorder With Depressed Mood
              309.4   Adjustment Disorder With Mixed Disturbance
                       of Emotions and Conduct
              300.4   Dysthymic Disorder
              _____   _____
              _____   _____

Axis II: 799.9   Diagnosis Deferred
              V71.09   No Diagnosis on Axis II
              _____   _____
              _____   _____

LOW SELF-ESTEEM

BEHAVIORAL DEFINITIONS

1. Verbalizes self-disparaging remarks; sees self as unattractive, worthless, stupid, a loser, a burden, unimportant; takes blame easily.
2. Inability to accept compliments.
3. Refuses to take risks associated with new experiences, as she/he expects failure.
4. Avoids social contact with adults and peers.
5. Seeks excessively to please or receive attention/praise of adults and/or peers.
6. Inability to identify or accept positive traits or talents about self.
7. Fear of rejection of others, especially peer group.
8. Acts out in negative, attention-seeking ways.
9. Difficulty saying no to others; fears not being liked by others.

__.__ _____
_____
_____

__.__ _____
_____
_____

__.__ _____
_____

LONG-TERM GOALS

1. Elevate self-esteem.
2. Increase social interaction, assertiveness, confidence in self, and reasonable risk taking.
3. Build a consistent positive self-image.

4. Demonstrate improved self-esteem by accepting compliments, by identifying positive characteristics about self, by being able to say no to others, and by avoiding self-disparaging remarks.
5. See self as lovable and capable.
6. Increase social skill level.

—. _____
   _____
—. _____
   _____
—. _____
   _____

SHORT-TERM OBJECTIVES

1. Attend and freely participate in play-therapy sessions. (1, 2, 3, 4)
2. Verbalize an increased awareness of self-disparaging statements. (5, 6, 7)
3. Decrease frequency of negative self-statements. (5, 7, 9, 10)
4. Decrease verbalized fear of rejection while increasing statements of self-acceptance. (8, 9, 10, 27)
5. Identify positive traits and talents about self. (9, 10, 11, 12, 13, 21)
6. Identify and verbalize feelings. (14, 15, 16, 17)
7. Increase eye contact with others. (6, 7, 18, 19)
8. Identify actions that can be taken to improve self-image. (16, 20, 22)

THERAPEUTIC INTERVENTIONS

1. Employ psychoanalytic play-therapy approaches (e.g., allow the client to take the lead with therapist in exploring the source of unconscious conflicts, fixations, or developmental arrests) to assist the client in developing trust in therapist and in letting go of negative thought patterns/beliefs or fears that impact his/her level of self-esteem.
2. Use puppets in a directed or nondirected way to play out scenes involving self-esteem, such as making friends, starting conversations, trying something new, working out a conflict, expressing feelings, or asking for something he/she needs.
3. Conduct sessions, either directed or nondirected, with Play-Doh (several colors)

9. Identify and verbalize needs. (2, 23, 24, 25)

10. Increase frequency of speaking up with confidence in social situations. (7, 26, 27, 28)

11. Identify instances of emotional, physical, or sexual abuse that have damaged self-esteem. (29)

12. Identify negative automatic thoughts and replace with positive self-talk messages to build self-esteem. (30, 31)

13. Take responsibility for daily self-care and household tasks that are developmentally age-appropriate. (32, 33)

14. Identify and discuss the feelings associated with successful task accomplishment. (34, 35, 36, 37)

15. Positively acknowledge and verbally accept praise or compliments from others. (38)

16. Parents attend a didactic series on positive parenting. (39)

17. Parents verbalize realistic expectations and discipline methods for the client. (33, 40)

18. Parents identify specific activities for client that will facilitate development of positive self-esteem. (41)

19. Parents increase positive messages to the client. (39, 42)

and assorted instruments (cookie cutters, scissors, toothpicks, rolling pin, etc.) to engage child by relaxing defenses and opening the avenues of expression, which will facilitate therapist in helping to enhance client's self-esteem.

4. Conduct a session using an expressive clay technique, either directed (see *Clay-scaper* by Hadley) or non-directed, to assist client's expression and communication of significant issues and to facilitate increased self-esteem.

5. Confront and reframe client's self-disparaging comments.

6. Assist client in becoming aware of how he/she expresses or acts out (lack of eye contact, social withdrawal, expectation of failure or rejection, etc.) negative feelings about self.

7. Refer client to a group therapy that is focused on ways to build self-esteem.

8. Probe parents' interactions with client in family sessions and redirect or rechannel any patterns of interaction or methods of discipline that are negative or critical of the client.

9. Ask client to make one positive statement about self daily and record it on a chart or in a journal.

__. _____

     _____

__. _____

     _____

__. _____

     _____

10. Assist client in developing positive self-talk as a way of boosting his/her confidence and positive self-image.

11. Develop with client a list of positive affirmations about himself/herself and ask that it be read three times daily.

12. Use the Positive Attitude Ball (available from Childswork/Childsplay, LLC) or a similar aid to identify and affirm with client positive things about him/her for the first five minutes of each session.

13. Reinforce verbally client's use of positive statements of confidence or identification of positive attributes about self.

14. Use a therapeutic game (e.g., Talking, Feeling, Doing, available from Creative Therapeutics; Let's See About Me, available from Childswork/Childsplay, LLC; or The Ungame available from The Ungame Company) to promote client becoming more aware of self and his/her feelings.

15. Use a feelings chart, feelings felt board, or card game to enhance client's ability to identify specific feelings.

16. Assign self-esteem-building exercises from a workbook such as *The Building Blocks of Self-Esteem* (available from Childswork/Childsplay, LLC).

17. Educate client in the basics of identifying and labeling feelings, and assist him/her in beginning to identify what they are feeling.

18. Focus attention on client's lack of eye contact; encourage and reinforce increased eye contact within sessions.

19. Ask client to increase eye contact with teachers, parents, and other adults; review and process reports of attempts and the feelings associated with them.

20. Read with client *Don't Feed the Monster on Tuesdays* (Moser). Afterward, assist him/her in identifying things from the book that can be used to keep the monster of self-critical messages away. Then help the client make a chart containing self-esteem-building activities and have him/her record progress on each. Monitor and provide encouragement and affirmation for reported progress.

21. Ask client to read *My Best Friend Is Me* (available from Childswork/Childsplay, LLC), then make a list of good qualities about self to share with therapist.

22. Assign client and parents to complete exercises "Dixie Overcomes Her Fears" and "Learn from Your Mistakes" from *Brief Child Therapy Homework Planner* (Jongsma, Peterson, and

McInnis) to help client try new activities and see failure as a learning experience.

23. Assist client in becoming capable of identifying and verbalizing his/her emotional needs, along with ways to increase the chances of their needs being met.

24. Conduct a family session in which client expresses his/her needs to family and vice versa.

25. Use therapeutic stories (e.g., *Dr. Gardener's Fairy Tales for Today's Children* by Gardner) to help client identify feelings or needs and to build self-esteem.

26. Use role playing and behavioral rehearsal to improve assertiveness and social skills.

27. Encourage client to use the Pretending to Know How (Theiss) method in attempting tasks and facing new situations. Process client's results, acknowledging his/her competence in following through and reinforcing the self-confidence gained from each experience.

28. Assign parents to read with the client *Good Friends Are Hard to Find* (Frankel) to help client build social skills.

29. Explore for incidents of abuse (emotional, physical, and sexual) and how they have impacted feelings

about self. (See Sexual Abuse Victim and/or Physical/Emotional Abuse Victim sections in this *Planner.*)

30. Help client identify distorted negative beliefs about self and the world.

31. Help client identify, and reinforce the use of, more realistic, positive messages about self and life events.

32. Help client find and implement daily self-care and household or academic responsibilities that are age-appropriate. Monitor follow-through and give positive verbal feedback when warranted.

33. Train parents in 3 R's (related, respectful, and reasonable) discipline techniques (see *Raising Self-Reliant Children in a Self-Indulgent World* by Glenn and Nelson) in order to eliminate discipline that results in rebellion, revenge, or reduced self-esteem. Assist in implementation, and coach parents as they develop and improve their skills using this method.

34. Have conversation(s) on phone with client about some recent accomplishment, allowing client to initiate the call if he/she chooses and tell about the accomplishment. Give positive feedback, praise, compliments.

35. Use Positive Thinking game (available from Childswork/ Childsplay, LLC) to promote healthy self-talk and thought patterns. Allow client to take game home to play with parent(s).

36. Ask client to participate in The Yarn Drawing Game (see *Directive Group Play Therapy* by Leben), in which a ball of yarn/string is shaped into words, numbers, objects, or a complete picture. Therapist will offer the directive that there is no wrong design to empower client and will also give encouragement and perspective on the various designs created.

37. Use a projective exercise such as "Magic Act" (Walker), whereby client selects a colored piece of paper and uses at least three colors of paint to make dots, lines, or a picture. Paper is then folded lengthwise and flattened, with therapist saying, "Magic picture, what will client draw today?" The client unfolds the paper and tells what he/she sees in the design. Therapist will emphasize that there is no possible way to make a bad picture.

38. Use neurolinguistic programming or reframing techniques in which messages about self are

changed to assist the client in accepting compliments from others.

39. Ask parents to attend a didactic series on positive parenting, afterward processing how they can begin to implement some of these techniques.

40. Explore parent's expectations of the client. Assist, if necessary, in making them more realistic.

41. Ask parents to involve client in esteem-building activities (scouting, experiential camps, music, sports, youth groups, enrichment programs, etc.).

42. Encourage parents to seek out opportunities to praise, reinforce, and recognize client's minor or major accomplishments.

__. _____
   _____
__. _____
   _____
__. _____
   _____

DIAGNOSTIC SUGGESTIONS

Axis I:	300.4	Dysthymic Disorder
	314.01	Attention-Deficit/Hyperactivity Disorder, Predominantly Hyperactive-Impulsive Type
	300.23	Social Phobia
	296.xx	Major Depressive Disorder
	307.1	Anorexia Nervosa

	309.21	Separation Anxiety Disorder
	300.02	Generalized Anxiety
	995.5	Physical Abuse of Child (Victim)
	V61.21	Sexual Abuse of Child, 995.5 Victim
	V61.21	Neglect of Child, 995.5 Victim
	303.90	Alcohol Dependence
	304.30	Cannabis Dependence
	_____	_____
	_____	_____
Axis II:	317	Mild Mental Retardation
	V62.89	Borderline Intellectual Functioning
	799.9	Diagnosis Deferred
	V71.09	No Diagnosis on Axis II
	_____	_____
	_____	_____

MEDICAL CONDITION

BEHAVIORAL DEFINITIONS

1. A diagnosis of a chronic illness that is not life threatening but necessitates changes in living.
2. A diagnosis of an acute, serious illness that is life threatening.
3. A diagnosis of chronic illness that eventually will be terminal.
4. Sad affect, social withdrawal, anxiety, loss of interest in activities, and low energy.
5. Suicidal ideation.
6. Denial of the seriousness of the medical condition.
7. Refusal to cooperate with recommended medical treatments.

—. _____
    _____
—. _____
    _____
—. _____
    _____

LONG-TERM GOALS

1. Accept the illness and adapt life to necessary changes.
2. Resolve emotional crisis and face terminal-illness implications.
3. Work through the grieving process and face the reality of own death with peace.
4. Accept emotional support from those who care without pushing them away in anger.
5. Resolve depression and find peace of mind in spite of the illness.
6. Live life to the fullest extent possible even though time may be limited.

7. Cooperate with medical treatment regimen without passive-aggressive or active resistance.

8. Become as knowledgeable as possible about the diagnosed condition and about living as normally as possible.

9. Reduce fear, anxiety, and worry associated with the medical condition.

—. _____

_____

—. _____

_____

—. _____

_____

SHORT-TERM OBJECTIVES

1. Describe history, symptoms, and treatment of medical condition. (1, 2)

2. Identify feelings associated with the medical condition. (3)

3. Family members share with each other feelings that are triggered by client's medical condition. (4)

4. Identify the losses or limitations that have been experienced due to the medical condition. (5)

5. Verbalize an increased understanding of the steps to grieving the losses brought on by the medical condition. (6, 7)

6. Identify the stages of grief that have been experienced in the continuum of the grieving process. (6, 7)

THERAPEUTIC INTERVENTIONS

1. Gather a history of the facts regarding client's medical condition, including symptoms, treatment, and prognosis.

2. With client's informed consent, contact treating physician and family members for additional medical information regarding client's diagnosis, treatment, and prognosis.

3. Assist client in identifying, sorting through, and verbalizing the various feelings generated by the medical condition.

4. Meet with family members to facilitate their clarifying and sharing possible feelings of guilt, anger, helplessness, and/or sibling attention jealousy associ-

7. Begin verbalizing feelings associated with the losses related to the medical condition. (3, 8)

8. Daily, decrease time spent focused on the negative aspects of the medical condition. (9, 10)

9. Implement acts of spiritual faith as a source of comfort and hope. (11)

10. Verbalize acceptance of the reality of the medical condition and its consequences while decreasing denial. (12, 13)

11. Verbally express fears about possible deterioration of physical condition and death. (14, 15)

12. Identify and verbally express feelings of depression or anxiety associated with medical condition. (16, 17)

13. Attend a support group of others diagnosed with a similar illness. (17)

14. Parents and family members attend a support group. (18)

15. Comply with medication regimen and necessary medical procedures, reporting any side effects or problems to physicians or therapists. (2, 19, 20, 21)

16. Identify enjoyable activities that can still be engaged in alone and with others. (22)

17. Implement engagement of social, productive, and recreational activities that

ated with client's medical condition.

5. Ask client to list the changes, losses, or limitations that have resulted from the medical condition.

6. Educate the patient on the stages of the grieving process and answer any questions.

7. Suggest client read *Don't Despair on Thursday* (Moser) or some other book on grief and loss.

8. Assign client to keep a daily grief journal to be shared in therapy sessions.

9. Suggest that the client set aside a specific time-limited period each day to focus on mourning the medical condition. After time period is up, have client resume regular daily activities with agreement to put off thoughts until next scheduled time. (Mourning times could include putting on dark clothing, listening to sad music, and so forth. Clothing would be changed at end of allotted time period.)

10. Challenge client to focus thoughts on positive aspects of life rather than on losses associated with medical condition; reinforce instances of such positive focus.

11. Encourage client to rely upon his/her spiritual faith promises, activities (prayer, meditation, worship, music,

are possible in spite of medical condition. (23)

18. Implement behavioral stress-reduction skills to terminate exacerbation of medical condition due to tension. (24, 25, 26)

19. Identify negative self-talk and catastrophizing that is associated with medical condition. (27)

20. Implement positive self-talk and positive imagery as means of triggering peace of mind and reduced tension. (28, 29)

21. Verbalize increased factual understanding of medical condition. (30, 31)

22. Identify the sources of emotional support that have been beneficial and additional sources that could be tapped. (32, 33)

23. Parents verbalize fears regarding the possible death or severely disabled life of their child. (34)

24. Family members share any conflicts that have developed between them as each person reacts to the child's illness in a unique way. (35, 36)

25. Parents verbalize an understanding of the healing potential of hope, faith, touch, love, and one's own personal positive presence with the sick child. (37)

etc.), and fellowship as sources of support.

12. Gently confront denial of the seriousness of condition and of the need for compliance with medical treatment procedures.

13. Reinforce acceptance of medical condition.

14. Explore and process fears associated with deterioration of physical health, death, and dying.

15. Normalize client's feelings of grief, sadness, or anxiety associated with medical condition. Encourage verbal expression of these emotions.

16. Assess for and treat depression and anxiety. (See Depression and Anxiety sections in this *Planner.*)

17. Refer client to a support group of others living with the same medical condition.

18. Refer family members to a community-based support group associated with client's medical condition.

19. Monitor and reinforce client's compliance with medical treatment regimen.

20. Explore and address misconceptions, fears, and situational factors that interfere with medical treatment compliance.

21. Confront any manipulation, passive-aggressive, and denial mechanisms that block compliance with medical regimen.

__· _____
    _____
__· _____
    _____
__· _____
    _____

22. Sort out with client activities that can still be enjoyed alone and with others.

23. Solicit a commitment to increase activity level by engaging in enjoyable and challenging activities; reinforce such engagement.

24. Teach deep-muscle relaxation and deep-breathing methods along with positive imagery to induce relaxation.

25. Utilize EMG biofeedback to monitor, increase, and reinforce client's depth of relaxation.

26. Develop and encourage a routine of physical exercise.

27. Assist client in identifying the cognitive distortions and negative automatic thoughts that contribute to a negative attitude and hopeless feelings associated with medical condition.

28. Generate with client a list of positive, realistic self-talk that can replace the cognitive distortions and catastrophizing regarding his/her medical condition and its treatment.

29. Teach client the use of positive, relaxing, healing imagery to reduce stress and promote peace of mind.

30. Provide client with accurate information regarding symptoms, causes, treatment, and prognosis for medical condition.

31. Refer client and parents to reading material and reliable Internet resources for medical information.

32. Probe and evaluate the parents' resources of emotional support.

33. Encourage parents to reach out for support from church leaders, extended family, hospital social services, community support groups, and God.

34. Draw out parents' unspoken fears about the child's possible death; empathize with their panic, helpless frustration, and anxiety. Reassure them of God's presence as the giver and supporter of life.

35. Explore how each parent is dealing with the stress and whether conflicts have developed between the parents because of differing response styles. Can they be supportive and accepting of each other?

36. Facilitate a spirit of tolerance for individual differences in each person's internal resources and response styles in the face of threat.

37. Stress the potent healing power in the family's constant presence with the ill child and emphasize that there is strong healing potential in creating a warm, caring, supportive, positive environment for the child.

___.   _____
       _____

___.   _____
       _____

___.   _____
       _____

DIAGNOSTIC SUGGESTIONS

Axis I: 316   Psychological Symptoms Affecting (Axis III
                          Disorder)
              309.0   Adjustment Disorder With Depressed Mood
              309.24   Adjustment Disorder With Anxiety
              309.28   Adjustment Disorder With Mixed Anxiety and
                          Depressed Mood
              309.3   Adjustment Disorder With Disturbance of
                          Conduct
              309.4   Adjustment Disorder With Mixed Disturbance
                          of Emotions and Conduct
              296.xx   Major Depressive Disorder
              311   Depressive Disorder NOS
              300.02   Generalized Anxiety Disorder
              300.00   Anxiety Disorder NOS

              _____   _____

              _____   _____

Axis II: 799.9   Diagnosis Deferred
              V71.09   No Diagnosis on Axis II

              _____   _____

              _____   _____

MENTAL RETARDATION

BEHAVIORAL DEFINITIONS

1. Significantly subaverage intellectual functioning as demonstrated by an IQ score of approximately 70 or below on an individually administered intelligence test.
2. Significant impairments in academic functioning, communication, self-care, home living, social skills, and leisure activities.
3. Difficulty understanding and following complex directions in home, school, or community settings.
4. Short- and long-term memory impairment.
5. Concrete thinking or impaired abstract reasoning abilities.
6. Impoverished social skills as manifested by frequent use of poor judgment, limited understanding of the antecedents and consequences of social actions, and lack of reciprocity in peer interactions.
7. Lack of insight and repeated failure to learn from experience or past mistakes.
8. Low self-esteem as evidenced by frequent self-derogatory remarks (e.g., "I'm so stupid").
9. Recurrent pattern of acting out or engaging in disruptive behaviors without considering the consequences of the actions.

__. _____
_____

__. _____
_____

__. _____
_____

LONG-TERM GOALS

1. Achieve all academic goals identified on the Individualized Educational Plan (IEP).
2. Function at an appropriate level of independence in home, residential, educational, or community settings.
3. Develop an awareness and acceptance of intellectual and cognitive limitations but consistently verbalize feelings of self-worth.
4. Parents and/or caregivers develop an awareness and acceptance of the client's intellectual and cognitive capabilities so that they place appropriate expectations on his/her functioning.
5. Consistently comply and follow through with simple directions in a daily routine at home, at school, and/or in a residential setting.
6. Significantly reduce the frequency and severity of socially inappropriate or acting-out behaviors.

—. _____

_____

—. _____

_____

—. _____

_____

SHORT-TERM OBJECTIVES

1. Complete a comprehensive intellectual and cognitive assessment. (1, 4, 7)
2. Complete psychological testing. (2, 4, 7)
3. Complete neuropsychological testing. (3, 4, 7)
4. Complete an evaluation by physical and occupational therapists. (5, 7)
5. Complete a speech/language evaluation. (6, 7)
6. Receive appropriate auxiliary services (e.g., physical,

THERAPEUTIC INTERVENTIONS

1. Arrange for a comprehensive intellectual and cognitive assessment to determine the presence of mental retardation and to gain greater insight into the client's learning strengths and weaknesses.
2. Arrange for psychological testing to assess whether emotional factors or ADHD are interfering with the client's intellectual and academic functioning.

speech/language, occupational therapy, and counseling). (5, 6, 7)

7. Client and parents comply with recommendations made by a multidisciplinary evaluation team at school regarding educational interventions. (7, 8, 15)

8. Move the client to appropriate classroom(s) in a school setting or residential program. (7, 8, 9, 15)

9. Move the client to an appropriate residential setting if warranted. (8, 9, 15)

10. Parents and teachers implement educational strategies that maximize client's learning strengths and compensate for learning weaknesses. (7, 8, 10, 11)

11. Parents maintain regular communication with client's teachers and other appropriate school officials. (10)

12. Complete school and homework assignments on a regular basis. (10, 11, 12)

13. Parents, teachers, and caregivers implement a token economy in the classroom or placement setting to reinforce on-task behaviors, completion of school assignments, good impulse control, and positive social skills. (10, 11, 12, 13)

14. Parents increase praise and other positive reinforcement toward the client in regard to his/her academic perfor-

3. Arrange for a neurological examination or neuropsychological testing to rule out possible organic factors that may be contributing to the client's intellectual or cognitive deficits.

4. Provide feedback to the client, his/her parents, school officials, and residential staff regarding the intellectual, psychological, or neuropsychological testing.

5. Refer the client to physical and occupational therapists to assess perceptual or sensory-motor deficits and determine the need for ongoing physical and/or occupational therapy.

6. Refer the client to a speech/language pathologist to assess deficits and determine the need for appropriate therapy.

7. Attend an Individualized Educational Planning Committee meeting with the client's parents, teachers, and other appropriate professionals to determine his/her eligibility for special education services. Design educational interventions and establish goals.

8. Consult with the client, his/her parents, teachers, and other appropriate school officials about designing effective learning programs or interventions that build on the client's

mance or social behaviors.
(12, 13, 22, 26)

15. Parents and family cease verbalizations of denial about the client's intellectual and cognitive deficits. (14, 15, 16)

16. Parents recognize and verbally acknowledge their unrealistic expectations of or excessive pressure on the client to function at an unrealistic level. (16, 17, 18, 20)

17. Parents recognize and verbally acknowledge that their pattern of overprotectiveness interferes with the client's intellectual, emotional, and social development. (15, 19, 20, 24)

18. Parents reduce the frequency of speaking for the client or performing activities that he/she is capable of doing independently. (19, 21, 24, 25)

19. Increase participation in family activities or outings. (20, 21, 22, 23)

20. Perform household chores (e.g., pick up toys, make bed, help put away clothes) on a daily or regular basis. (26, 29, 30, 31)

21. Parents consistently implement behavior management techniques to reduce the client's frequency and severity of temper outbursts and disruptive or aggressive behaviors. (27, 28, 32, 33)

strengths and compensate for weaknesses.

9. Consult with the client's parents, school officials, or mental health professionals about the need for placement in a foster home, group home, or residential program.

10. Encourage the parents to maintain regular communication with the client's teacher or school officials to monitor his/her academic, behavioral, emotional, and social progress.

11. Design a token economy for the classroom or residential program to improve the client's academic performance, impulse control, and social skills.

12. Encourage the parents to provide frequent praise and other reinforcement for positive social behaviors and academic performance.

13. Design a reward system or contingency contract to reinforce client's adaptive or social behaviors.

14. Educate parents about the symptoms and characteristics of mental retardation.

15. Confront and challenge the parents' denial surrounding their child's intellectual deficits so they cooperate with recommendations regarding placement and educational interventions.

22. Parents agree to and implement an allowance program that helps the client learn to manage money more effectively. (29, 30)

23. Take a bath or shower, comb hair, wash hands before meals, and brush teeth on a daily basis. (20, 30, 31)

24. Dress self independently, with either preselected clothes or clothes of own choosing. (20, 30, 31)

25. Initiate appropriate social greetings, smile, and make eye contact when entering a social situation. (34, 35, 37)

26. Recognize and verbally identify appropriate and inappropriate social behaviors. (34, 35, 37)

27. Increase the frequency of making positive self-descriptive statements. (12, 34, 36)

28. Increase ability to identify and express feelings. (38, 39, 40, 41)

29. Express feelings of sadness, anxiety, and insecurity that are related to cognitive and intellectual limitations. (43, 44, 45)

30. Express feelings through play therapy, mutual story-telling, and artwork. (41, 42, 46)

31. Take medication as prescribed by a physician. (2, 3, 47)

16. Conduct family therapy sessions to assess whether the parents are placing excessive pressure on the client to function at level that he/she is not capable of achieving.

17. Confront and challenge the parents about placing excessive pressure on the client.

18. Instruct client to complete family kinetic drawing to assess how client perceives his/her role or place in family system.

19. Observe parent-child interactions to assess whether the parents' overprotectiveness or infantilization of the client interferes with his/her intellectual, emotional, or social development.

20. Assist parents or caregivers in developing realistic expectations of client's intellectual capabilities and level of adaptive functioning.

21. Encourage parents and family members to regularly include the client in outings or activities (e.g., attending sporting events, going ice skating, visiting a child's museum).

22. Instruct family members to observe positive behaviors by the client in between therapy sessions. Reinforce positive behaviors and encourage client to continue to exhibit these behaviors.

23. Encourage parents to use "You Belong Here" exercise

—. _____
    _____
    _____
—. _____
    _____
—. _____
    _____

in *Brief Child Therapy Homework Planner* (Jongsma, Peterson, and McInnis) to promote client's feelings of acceptance and sense of belonging in the family.

24. Assign the client a task in the family (e.g., vacuuming, dusting, taking out recyclables) that is appropriate for his/her level of functioning and provides him/her with a sense of responsibility or belonging.

25. Consult with school officials or residential staff about the client performing a job (e.g., raising the flag, helping run video equipment) to build self-esteem and provide him/her with a sense of responsibility.

26. Explore instances in which client achieved success or accomplished a goal; reinforce positive steps that client took to successfully accomplish goals.

27. Teach the parents effective behavior management techniques (e.g., time-outs, removal of privileges) to decrease the frequency and severity of the client's temper outbursts, acting-out, and aggressive behaviors.

28. Encourage the parents to utilize natural, logical consequences for the client's inappropriate social or maladaptive behaviors.

29. Counsel the parents about setting up an allowance plan that seeks to increase the client's responsibilities and to help him/her learn simple money management skills.

30. Design a reward system at home to improve the client's personal hygiene and self-help skills.

31. Utilize "Activities of Daily Living Program" in *Brief Child Therapy Homework Planner* (Jongsma, Peterson, and McInnis) to increase client's level of independence and improve personal hygiene or self-care skills.

32. Teach the client basic mediational and self-control strategies (e.g., "stop, look, listen, and think") to delay gratification and inhibit impulses.

33. Train client in use of guided imagery or relaxation techniques to calm himself/herself down and develop greater control of anger.

34. Identify and reinforce the client's positive social behaviors.

35. Use role play, modeling, and puppets to teach the client social skills.

36. Encourage the client to participate in the Special Olympics to build self-esteem.

37. Use puppets, dolls, or stuffed animals to model so-

cially appropriate ways of expressing emotions or relating to others.

38. Teach the client effective communication skills (i.e., proper listening, good eye contact, "I" statements) to improve his/her ability to express thoughts, feelings, and needs more clearly.

39. Teach the client how to identify and label different emotions.

40. Use Feelings Poster, available from Childswork/ Childsplay, LLC, to help client identify and express different emotions.

41. Instruct client to draw faces of different emotions; have client tell of times when he/she experienced these different emotions.

42. Conduct filial play-therapy sessions (i.e., parents are present) to increase parents' awareness of client's thoughts and feelings and to strengthen parent-child bond.

43. Employ child-centered principles (e.g., demonstrate genuine interest, provide unconditional positive regard, reflect feelings in nonjudgmental manner) in play-therapy sessions to help client develop greater awareness of self and his/her unique thoughts, feelings, and needs.

44. Assist the client in coming to an understanding and acceptance of the limitations surrounding his/her intellectual deficits and adaptive functioning.

45. Read *Don't Look at Me* (Sanford) to client to help him/her gain acceptance of his/her limitations while at the same time developing an awareness of his/her own unique strengths or talents.

46. Use art therapy (drawing, painting, sculpting) with client in foster care or residential program to help him/her express basic emotions related to issues of separation, loss, or abandonment by parental figures.

47. Arrange a medication evaluation for the client.

__. _____
   _____

__. _____
   _____

__. _____
   _____

DIAGNOSTIC SUGGESTIONS

Axis I:	299.00	Autistic Disorder
	299.80	Rett's Disorder
	299.80	Asperger's Disorder
	299.10	Childhood Disintegrative Disorder
	_____	_____
	_____	_____

Axis II: 317   Mild Mental Retardation
318.0   Moderate Mental Retardation
318.1   Severe Mental Retardation
318.2   Profound Mental Retardation
319   Mental Retardation, Severity Unspecified
V62.89   Borderline Intellectual Functioning
799.9   Diagnosis Deferred
V71.09   No Diagnosis on Axis II

_____   _____

_____   _____

OPPOSITIONAL DEFIANT

BEHAVIORAL DEFINITIONS

1. Displays a pattern of negativistic, hostile, and defiant behavior toward most adults.
2. Often acts as if parents, teachers, and other authority figures are the "enemy."
3. Erupts in temper tantrums (e.g., screaming, crying, throwing objects, thrashing on ground, or refusing to move) in defiance of direction from an adult caregiver.
4. Consistently argues with adults.
5. Often defies or refuses to comply with requests and rules, even when they are reasonable.
6. Deliberately annoys people and is easily annoyed by others.
7. Often blames others for his/her mistakes or misbehavior.
8. Consistently is angry and resentful.
9. Often is spiteful or vindictive.
10. Has experienced significant impairment in either social, academic, or occupational functioning.

__. _____
   _____
   _____
__. _____
   _____
   _____
__. _____
   _____

LONG-TERM GOALS

1. Marked reduction in the intensity and frequency of hostile and defiant behaviors toward adults.

2. Terminate temper tantrums and replace with calm, respectful compliance with adult directions.
3. Begin to consistently interact with adults in a mutually respectful manner.
4. Bring hostile, defiant behaviors within socially acceptable standards.
5. Replace hostile, defiant behaviors toward adults with those of respect and cooperation.
6. Resolution of the conflict that underlies the anger, hostility, and defiance.
7. Reach a level of reduced tension, increased satisfaction, and improved communication with family and/or other authority figures.

—. _____

_____

—. _____

_____

—. _____

_____

SHORT-TERM OBJECTIVES

1. Describe perception of own behavior and feelings toward rules and authority figures. (1, 2)

2. Attend and freely participate in play-therapy sessions. (3, 4, 5)

3. Participate in family therapy with focus on changes necessary to produce harmony. (6, 7)

4. Decrease the frequency and intensity of hostile, negativistic, and defiant interactions with parents/adults. (8, 9, 10, 11)

THERAPEUTIC INTERVENTIONS

1. Actively build the level of trust with client through consistent eye contact, active listening, unconditional positive regard, and warm acceptance to help increase his/her disclosure of thoughts and feelings.

2. Explore client's own perception of oppositional pattern toward rules and authority figures.

3. Employ A.C.T. model (Landreth) in play therapy to *acknowledge* feelings, *communicate* limits, and *target* and reinforce prosocial and cooperative behavior.

5. Identify preferred treatment by parents/adults. (12, 13, 20)

6. Parents demonstrate the ability to give effective commands. (14, 15)

7. Recognize and verbalize hurt or angry feelings in constructive ways. (5, 16, 17)

8. Verbalize the connection between feelings and behavior. (9, 18, 19)

9. Identify and verbalize what is needed from parents and other adults. (17, 20)

10. Increase the frequency of civil, respectful interactions with parents/adults. (12, 14, 20, 21)

11. Identify targets and causes for angry feelings. (10, 16, 17, 22)

12. Parents identify new child behavior management techniques they will try. (23, 24)

13. Demonstrate the ability to play by the rules in a cooperative fashion. (25, 26)

14. Parents clearly state what is acceptable and unacceptable behavior in the family and identify positive and negative consequences of client's behavior. (6, 27, 28, 29)

15. Parents ignore inappropriate behaviors and reduce unproductive oververbalizing to client (30, 31, 32)

16. Parents revise previous responses to client's misbehavior and implement

4. Employ psychoanalytic play-therapy approach (e.g., explore and gain understanding of the etiology of the unconscious conflicts and defiance; interpret resistance, transference, or care anxieties) to help client resolve conflicts and exhibit more prosocial behaviors.

5. Interpret the feelings expressed in play-therapy sessions and relate them to the problems and conflicts that are daily occurring in client's life.

6. Read and process in a family session the story "The Little Crab" from *Stories for the Third Ear* (Wallas). Follow up by using the metaphor of the story as a basis for family/client change, referencing it regularly in future sessions.

7. Facilitate family therapy sessions in which the issues of respect, cooperation, and conflict resolution are addressed and in which possible solutions are reached and implemented.

8. Play with client the Don't Be Difficult game (available from Childswork/Childsplay, LLC) to decrease uncooperative behaviors and to demonstrate prosocial behaviors and their rewards.

9. In session, read and process with client the book *Everything I Do You Blame On Me* (Abern) to help him/her

significantly different reactions. (33, 34)

17. Parents acknowledge their own conflicts that influence the client's misbehavior. (35, 36)

18. Parents verbalize clear rules, boundaries, and behavioral expectations and implement time-out and other behavior-modification consequences. (15, 37, 38, 39)

19. Parents implement the Barkley method of oppositional child behavior control. (40)

20. Identify preferred relational patterns between family members. (41, 42)

—. _____
   _____

—. _____
   _____

—. _____
   _____

develop insight regarding his/her behavior.

10. In an open, accepting, and understanding manner, encourage client's verbalization of negative, hostile feelings in individual sessions.

11. Assist client in identifying negative, hostile, and defiant behaviors; then offer a paradoxical interpretation or reframing for each (e.g., if child and parents argue, select topics for them to argue about and set the time for arguing, or reframe the arguing as client's way to get parents to talk to him/her).

12. Establish with client the basics of treating others respectfully. Teach the principle of reciprocity, asking him/her to agree to treat everyone in a respectful manner for a one-week period to see if others will reciprocate by treating him/her with more respect.

13. Ask client to complete the exercise "If I Could Run My Family" from *Brief Child Therapy Homework Planner* (Jongsma, Peterson, and McInnis) to confront client with the challenges of being in control.

14. Ask parents to read *Winning Cooperation from Your Child* (Wenning) to expand their knowledge of difficult children. Give new suggestions for ways of interven-

ing with their child more effectively and with less frustration.

15. Assign parents to do the exercise "Switching from Defense to Offense" from *Brief Child Therapy Homework Planner* (Jongsma, Peterson, and McInnis) to help parents in identifying and implementing new methods of intervention in client's behaviors. Monitor parents' follow-through, coaching and giving encouragement as needed.

16. Use a therapeutic game (Talking, Feeling, Doing, available from Creative Therapeutics, or The Ungame, available from The Ungame Company) to expand client's ability to express feelings respectfully.

17. Assist client in becoming able to recognize needs and feelings and express them in constructive, respectful ways.

18. Help client make connections between feelings and behaviors.

19. Use a set of dominoes and/or Domino Rally to help client build an awareness of consequences and a sense of internal control. Play dominoes with client using an established set of rules. Use Domino Rally by setting it up and allowing the client to start the domino chain reactions. Emphasize the

behavioral chain of events
that occur and explain how
feelings lead to a chain of
behavioral events. (See
chapter by Case in *101 Favorite Play Therapy Tech-
niques.*)

20. Assign client to complete
exercise "Filing a Com-
plaint" from *Brief Child
Therapy Homework Planner*
(Jongsma, Peterson, and
McInnis) to assist him/her in
reframing complaints into
requests for positive change.

21. Videotape a family session,
using appropriate portions
to show the family interaction patterns that are destructive; teach family
members, using role play,
role reversal, and modeling,
to implement more respectful patterns.

22. Ask client to list all individuals with whom he/she feels
angry and the reasons for
the anger.

23. Assign parents to read the
chapters on defiant chil-
dren in *The Challenging
Child* (Greenspan), selecting key management tech-
niques they would like to
implement.

24. Assist parents in implementing new management
techniques (behavior-
modification principles,
*1-2-3 Magic: Training Your
Preschoolers and Preteens to
Do What You Want* by Phe-
lan, *8 Weeks to a Well-*

Behaved Child by Windell, etc.) and coach and encourage parents to consistently follow through on selected techniques.

25. Play checkers, first with client determining the rules (and therapist holding client to those rules) and then with rules determined by the therapist. Process the experience and give positive verbal praise to client for following established rules.

26. Utilize "Tearing Paper" exercise (see Davies in *101 Favorite Play Therapy Techniques*): Therapist places several phone books and Sunday papers in the center of family group and instructs the family to tear the paper into small pieces and throw them in the air. The only two conditions are not to throw paper anywhere but up in the air and that they must clean up at the end. During cleanup, the therapist will reenforce verbally their follow-through in cleaning up and process what it was like to release the energy in this way and to do something together without conflict.

27. Have parents read to client *The Girls and Boys Book About Good & Bad Behavior* (Gardner) to help the client develop conscience and behavior modification.

28. Institute with parents and teachers a system of positive consequences (see Selekman's *Solution-Focused Therapy with Children*) for client's prosocial and cooperative behaviors (e.g., writing a card to a relative, mowing a neighbor's lawn, doing a good deed for an elderly neighbor).

29. Help parents clarify and communicate to client what constitutes acceptable and unacceptable behavior in the family. Then ask them to implement as a consequence temporary "excommunication" of the child from the family (i.e., denial of interactions and privileges) when unacceptable behavior is exhibited, reinstating the child to good standing (interaction and privileges occurring again naturally) in the presence of acceptable behavior.

30. Conduct family sessions during which therapist models child-interaction techniques for parents.

31. Instruct parents to reduce their own unproductive ververbalizations to child and to ignore nondestructive abusive/negative behaviors.

32. Monitor parents' use of new techniques, giving feedback and suggesting adjustments as needed.

33. Conduct a family session in which the family is given a

task or problem to solve together (e.g., making a family coat of arms or collage). Observe and give feedback on more constructive intervention behaviors.

34. Teach parents to utilize the brief solution exercise (de Shazer or Selekman) "Do Something Different," in which parents break their predictable response with client to reestablish control in positive, fun, and novel ways. Brainstorm with parents possible options (Selekman suggests parents dancing a strange dance or starting to hug and kiss when client begins a temper tantrum) and select one to use.

35. In family sessions, expose the parental conflict that underlies the client's behavior; refer the parents to conjoint sessions to begin to resolve their issues of conflict.

36. Use a family-systems approach in individual sessions to assist client in seeing the family from a different perspective and in moving toward disengaging from dysfunction.

37. Assist parents in defining acceptable and unacceptable behaviors and in developing time-outs (either a set amount of time or until the behavior is under control) to reinforce these limits.

38. Help parents develop and implement a behavior-modification contract in which appropriate behaviors would be rewarded with money or special privileges (attending an event, going on a family outing), while inappropriate behaviors would result in fines (losing money and privileges).

39. Monitor parents' follow-through in administering the behavior-modification contract and/or time-outs. Give feedback, support, and praise as appropriate.

40. Ask parents to watch the video *Techniques for Working with Oppositional Defiant Disorder in Children* (Barkley), or read *Your Defiant Child: Eight Steps to Better Behavior* (Barkley and Benton), to develop understanding of the condition and the ways to intervene in the most effective ways; encourage implementation and monitor effectiveness.

41. Facilitate a family session in which the family is sculpted (Satir). Process the experience with family. Then sculpt them as they would like to be.

42. Conduct family sessions during which the family system and its interactions are analyzed. Develop and implement a strategic/structural/experiential intervention.

—.   _____
       _____
—.   _____
       _____
—.   _____
       _____

DIAGNOSTIC SUGGESTIONS

Axis I: 313.81   Oppositional Defiant Disorder
                 312.8   Conduct Disorder
                 312.9   Disruptive Behavior Disorder NOS
                 314.01   Attention-Deficit/Hyperactivity Disorder,
                                Predominantly Hyperactive-Impulsive Type
                 314.9   Attention-Deficit/Hyperactivity Disorder NOS
                 V62.81   Relational Problem NOS

                 _____   _____

Axis II: 799.9   Diagnosis Deferred
                 V71.09   No Diagnosis on Axis II

                 _____   _____
                 _____   _____

PEER/SIBLING CONFLICT

BEHAVIORAL DEFINITIONS

1. Frequent, overt, intense fighting (verbal and/or physical) with peers and/or siblings.
2. Projects responsibility for conflicts onto others.
3. Believes that he/she is treated unfairly and/or that parents favor sibling(s) over himself/herself.
4. Peer and/or sibling relationships are characterized by bullying, defiance, revenge, taunting, and incessant teasing.
5. Has virtually no friends, or only a few, who exhibit similar socially disapproved behavior.
6. Exhibits a general pattern of behavior that is impulsive, intimidating, and unmalleable.
7. Behaviors toward peers are aggressive and lack a discernable empathy for others.
8. Does not respond to praise and encouragement as do his/her peers.
9. Parents are hostile toward client, demonstrating a familial pattern of rejection, quarreling, lack of respect, and affection.

—. _____
_____
_____
—. _____
_____
_____
—. _____
_____

LONG-TERM GOALS

1. Compete, cooperate, and resolve conflict appropriately with peers and siblings.

2. Develop healthy mechanisms for handling anxiety, tension, frustration, and anger.
3. Obtain the skills required to build positive peer relationships.
4. Terminate aggressive behavior and replace with assertiveness and empathy.
5. Form respectful, trusting peer and sibling relationships.
6. Parents acquire the necessary parenting skills to model respect, kindness, nurturance, and lack of aggression.

—. _____
    _____
—. _____
    _____
—. _____
    _____

SHORT-TERM OBJECTIVES

1. Describe relationship with siblings and friends. (1, 2)
2. Attend and freely participate in play-therapy session. (3, 4, 5, 6)
3. Decrease the frequency and intensity of aggressive actions toward peers or siblings. (7, 8, 9, 10)
4. Identify verbally and in writing how he/she would like to be treated by others. (11, 12, 13, 14)
5. Recognize and verbalize the feelings of others as well as her/his own. (11, 15, 16)
6. Increase socially appropriate behavior with peers and siblings. (17, 18, 19)

THERAPEUTIC INTERVENTIONS

1. Actively build level of trust with client through consistent eye contact, active listening, unconditional positive regard, and warm acceptance to help increase client's ability to identify and express feelings.
2. Explore client's perception of the nature of his/her relationships with siblings and peers; assess degree of denial regarding conflict and projection of responsibility for conflict onto others.
3. Employ A.C.T. model (Landreth) in play-therapy sessions to *acknowledge* client's feelings, to *communicate* limits, and to *target* more appropriate alternatives to ongoing conflicts

7. Participate in peer group activities in a cooperative manner. (20, 21)

8. Parents facilitate client's social network building. (22)

9. Identify feelings associated with perception that parent(s) have special feelings of favoritism toward a sibling. (23)

10. Respond positively to praise and encouragement as evidenced by smiling and expressing gratitude. (24, 25)

11. Parents increase verbal and physical demonstrations of affection and praise to the client. (24, 25, 26)

12. Verbalize an understanding of the pain that underlies the anger. (5, 27)

13. Family decrease the frequency of quarreling and messages of rejection. (26, 28, 29, 30)

14. Parents attend a didactic series on positive parenting. (31)

15. Parents implement a behavior-modification plan designed to increase the frequency of cooperative social behaviors. (32, 33)

16. Parents terminate alliances with children that foster sibling conflict. (28, 34)

17. Family members engage in conflict resolution in a respectful manner. (35)

and aggression with peers and/or siblings.

4. Employ psychoanalytic play-therapy approaches (e.g., explore and gain understanding of the etiology of unconscious conflicts, fixations, or arrests; interpret resistance, transference, or core anxieties) to help clients work through and resolve the sibling and/or peer conflicts.

5. Interpret the feelings expressed in play therapy and relate them to anger and aggressive behaviors toward sibling and/or peers.

6. Create scenarios with puppets, dolls, or stuffed animals that model and/or suggest constructive ways to handle/manage conflicts with siblings or peers.

7. Guide parents in utilizing the Playing Baby game (see Schaefer in *101 Favorite Play Therapy Techniques*), in which the child is given an allotted time each day (30 minutes) to be a baby and have mother/parents cater to his/her every need. After the allotted time, client is again treated in an age-appropriate manner as a regular member of the family.

8. Utilize the "Tearing Paper" exercise (see Daves in *101 Favorite Play Therapy Techniques*), in which therapist places several phone books

18. Complete the recommended psychiatric or psychological testing/evaluation. (36)

19. Comply with the recommendations of the mental health evaluations. (36, 37)

—. _____
_____

—. _____
_____

—. _____
_____

and Sunday papers in center of room and instructs the family to tear the paper into small pieces and throw them in the air. The only two conditions are that they must clean up and not throw paper at one another. During cleanup, therapist reinforces verbally their follow-through in cleaning up and processes how it felt for family/siblings to release energy in this way and how could they do it in other situations at home.

9. Teach the client the Stamping Feet and Bubble Popping method (see Wunderlich in *101 Favorite Play Therapy Techniques*) of releasing angry and frustrating feelings by popping plastic bubble wrap while acknowleding that these feelings are part of everyday life and what is important is how we choose to handle them. Then talk about how the "anger goes through his/her fingers into the air."

10. Instruct parents and teachers in social learning techniques of ignoring client's aggressive acts, except when there is danger of physical injury, while making a concerted effort to attend to and praise all nonaggressive, cooperative, and peaceful behavior.

11. Educate client about feelings, focusing on how others

feel when they are the focus of aggressive actions and then asking how client would like to be treated by others.

12. Assign client and parents to complete the exercise "Negotiating a Peace Treaty" from *Brief Child Therapy Homework Planner* (Jongsma, Peterson, and McInnis), in which client must stipulate the problems that exist with siblings and suggest concrete solutions.

13. Play with client and/or family The Helping, Sharing, and Caring Game (Gardner) to develop and expand feelings of respect for self and others.

14. Use therapeutic stories (e.g., *Dr. Gardner's Fairy Tales for Today's Children* by Gardner) to increase awareness of feelings and ways to cooperate with others.

15. Refer client to a peer therapy group whose objectives are to increase social sensitivity and behavioral flexibility through the use of group exercises (strength bombardment, trust walk, expressing negative feelings, etc.).

16. Use Talking, Feeling, Doing game (available from Creative Therapeutics) to increase awareness of self and others.

17. Use Anger Control game (Berg) or a similar game to

expand client's ways to manage aggressive feelings.

18. Play with client The Social Conflict Game (Berg) to assist him/her in developing behavioral skills to decrease interpersonal antisocialism with others.

19. Conduct or refer to a behavioral contracting group therapy in which contracts for positive peer interaction are developed each week and reviewed. Positive reinforcers are verbal feedback and small concrete rewards.

20. Direct parents to involve client in cooperative activities (sports, scouts, etc.).

21. Refer client to an alternative summer camp that focuses on self-esteem and cooperation with peers.

22. Have parents read *Helping Your Child Make Friends* (Neviek). Then assist them in implementing several of the suggestions with the client to build his/her skills in connecting with others.

23. Ask client to complete "Joseph, His Amazing Technicolor Coat and More" from *Brief Child Therapy Homework Planner* (Jongsma, Peterson, and McInnis) to help client work through his/her perception that his/her parents have a favorite child.

24. Use role playing, modeling, and behavior rehearsal to

teach client to become open
and responsive to praise
and encouragement.

25. Assist parents in developing
their ability to verbalize affection and appropriate
praise to client in family
sessions.

26. Work with parents in family
sessions to reduce parental
aggression, messages of rejection, and quarreling
within the family.

27. Probe causes for anger in
rejection experiences with
family and friends.

28. Ask parents to read *How to
End the Sibling Wars* (Bieniek), and then coach them
into implementing several
of the suggestions. Therapist will follow up by monitoring, encouraging, and
redirecting as needed.

29. Assign parents to read *Siblings Without Rivalry* (Faber
and Mazish) and process
key concepts with therapist.
Then have parents choose
two suggestions from the
reading and implement
them with their children.

30. Assign parents to read *Between Parent and Child*
(Ginott), especially the
chapters "Jealousy" and
"Children in Need of Professional Help." Process the
reading with therapist,
identifying key changes in
family structure or personal
interactions that will need

to occur to decrease the level of rivalry.

31. Refer parents to a positive parenting class.

32. Assist parents in developing and implementing a behavior-modification plan in which client's positive interaction with peers and siblings is reinforced immediately with tokens that can be exchanged for preestablished rewards. Monitor and give feedback as indicated.

33. Conduct weekly contract sessions with client and parents in which past week's behavior-modification contract is reviewed and revised for the following week. Give feedback and model praise and positive encouragement when appropriate.

34. Hold family therapy sessions to assess dynamics and alliances that may underlie peer or sibling conflict.

35. Confront disrespectful expression of feelings in family session and use modeling, role play, and behavior rehearsal to teach cooperation, respect, and peaceful resolution of conflict.

36. Assess and refer client for a psychiatric or psychological evaluation.

37. Assist and monitor client and parents in implement-

ing the recommendations of
the psychiatric assessment.

—. _____
_____

—. _____
_____

—. _____
_____

DIAGNOSTIC SUGGESTIONS

Axis I: 313.81 Oppositional Defiant Disorder
312.8   Conduct Disorder
312.9   Disruptive Behavior Disorder NOS
314.01 Attention-Deficit/Hyperactivity Disorder,
Predominantly Hyperactive-Impulsive Type
314.9   Attention-Deficit/Hyperactivity Disorder NOS
V62.81 Relational Problem NOS
V71.02 Child or Adolescent Antisocial Behavior
315.00 Reading Disorder
315.9   Learning Disorder NOS

_____ _____

Axis II: 799.9   Diagnosis Deferred
V71.09 No Diagnosis on Axis II

_____ _____
_____ _____

PHYSICAL/EMOTIONAL ABUSE VICTIM

BEHAVIORAL DEFINITIONS

1. Confirmed self-report or account by others of assault (e.g., hitting, burning, kicking, slapping, or torture) by an older person.
2. Bruises or wounds as evidence of victimization.
3. Self-reports of being injured by a supposed caregiver coupled with feelings of fear and social withdrawal.
4. Significant increase in the frequency and severity of aggressive behaviors toward peers or adults.
5. Recurrent and intrusive distressing recollections of the abuse.
6. Feelings of anger, rage, or fear when in contact with the perpetrator.
7. Frequent and prolonged periods of depression, irritability, anxiety, and/or apathetic withdrawal).
8. Appearance of regressive behaviors (e.g., thumb sucking, baby talk, bed-wetting).
9. Sleep disturbances (e.g., difficulty falling asleep, refusal to sleep alone, night terrors, recurrent distressing nightmares).
10. Running away from home to avoid further physical assaults.

___. _____

_____

___. _____

_____

___. _____

_____

LONG-TERM GOALS

1. Terminate the physical abuse.
2. Remove the client from the environment where the abuse is occurring and provide him/her with a safe haven.
3. Rebuild sense of self-worth and remove the overwhelming sense of fear, shame, and sadness.
4. Resolve feelings of fear and depression while the family improves communication and setting the boundaries of respect.
5. Caregivers establish limits on the punishment of the client such that no physical harm can occur and that respect for his/her rights is maintained.
6. Eliminate denial in self and the family, putting the responsibility for the abuse on the perpetrator and allowing the victim to feel supported.
7. Reduce displays of aggression that reflect abuse and keep others at an emotional distance.
8. Build self-esteem and a sense of empowerment as manifested by an increased number of positive self-descriptive statements and greater participation in extracurricular activities.

—. _____

_____

—. _____

_____

—. _____

_____

SHORT-TERM OBJECTIVES

1. Tell the entire account of the most recent abuse. (1, 2, 3, 4, 5)
2. Identify the nature, frequency, and duration of the abuse. (3, 4, 5, 6, 7)
3. Identify and express the feelings connected to the abuse. (1, 3, 8, 9)

THERAPEUTIC INTERVENTIONS

1. Actively build the level of trust with the client through consistent eye contact, active listening, unconditional positive regard, and warm acceptance to help him/her increase the ability to identify and express facts and feelings about the abuse.

4. Demonstrate a stabilized mood and decreased emotional intensity connected to the abuse. (1, 8, 9, 10)

5. Terminate verbalizations of excuses for the perpetrator. (11, 12, 13)

6. Affirm the perpetrator as responsible for the abuse. (8, 11, 13, 14)

7. Perpetrator takes responsibility for the abuse. (11, 15, 16)

8. Perpetrator asks for forgiveness and pledges respect for disciplinary boundaries. (15, 16, 17)

9. Perpetrator agrees to seek treatment. (11, 18, 19)

10. Parents/caregivers verbalize the establishment of appropriate disciplinary boundaries to ensure protection of the client. (7, 17, 20)

11. Perpetrator verbalizes an understanding of how poor anger control continues the cycle of violence and distrust present in the extended family. (11, 21)

12. Perpetrator identifies stressors or other factors that may trigger violence. (22, 23)

13. Perpetrator acknowledges substance abuse and accepts referral for treatment. (23, 24)

14. Express forgiveness of the perpetrator and others connected with the abuse while

2. Explore, encourage, and support the client in verbally expressing and clarifying the facts associated with the abuse.

3. Use individual play-therapy sessions to provide the client with the opportunity to reveal facts and feelings regarding the abuse.

4. Report physical abuse to the appropriate child-protection agency, criminal justice officials, or medical professionals.

5. Consult with the family, a physician, criminal justice officials, or child-protection case managers to assess the veracity of the physical abuse charges.

6. Assess whether the perpetrator or the client should be removed from the client's home.

7. Implement the necessary steps (e.g., removal of the client from the home, removal of the perpetrator from the home) to protect the client and other children in the home from future physical abuse.

8. Explore, encourage, and support the client in expressing and clarifying his/her feelings toward perpetrator and self.

9. Assign client the homework of completing "My Thoughts and Feelings" in *Brief Child Therapy Homework Planner*

insisting on respect for own right to safety in the future. (15, 25, 26)

15. Reduce the expressions of rage and aggressiveness that stem from feelings of helplessness related to physical abuse. (15, 25, 26, 27, 28)

16. Reduce the depressive behaviors of flat affect, poor concentration, low energy, and social withdrawal. (29, 30, 31, 43, 44)

17. Increase the frequency of positive self-descriptive statements, eye contact, and use of a stronger voice. (30, 32, 33)

18. Increase socialization with peers and family. (31, 33, 34)

19. Decrease statements of being a victim while increasing statements that reflect personal empowerment. (35, 36)

20. Verbalize an understanding of the loss of trust in all relationships that results from abuse by a parent. (3, 8, 25, 37)

21. Increase the level of trust of others as shown by increased socialization and a greater number of friendships. (37, 38, 39, 43, 44)

22. Attend a victim support group. (40)

23. Verbalize how abuse has affected feelings toward self. (8, 41, 42, 43, 44)

(Jongsma, Peterson, and McInnis) to promote openness of expression.

10. Reassure client repeatedly of concern and caring on the part of the therapist and others who will protect client from any further abuse.

11. Actively confront and challenge denial within the perpetrator and the entire family system.

12. Confront the client about making excuses for the perpetrator's abuse and accepting blame for it.

13. Reassure the client that he/she did not deserve the abuse but that he/she deserves respect and a controlled response even in punishment situations.

14. Reinforce any and all client statements that put responsibility clearly on the perpetrator for the abuse, regardless of any misbehavior by the child.

15. Hold a family therapy session in which the client and/or therapist confront the perpetrator with the abuse.

16. Hold a family session in which the perpetrator apologizes to the client and/or other family member(s) for the abuse.

17. Counsel the client's family about appropriate disciplinary boundaries.

___. _____
      _____

___. _____
      _____

___. _____
      _____

18. Require the perpetrator to participate in a child abuser's group.

19. Refer the perpetrator for psychological evaluation and treatment.

20. Ask the parents/caregivers to list appropriate means of discipline or correction; reinforce reasonable actions and appropriate boundaries that reflect respect for the rights and feelings of the child.

21. Construct a multigenerational family genogram that identifies physical abuse within the extended family to help the perpetrator recognize the cycle of violence.

22. Assess the family dynamics and identify the stress factors or precipitating events that contributed to the emergence of the abuse.

23. Evaluate the possibility of substance abuse within the family.

24. Refer perpetrator for substance abuse treatment.

25. Assign the client to write a letter expressing feelings of hurt, fear, and anger to the perpetrator; process the letter.

26. Assign the client to write a forgiveness letter and/or complete a forgiveness exercise in which he/she verbalizes forgiveness to the perpetrator and/or significant family member(s)

while asserting the right to safety. Process this letter.

27. Assign the client a letting-go exercise in which a symbol of the abuse is disposed of or destroyed. Process this experience.

28. Interpret child's generalized expressions of anger and aggression as triggered by feelings toward the perpetrator.

29. Elicit and reinforce support and nurturance for the client from other key family members.

30. Assist the client in identifying a basis for self-worth by reviewing his/her talents, importance to others, and intrinsic spiritual value.

31. Encourage the client to make plans for the future that involve interacting with his/her peers and family.

32. Reinforce positive statements that the client has made about himself/herself and the future.

33. Reinforce the client's self-worth by relating to him/her with unconditional positive regard, genuine warmth, and active listening.

34. Encourage the client to participate in positive peer groups or extracurricular activities.

35. Empower the client by identifying sources of help against abuse (phone numbers to call, a safe place to

run to, asking for tempo-
rary alternate protective
placement, etc.).

36. Assign the exercise "Letter
of Empowerment" in *Brief
Child Therapy Homework
Planner* (Jongsma, Peterson,
and McInnis) to help client
express thoughts and feelings regarding the abuse.

37. Facilitate client expressing
loss of trust in adults and
relate this loss to the perpetrator's abusive behavior
and the lack of protection
provided.

38. Assist the client in making
discriminating judgments
that allow for the trust of
some people rather than
distrust of all.

39. Teach the client the share-
check method of building
trust, in which a degree of
shared information is re-
lated to a proven level of
trustworthiness.

40. Refer the client to a victim
support group with other
children to assist him/her in
realizing that he/she is not
alone in this experience.

41. Assign client to draw pictures that represent how
he/she feels about self.

42. Ask client to draw pictures
of own face that represent
how client felt about self before, during, and after
abuse occurred.

43. Use child-centered play-
therapy approaches (e.g.,

demonstrate genuine interest, provide unconditional positive regard, reflect feelings, profess trust in client's inner direction) to promote resolution of self-esteem, fear, grief, and rage.

44. Using psychoanalytic playtherapy principles (e.g., allowing client to take the lead, explore etiology of unconscious conflicts, fixations, or developmental arrests; interpret resistance, transference, and core depression), assist client in overcoming fear, low self-worth, and rage.

___. _____

_____

___. _____

_____

___. _____

_____

DIAGNOSTIC SUGGESTIONS

Axis I: 309.81   Posttraumatic Stress Disorder
308.3   Acute Stress Disorder
300.4   Dysthymic Disorder
296.xx   Major Depressive Disorder
311   Depressive Disorder NOS
300.02   Generalized Anxiety Disorder
307.47   Nightmare Disorder
313.81   Oppositional Defiant Disorder
312.8   Conduct Disorder/Childhood-Onset Type
300.6   Depersonalization Disorder
300.15   Dissociative Disorder NOS

_____   _____

_____   _____

Axis II: 799.9   Diagnosis Deferred
               V71.09   No Diagnosis on Axis II

               _____   _____

               _____   _____

POSTTRAUMATIC STRESS DISORDER

BEHAVIORAL DEFINITIONS

1. Exposure to threats of death or serious injury, or subjected to actual injury, that resulted in an intense emotional response of fear, helplessness, or horror.
2. Experiences intrusive, distressing thoughts or images that recall the traumatic event.
3. Disturbing dreams associated with the traumatic event.
4. A sense that the event is recurring, as in illusions or flashbacks.
5. Intense distress when exposed to reminders of the traumatic event.
6. Physiological reactivity when exposed to internal or external cues that symbolize the traumatic event.
7. Avoidance of thoughts, feelings, or conversations about the traumatic event.
8. Avoidance of activity, places, or people associated with the traumatic event.
9. Inability to recall some important aspect of the traumatic event.
10. Lack of interest and participation in significant activities.
11. A sense of detachment from others.
12. Inability to experience the full range of emotions, including love.
13. A pessimistic, fatalistic attitude regarding the future.
14. Sleep disturbance.
15. Irritability.
16. Lack of concentration.
17. Hypervigilance.
18. Exaggerated startle response.
19. Symptoms have been present for more than one month.
20. Sad or guilty affect and other signs of depression.
21. Verbally and/or physically violent threats or behavior.

__. _____

_____

—. _____

_____

—. _____

_____

LONG-TERM GOALS

1. Interact normally with friends and family without irrational fears that control behavior.
2. Return to pretrauma level of functioning without avoiding people or places associated with the traumatic event.
3. Display a full range of emotions without experiencing loss of control.
4. Reduce the negative impact that the traumatic event has had on many aspects of life and return to pretrauma level of functioning.
5. Develop and implement effective coping skills that allow for carrying out normal responsibilities and participating constructively in relationships.
6. Recall the traumatic event without becoming overwhelmed with negative emotions.

—. _____

_____

—. _____

_____

—. _____

_____

SHORT-TERM OBJECTIVES

1. Describe in as much detail as possible the traumatic event. (1, 2, 3)
2. Describe the feelings that were experienced at the time of the trauma. (1, 3)
3. Identify the symptoms of PTSD that have caused dis-

THERAPEUTIC INTERVENTIONS

1. Actively build the level of trust with the client through consistent eye contact, active listening, unconditional positive regard, and warm acceptance to help him/her increase the ability to identify and express feelings.

tress and impaired functioning. (4)

4. Describe how PTSD symptoms have affected personal relationships, functioning at school, and social/recreational life. (5)

5. Identify instances of uncontrollable anger. (6)

6. Implement anger-control techniques. (7)

7. Practice and implement relaxation training as a coping mechanism for tension, panic, stress, anger, and anxiety. (8, 9, 10)

8. Report increased comfort and ability to talk and/or think about the traumatic incident without emotional turmoil. (11, 12)

9. Identify negative self-talk and catastrophizing that is associated with past trauma and current stimulus triggers for anxiety. (13)

10. Replace negative, self-defeating thinking with positive, accurate, self-enhancing self-talk. (14)

11. Approach actual stimuli (*in vivo*) that trigger memories and feelings associated with past trauma, staying calm by using relaxation techniques and positive self-talk. (8, 14, 15)

12. Sleep without being disturbed by dreams of the trauma. (8, 10, 16)

13. Cooperate with EMDR technique to reduce emotional

2. Gently and sensitively explore recollection of the facts of the traumatic incident.

3. Explore the client's emotional reaction at the time of the trauma.

4. Ask client to identify how the traumatic event has negatively impacted his/her life, comparing pretrauma functioning to current functioning.

5. Explore the effect that the PTSD symptoms have had on personal relationships, functioning at school, and social/recreational life.

6. Assess for instances of poor anger management that have led to threats of or actual violence against property and/or people.

7. Teach anger management control techniques. (See Anger Management in this *Planner.*)

8. Teach deep-muscle relaxation, deep-breathing exercises, and positive imagery to induce relaxation.

9. Use EMG biofeedback to increase client's depth of relaxation.

10. Train client to calm self as preparation for sleep using relaxation tapes (e.g., *Relaxation Imagery for Children* by Weinstock or *Magic Island: Relaxation for Kids* by Mehling, Highstein, and Delamarter).

reaction to the traumatic event. (17)

14. Participate in group therapy session focused on PTSD. (18)

15. Cooperate with an evaluation for medication intervention. (19)

16. Take medication as prescribed and report on effectiveness and side effects. (19, 20)

17. Participate in family therapy sessions. (21, 22)

18. Parents verbalize understanding of how PTSD develops and how it impacts survivors. (21, 22)

19. Express facts and feelings surrounding the trauma through play therapy and mutual storytelling. (23, 24, 25)

20. Express facts and feelings through painting or drawing. (26)

—. _____
   _____

—. _____
   _____

—. _____
   _____

11. Gradually expose client to the traumatic event through imaginal systematic desensitization and positive guided imagery to reduce emotional reactivity to the traumatic event.

12. Explore in detail the client's feelings surrounding the traumatic incident, allowing for a gradual reduction in the intensity of the emotional response with repeated retelling.

13. Explore the negative self-talk that is associated with the past trauma and the predictions of unsuccessful coping or catastrophizing.

14. Assist client in replacing distorted, negative, self-defeating thoughts with positive, reality-based self-talk.

15. Encourage the client to gradually approach previously avoided stimuli that trigger thoughts and feelings associated with the past trauma. Urge use of relaxation, deep breathing, and positive self-talk during approach to stimulus.

16. Monitor client's sleep patterns and encourage use of relaxation and positive imagery as aids to sleep. (See Sleep Disturbance in this *Planner.*)

17. Use eye movement desensitization and reprocessing (EMDR) technique to reduce emotional reactivity to traumatic event.

18. Refer to or conduct group therapy sessions that focus on sharing traumatic events and its effects with other PTSD survivors.

19. Assess the need for medication (e.g., selective serotonin reuptake inhibitors) and arrange for prescription if appropriate.

20. Monitor and evaluate medication compliance and its effectiveness on level of functioning.

21. Conduct family therapy sessions to facilitate family members giving emotional support to client.

22. Teach client and family members the facts about trauma and its impact on survivors and their subsequent adjustment.

23. Use child-centered play-therapy principles (e.g., provide unconditional positive regard, offer nonjudgmental reflection of feelings, display trust in child's capacity for growth) to help client identify and express feelings surrounding the traumatic incident.

24. Employ psychoanalytic play-therapy approaches (e.g., allow child to take lead; explore etiology of unconscious conflicts, fixations, or developmental arrests; interpret resistance, transference, and core anxieties) to help client express and work through

feelings surrounding the traumatic incident.

25. Utilize mutual storytelling technique whereby client and therapist alternate telling stories through the use of puppets, dolls, or stuffed animals: Therapist first models constructive steps to take to protect self and feel empowered; then client follows by creating a story with similar characters or themes.

26. Provide client with materials and ask him/her to draw/paint pictures depicting the trauma and of self depicting emotions associated with the trauma.

—. _____
   _____

—. _____
   _____

—. _____
   _____

DIAGNOSTIC SUGGESTIONS

Axis I:

309.81	Posttraumatic Stress Disorder
309.xx	Adjustment Disorder
995.5	Physical Abuse of Child (Victim)
995.5	Sexual Abuse of Child (Victim)
308.3	Acute Stress Disorder
296.xx	Major Depressive Disorder
_____	_____

Axis II:

799.9	Diagnosis Deferred
V71.09	No Diagnosis on Axis II
_____	_____
_____	_____

SCHOOL REFUSAL

BEHAVIORAL DEFINITIONS

1. Persistent reluctance or refusal to attend school because of a desire to remain at home with the parent(s).
2. Marked emotional distress and repeated complaints (e.g., crying, temper outbursts, pleading with parent(s) not to go to school) when anticipating separation from home to attend school or after arrival at school.
3. Frequent somatic complaints (e.g., headaches, stomachaches, nausea) associated with attending school or in anticipation of school attendance.
4. Excessive clinging or shadowing of parent(s) when anticipating leaving home for school or after arriving at school.
5. Frequent negative comments about school and/or repeated questioning of the necessity of going to school.
6. Persistent and unrealistic expression of fear that a future calamity will cause a separation from his/her parent(s) if he/she attends school (e.g., he/she or parent(s) will be lost, kidnapped, killed, or the victim of an accident).
7. Verbalizations of low self-esteem and lack of confidence that contribute to the fear of attending school and being separated from the parent(s).
8. Verbalization of a fear of failure, ridicule, or anxiety regarding academic achievement accompanying the refusal to attend school.
9. Excessive shrinking or avoidance of contact with unfamiliar people for extended periods of time.

—. _____
   _____
—. _____
   _____

—. _____

_____

LONG-TERM GOALS

1. Attend school on a consistent, full-time basis.
2. Eliminate anxiety and the expression of fears prior to leaving home and after arriving at school.
3. Cease the temper outbursts, regressive behaviors, complaints, and pleading associated with attending school.
4. Eliminate the somatic complaints associated with attending school.
5. Resolve the core conflicts or traumas contributing to the emergence of the school refusal.
6. Verbalize positive statements about accomplishments and experiences at school.
7. Increase the frequency of independent behaviors.
8. Parents establish and maintain appropriate parent-child boundaries, setting firm, consistent limits when the client exhibits temper tantrums and passive-aggressive behaviors associated with attending school.

—. _____

_____

—. _____

_____

—. _____

—. _____

SHORT-TERM OBJECTIVES

1. Describe the fears associated with school attendance and state any known reasons for the fear. (1, 11, 12)
2. Complete psychological testing and an assessment interview. (2, 4)
3. Complete psychoeducational testing. (3, 4)

THERAPEUTIC INTERVENTIONS

1. Actively build the level of trust with the client through consistent eye contact, active listening, unconditional positive regard, and warm acceptance to help increase his/her ability to identify and express feelings regarding school atten-

4. Parents and school officials effectively implement a systematic desensitization program. (5, 6, 7)

5. Comply with a systematic desensitization program and begin to attend school for increasingly longer periods of time. (5, 6, 7)

6. Parents agree to and follow through with implementing a reward system, contingency contract, or token economy. (6, 7, 8)

7. Parents and school officials implement a contingency plan to deal with temper tantrums, crying spells, or excessive clinging after arriving at school. (6, 9, 10, 25)

8. Decrease the intensity of the crying spells and temper outbursts associated with attending school. (6, 8, 23, 25)

9. Verbally acknowledge how the fears related to attending school are irrational or unrealistic. (11, 12, 13)

10. Implement relaxation and guided imagery to reduce anxiety. (14)

11. Increase positive statements about accomplishments and experiences at school. (6, 9, 15)

12. Decrease the frequency of negative comments and questions about attending school. (11, 13, 15)

13. Parents and school officials follow through with a con-

dance and any know reasons for them.

2. Arrange for psychological testing of the client to assess the severity of anxiety, depression, or gross psychopathology and to gain greater insight into the underlying dynamics contributing to school refusal.

3. Arrange for psychoeducational testing to rule out the presence of learning disabilities.

4. Give feedback to the client and his/her family regarding the results of the psychological testing.

5. Design and implement a systematic desensitization program to help the client manage his/her anxiety and gradually attend school for longer periods of time.

6. Consult with the parents and school officials to develop a plan to manage the client's emotional distress and negative outbursts after arriving at school (e.g., the parent ceases lengthy good-bye, the client goes to the principal's office to calm down).

7. Develop a reward system or contingency contract to reinforce attending school for increasingly longer periods of time.

8. Design and implement a token economy to reinforce client's school attendance.

tingency plan to manage the client's somatic complaints. (16, 17, 18)

14. Decrease the frequency of verbalized somatic complaints. (16, 17, 18)

15. Understand and verbally recognize the secondary gain that results from somatic complaints. (17, 18, 19)

16. Increase the time spent between the client and the disengaged parent in play, school, or work activities. (20, 21, 22)

17. Parents reinforce the client's autonomous behaviors and set limits on overly dependent behaviors. (20, 23, 24, 25, 26)

18. Parents cease sending inconsistent messages about school attendance and begin to set firm, consistent limits on excessive clinging, pleading, crying, and temper tantrums. (23, 26, 29, 31)

19. Enmeshed or overly protective parent identifies and verbally recognizes overly dependent behaviors. (20, 23, 26, 30)

20. Identify positive coping strategies to help decrease anxiety, fears, and emotional distress. (27, 28)

21. Increase communication, intimacy, and consistency between parents. (19, 32)

22. Verbalize an understanding of how current fears and

9. Consult with the teacher in the initial stages of treatment about planning an assignment that will provide the client with an increased chance of success.

10. Use the teacher's aide or a positive peer role model to provide one-on-one attention for the client and help decrease the fear and anxiety about attending school.

11. Explore the irrational negative cognitive messages that produce the client's anxiety or fear.

12. Assist the client in realizing that his/her fears about attending school are irrational or unrealistic.

13. Assist the client in developing reality-based positive cognitive messages that increase his/her self-confidence to cope with anxiety or fear.

14. Teach the client relaxation techniques or guided imagery to reduce his/her anxiety and fears.

15. Assist the client in developing and implementing positive self-talk as a means of managing the anxiety or fears associated with school refusal.

16. Consult with the parents and school officials to develop a contingency plan to manage the client's somatic complaints (e.g., ignore them, take the client's tem-

anxiety about attending school are associated with past separation, loss, or trauma. (33, 34, 35, 36)

23. Identify and express the feelings connected with past unresolved separation, loss, or trauma.
    (34, 35, 36, 43, 44)

24. Implement assertiveness skills to reduce social anxiety and cope with ridicule. (37, 38, 39)

25. Increase the frequency and duration of time spent in independent play or activities away from the parents or home. (39, 40, 41)

26. Agree to initiate three social contacts per week. (39, 40, 41)

27. Increase the participation in school or positive peer group activities. (39, 40, 41, 42)

28. Express feelings about attending school through play, mutual storytelling, and art. (43, 44, 45, 46, 47)

29. Parents follow through with recommendations regarding medication and therapeutic interventions. (32, 48)

30. Take medication as prescribed by the physician and comply with any recommendations regarding medical treatment. (49, 50, 51)

—. _____

_____

perature matter-of-factly, redirect the client to task, send the client to the nurse's office).

17. Refocus the client's discussion from physical complaints to emotional conflicts and the expression of feelings.

18. Assist the client and his/her parents in developing insight into the secondary gain received from physical illnesses, complaints, and the like.

19. Conduct family therapy sessions to assess the dynamics, including secondary gain, that may be contributing to the emergence of the school refusal.

20. Use a family-sculpting technique, in which the client describes the behavior of each family member in a specific scene of his/her choosing, to assess the family dynamics.

21. Ask the client to draw a picture of a house; then instruct client to pretend that he/she lives in the house and describe what it is like to live there; process client's responses to assess family dynamics, focusing on role of disengaged parent.

22. Give a directive to the disengaged parent to transport the client to school in the morning; contact the parent's employer, if necessary, to gain permission for this.

—. _____

_____

—. _____

_____

23. Encourage the parents to reinforce the client's autonomous behaviors (e.g., attending school, working alone on school assignments) and set limits on overly dependent behaviors (e.g., client insisting that the parent enter the classroom).

24. Stress to parents the importance of remaining calm and not communicating anxiety to client.

25. Praise and reinforce parents for taking positive steps to help client overcome his/her fears or anxieties about attending school.

26. Counsel the parents about setting firm, consistent limits on the client's temper outbursts, manipulative behaviors, or excessive clinging.

27. Assess days or periods of time in which client was able to attend school without exhibiting significant distress. Identify and reinforce coping strategies that client used to attend school without displaying excessive fear or anxiety.

28. Anticipate possible stressors or events (e.g., illness, school holidays, vacations) that might cause fears and anxiety about attending school to reappear. Identify coping strategies and contingency plans (e.g., relaxation techniques, positive

self-talk, disengaged parent transporting client to school) that client and family can use to overcome fears or anxiety.

29. Instruct parents to write a letter (see "Letter of Encouragement" in *Brief Child Therapy Homework Planner* by Jongsma, Peterson, and McInnis) to client that sends a clear message about the importance of attending school and reminds him/her of coping strategies that he/she can use to calm fears or anxieties. Place letter in notebook and have client read letter at appropriate times during school day when he/she begins to feel afraid or anxious.

30. Identify how enmeshed or overly protective parents reinforce the client's dependency and irrational fears.

31. Use a paradoxical intervention (e.g., instruct the enmeshed parent to spoon-feed the client each morning) to work around the family's resistance and disengage the client from an overly protective parent.

32. Assess the marital dyad for possible conflict and the triangulation that deflects the focus away from the discord and onto the client's symptoms.

33. Assess whether the client's anxiety and fear about attending school are associ-

ated with a previously unresolved separation, loss, trauma, or realistic danger.

34. Explore, encourage, and support the client in verbally expressing and clarifying his/her feelings associated with a past separation, loss, trauma, or realistic danger.

35. Assign the older child to write a letter to express his/her feelings about a past separation, loss, trauma, or danger; process it with the therapist.

36. Request that the client perform a letting-go exercise in which a symbol of a past separation, loss, or trauma is destroyed; process this with the therapist.

37. Train the client in assertiveness to reduce social anxiety and/or fear of ridicule.

38. Use Stand Up for Yourself (Shapiro) game in therapy sessions to help teach assertiveness skills that can be used at school.

39. Encourage the client's assertive participation in extracurricular and positive peer group activities.

40. Give the client a directive to spend a specified period of time with his/her peers after school or on weekends.

41. Give directive of initiating three social contacts per week with unfamiliar peo-

ple or when placed in new social settings.

42. Assign reading of *Why Is Everybody Always Picking on Me? A Guide to Understanding Bullies for Young People* (Webster-Doyle) to teach client effective ways to deal with aggressive or intimidating peers at school; process reading with therapist in session.

43. Use child-centered play-therapy principles (e.g., provide unconditional positive regard, offer nonjudgmental reflection of feelings, demonstrate trust in client's capacity for self-growth) to help client express his/her feelings and work through fears about attending school.

44. Employ psychoanalytic play-therapy approaches (e.g., allow child to take lead; explore etiology of unconscious conflicts, fixations, or developmental arrests; interpret resistance, transference, and core anxieties) to help client work through and resolve issues contributing to school refusal.

45. Use mutual storytelling technique: The client and therapist alternate telling stories through the use of puppets, dolls, or stuffed animals. Therapist first models appropriate ways to overcome fears or anxieties to face separation or aca-

demic challenges; then client follows by creating a story with similar characters or themes.

46. Direct client to draw picture or create sculpture about what he/she fears will happen when he/she goes to school; discuss whether client's fears are realistic or unrealistic.

47. Use the Angry Tower technique (Saxe) to help client identify and express underlying feelings of anger that contribute to school refusal: Build tower out of plastic containers or buckets; place doll on top of tower (doll represents object of anger); instruct client to throw small fabric ball at tower while verbalizing feelings of anger.

48. Assess overly enmeshed parent for the possibility of having either an anxiety or a depressive disorder that may be contributing to client's refusal to attend school. Refer parent for medication evaluation and/or individual therapy if it is found that parent has an anxiety or a depressive disorder.

49. Arrange for psychotropic medication for the client.

50. Monitor the client for medication compliance, side effects, and effectiveness.

51. Refer the client for a medi-
    cal examination to rule out
    genuine health problems.

—. _____
   _____

—. _____
   _____

—. _____
   _____

DIAGNOSTIC SUGGESTIONS

Axis I: 309.21   Separation Anxiety Disorder
             300.02   Generalized Anxiety Disorder
             300.23   Social Phobia
             296.xx   Major Depressive Disorder
             300.4   Dysthymic Disorder
             300.81   Somatization Disorder
             300.81   Undifferentiated Somatoform Disorder
             309.81   Posttraumatic Stress Disorder

             _____   _____
             _____   _____

Axis II: 799.9   Diagnosis Deferred
             V71.09   No Diagnosis on Axis II

             _____   _____
             _____   _____

SEPARATION ANXIETY

BEHAVIORAL DEFINITIONS

1. Excessive emotional distress and repeated complaints (e.g., crying, regressive behaviors, pleading with parents to stay, temper tantrums) when anticipating separation from home or major attachment figures.
2. Persistent and unrealistic worry about possible harm occurring to major attachment figures or excessive fear that they will leave and not return.
3. Persistent and unrealistic fears expressed that a future calamity will separate the client from a major attachment figure (e.g., the client or his/her parent will be lost, kidnapped, killed, or the victim of an accident).
4. Repeated complaints and heightened distress (e.g., pleading to go home, demanding to see or call a parent) after separation from home or the attachment figure has occurred.
5. Persistent fear or avoidance of being alone as manifested by excessive clinging and shadowing of a major attachment figure.
6. Frequent reluctance or refusal to go to sleep without being near a major attachment figure; refusal to sleep away from home.
7. Recurrent nightmares centering around the theme of separation.
8. Frequent somatic complaints (e.g., headaches, stomachaches, nausea) when separation from home or the attachment figure is anticipated.
9. Excessive need for reassurance about safety and protection from possible harm or danger.
10. Low self-esteem and lack of self-confidence that contributes to the fear of being alone or participating in social activities.
11. Excessive shrinking from unfamiliar or new situations.

—. _____

_____

—. _____
_____
—. _____
_____

LONG-TERM GOALS

1. Eliminate the anxiety and expression of fears when a separation is anticipated or occurs.
2. Tolerate separation from attachment figures without exhibiting heightened emotional distress, regressive behaviors, temper outbursts, or pleading.
3. Eliminate the somatic complaints associated with separation.
4. Manage nighttime fears effectively as evidenced by remaining calm, sleeping in own bed, and not attempting to go into the attachment figure's room at night.
5. Resolve the core conflicts or traumas contributing to the emergence of the separation anxiety.
6. Participate in extracurricular or peer group activities and spend time in independent play on a regular, consistent basis.
7. Parents establish and maintain appropriate parent-child boundaries and set firm, consistent limits when the client exhibits temper outbursts or manipulative behaviors around separation points.

—. _____
_____
—. _____
_____
—. _____
_____

SHORT-TERM OBJECTIVES

1. Complete psychological testing. (1, 2, 28)
2. Describe the fear and the circumstances that precipitate it. (3, 4, 5)

THERAPEUTIC INTERVENTIONS

1. Arrange for psychological testing to assess the severity of the client's anxiety and gain greater insight into the underlying dynam-

3. Verbally acknowledge how the fears are irrational or unrealistic. (4, 5, 6, 7)

4. Develop and implement behavioral and cognitive strategies to reduce or eliminate irrational anxiety or fears. (6, 7, 8, 9)

5. Reduce the frequency and severity of crying, clinging, temper tantrums, and verbalized fears when separated from attachment figures. (8, 9, 10, 11)

6. Parents begin to set limits on the client's excessive clinging, whining, pleading, and temper tantrums. (11, 12, 30, 31)

7. Decrease the frequency of crying spells and temper outbursts at times of separation. (8, 11, 12, 31)

8. Increase the frequency and duration of time spent in independent play away from major attachment figures. (13, 14, 19, 20)

9. Increase the participation in extracurricular or positive peer group activities away from home. (15, 16, 17, 18)

10. Increase the frequency and duration of contacts with peers away from the presence of attachment figure. (18, 20, 21)

11. Decrease the frequency of verbalized, somatic complaints. (22, 23, 24)

ics contributing to the symptoms.

2. Give feedback to the client and his/her family regarding the results of the psychological testing.

3. Actively build the level of trust with the client through consistent eye contact, active listening, unconditional positive regard, and warm acceptance to help him/her increase the ability to identify and express feelings.

4. Explore the origins, strengths, triggers, and feared consequence of the client's fears.

5. Explore the irrational cognitive messages that produce anxiety or fear.

6. Assist in developing reality-based cognitive messages that increase self-confidence to cope with the anxiety or fears.

7. Assist the client in realizing how his/her fears are irrational or unrealistic by helping him/her examine experience objectively regarding the low probability of danger, harm, or other feared consequence occurring.

8. Train in relaxation techniques or guided imagery to reduce anxiety.

9. Assist the client in developing positive self-talk as a means of managing the

12. Understand and verbally recognize the secondary gain that results from somatic complaints. (22, 23)

13. Increase school attendance as evidenced by a decreased frequency of unexcused absences. (11, 22, 23)

14. Begin to manage nighttime fears more effectively as evidenced by fewer visits to the attachment figure's room at night. (25, 26)

15. Decrease frequency of nightmares reported by client. (8, 25, 26)

16. Parents reinforce the client's autonomous behavior and set limits on overly dependent behaviors. (21, 27, 30, 31, 34)

17. Enmeshed or overly protective parents identify how they reinforce client's irrational fears or dependent behaviors. (29, 31, 33, 35)

18. Increase the time spent between the client and the disengaged parent in play, school, or work activities. (29, 36)

19. Parents comply and follow through with recommendations regarding therapy and/or medication evaluations. (32, 37)

20. Increase communication and intimacy between the parents. (21, 37, 48)

21. Verbalize how current anxiety and fears are associated with past separation, loss,

anxiety or fears associated with separation.

10. Use biofeedback techniques to increase relaxation skills and decrease the level of anxiety and resultant somatic ailments.

11. Counsel the parents about setting firm, consistent limits on the client's temper tantrums and excessive clinging or whining.

12. Design a reward system or establish a contingency contract that reinforces the client for being able to manage separation from his/her parents without displaying excessive emotional distress.

13. Direct the client to spend gradually longer periods of time in independent play or with friends after school.

14. Inquire into what client does differently on days that he/she is able to separate from parents without displaying excessive clinging, pleading, crying, or protesting; process client's response and reinforce any positive coping mechanisms that are used to manage separations.

15. Encourage participation in extracurricular or peer group activities.

16. Utilize behavioral rehearsal and role play of peer group interaction to teach social skills and reduce social anxiety.

abuse, or trauma.
(38, 39, 41)

22. Identify and express feelings connected with a past separation, loss, abuse, or trauma. (39, 41, 42)

23. Parents comply with recommendations to protect client from ongoing danger, abuse, or trauma. (38, 40)

24. Express feelings and fears in play therapy, mutual storytelling, and art.
(41, 42, 45, 46, 47)

25. Increase the frequency of positive self-descriptive statements. (3, 9, 19, 43)

26. Increase assertive behaviors to deal more effectively and directly with stress, conflict, or responsibilities. (49, 50)

27. Take prescribed medication as directed by the physician. (51, 52)

—. _____
   _____

—. _____
   _____

—. _____
   _____

17. Use Draw Me Out game (Shapiro) in therapy sessions to help child overcome shyness and communicate more effectively with peers.

18. Encourage the client to invite a friend for an overnight visit and/or set up an overnight visit at a friend's home; process any fears that arise and reinforce independence.

19. Assign a task (e.g., doing a special chore at home, writing a school paper on a topic of interest) that facilitates autonomy and reinforces confidence and a sense of empowerment.

20. Assign "Explore Your World" exercise in *Brief Child Therapy Homework Planner* (Jongsma, Peterson, and McInnis) to have client explore immediate neighborhood and foster autonomy.

21. Direct the parents to go on a weekly outing without the client. Begin with 30- to 45-minute outing and gradually increase duration. Teach client effective coping strategies (e.g., relaxation techniques, deep breathing, calling a friend, playing with sibling) to help reduce separation anxiety while parents are away on outing.

22. Refocus discussion from physical complaints to emo-

tional conflicts and the expression of feelings.

23. Assist the client and his/her parents in developing insight into the secondary gain received from physical illnesses, complaints, and the like.

24. Refer the client for a medical examination to rule out genuine health problems.

25. Establish contract to reward client for being able sleep in his/her own bedroom without exhibiting excessive distress or going into parent's room at night.

26. Require the client to perform a ritual at night (e.g., reassuringly putting a stuffed animal or doll to bed, reading a story with a parent, placing a bad-dream catcher in the room) to manage fears and facilitate autonomy.

27. Conduct family therapy sessions to assess the dynamics contributing to the emergence of separation anxiety and fears.

28. Ask the client to draw a picture of a house; then instruct client to pretend that he/she lives in that house and describe what it is like to live there; process client's responses to help assess family dynamics.

29. Use a family-sculpting technique, in which the client

defines the role and behavior of each family member in a scene of his/her choosing to assess family dynamics.

30. Counsel family members about the need for appropriate boundaries, space, and privacy.

31. Identify how the enmeshed or overly protective parent reinforces the client's dependency and irrational fears.

32. Assess overly enmeshed parent for the possibility of having either an anxiety or affective disorder; refer parent for medication evaluation and/or individual therapy if he/she is exhibiting symptoms of either an anxiety or affective disorder.

33. Encourage the parents to reinforce the client's autonomous behaviors (e.g., independent play, socializing with friends) and set limits on overly dependent behaviors (e.g., insisting that the parent be in the same room, going into the parents' room at night).

34. Assign "Parents' Time Away" exercise in *Brief Child Therapy Homework Planner* (Jongsma, Peterson, and McInnis) to decrease enmeshment between client and parents and help him/her manage separation more effectively.

35. Use a paradoxical intervention (e.g., instruct the client and his/her parent to tie a

six-foot string to each other every day so they can never be separated) to work around the family's resistance and disengage the client from overly protective parent.

36. Direct the disengaged or distant parent to spend more time or perform a specific task with the client (e.g., working on a project around the home, assisting the client with homework, going on an outing together).

37. Assess the marital dyad for possible conflict and triangulation of the client into discord. Refer parents for marital counseling if discord is present.

38. Assess whether the client's anxiety and fears are associated with a separation, loss, abuse, trauma, or unrealistic danger.

39. Explore, encourage, and support the client in verbally expressing and clarifying the feelings associated with the separation, loss, trauma, or realistic danger.

40. Identify and implement the steps necessary to protect the client from ongoing danger, abuse, or trauma.

41. Assign the client to write a letter to express his/her feelings about a past separation, loss, trauma, or danger; process the letter with therapist.

42. Request that the client perform a letting-go exercise in which a symbol of a past separation, loss, or trauma is destroyed; process this with the therapist.

43. Use child-centered play-therapy principles (e.g., display genuine interest in unconditional positive regard, reflect feelings in nonjudgmental manner, demonstrate trust in client's capacity to grow) to promote greater awareness of self and increase motivation to overcome fears about separation.

44. Employ psychoanalytic play-therapy approaches (e.g., explore and help client understand the etiology of unconscious conflicts, fixations, or arrests; interpret resistance, transference, or core anxieties) to help client work through and resolve issues contributing to his/her separation anxiety.

45. Utilize mutual storytelling technique: The client and therapist alternate telling stories through the use of puppets, dolls, or stuffed animals; therapist first models appropriate ways to overcome fears or anxieties; then client follows by creating a story with similar characters or themes.

46. Direct client and detached parent to create mutual

story of fear reduction through the use of puppets, dolls, or stuffed animals, first in filial play-therapy sessions and later at home, to facilitate closer parent-child relationship.

47. Direct client to draw picture or create sculpture about what he/she fears will happen upon separation from major attachment figures; assess whether client's fears are irrational or unrealistic.

48. Teach effective communication skills to the client and his/her parents.

49. Play Stand Up for Yourself (Shapiro) game in therapy sessions to teach client assertiveness skills.

50. Refer to group therapy to help client develop positive social skills and overcome social anxieties.

51. Arrange for medication evaluation for the client.

52. Monitor the client for compliance, side effects, and overall effectiveness of the medication.

__. _____
   _____

__. _____
   _____

__. _____
   _____

DIAGNOSTIC SUGGESTIONS

Axis I:	309.21	Separation Anxiety Disorder
	300.02	Generalized Anxiety Disorder
	300.23	Social Phobia
	296.xx	Major Depressive Disorder
	300.81	Somatization Disorder
	301.47	Nightmare Disorder
	307.46	Sleep Terror Disorder
	309.81	Posttraumatic Stress Disorder
	_____	_____
	_____	_____
Axis II:	799.9	Diagnosis Deferred
	V71.09	No Diagnosis on Axis II
	_____	_____
	_____	_____

SEXUAL ABUSE VICTIM

BEHAVIORAL DEFINITIONS

1. Self-report of being sexually abused.
2. Physical signs of sexual abuse (e.g., red or swollen genitalia, blood in the underwear, constant rashes, a tear in the vagina or rectum, venereal disease, hickeys on the body).
3. Strong interest in or curiosity about advanced knowledge of sexuality.
4. Sexual themes or sexualized behaviors emerge in play or artwork.
5. Recurrent and intrusive distressing recollections or nightmares of the abuse.
6. Acting or feeling as if the sexual abuse were recurring (including delusions, hallucinations, dissociative flashback experiences).
7. Unexplainable feelings of anger, rage, or fear when coming into contact with the perpetrator or after exposure to sexual topics.
8. Pronounced disturbance of mood and affect (e.g., frequent and prolonged periods of depression, irritability, anxiety, and fearfulness).
9. Appearance of regressive behaviors (e.g., thumb sucking, baby talk, bed-wetting).
10. Marked distrust in others as manifested by social withdrawal and problems with establishing and maintaining close relationships.
11. Feelings of guilt, shame, and low self-esteem.

—. _____
   _____

—. _____
   _____

—. _____
   _____

LONG-TERM GOALS

1. Obtain protection from all further sexual victimization.
2. Work successfully through the issue of sexual abuse with consequent understanding and control of feelings and behavior.
3. Resolve the issues surrounding the sexual abuse, resulting in an ability to establish and maintain close interpersonal relationships.
4. Establish appropriate boundaries and generational lines in the family to greatly minimize the risk of sexual abuse ever occurring in the future.
5. Achieve healing within the family system as evidenced by the verbal expression of forgiveness and a willingness to let go and move on.
6. Eliminate denial in self and the family, placing responsibility for the abuse on the perpetrator and allowing the survivor to feel supported.
7. Eliminate all inappropriate sexual behaviors.
8. Build self-esteem and a sense of empowerment as manifested by an increased number of positive self-descriptive statements and greater participation in extracurricular activities.

—. _____
_____

—. _____
_____

—. _____
_____

SHORT-TERM OBJECTIVES

1. Tell the entire story of the abuse. (1, 2, 3, 6, 14, 45)

2. Identify the nature, frequency, and duration of the abuse. (1, 2, 3, 4, 6)

3. Identify and express feelings connected to the abuse. (2, 21, 22, 23, 24)

4. Decrease secrecy in the family by informing key

THERAPEUTIC INTERVENTIONS

1. Actively build the level of trust with the client through consistent eye contact, active listening, unconditional positive regard, and warm acceptance to help increase his/her ability to identify and express feelings connected to the abuse.

2. Explore, encourage, and support the client in ver-

members about the abuse.
(6, 10, 25, 28)

5. Verbally demonstrate a knowledge of sexual abuse and its effects. (13, 17, 21, 38)

6. Verbalize the way sexual abuse has impacted life. (2, 20, 21, 22, 23)

7. Verbally identify the perpetrator as being responsible for the sexual abuse. (7, 10, 28, 29, 30)

8. Decrease expressed feelings of shame and guilt and affirm self as not being responsible for the abuse. (2, 18, 23, 25, 29)

9. Stabilize the mood and decrease the emotional intensity connected to the abuse. (8, 11, 48, 49)

10. Increase the willingness to talk about sexual abuse in the family. (6, 10, 13, 25, 27)

11. Agree to actions taken to protect self and provide boundaries against any future abuse or retaliation. (5, 7, 8, 9, 12)

12. Parents establish and adhere to appropriate intimacy boundaries within the family. (5, 7, 8, 9, 12, 13, 16, 17)

13. Nonabusive parent and other key family members increase support and acceptance of client. (10, 13, 25, 26, 37)

14. Nonabusive parent follows through with recommendations to spend greater qual-

bally expressing the facts and clarifying his/her feelings associated with the abuse.

3. Report sexual abuse to the appropriate child protection agency, criminal justice officials, or medical professionals.

4. Consult with physician, criminal justice officials, or child protection case managers to assess the veracity of the sexual abuse charges.

5. Consult with a physician, criminal justice officials, and child protection case managers to develop appropriate treatment interventions.

6. Facilitate conjoint sessions to reveal the sexual abuse to key family members or caregivers.

7. Assess whether the perpetrator should be removed from the home.

8. Implement the necessary steps to protect the client and other children in the home from future sexual abuse.

9. Assess whether the client is safe to remain in the home or should be removed.

10. Actively confront and challenge denial within the family system.

11. Empower the client by reinforcing the steps necessary to protect himself/herself.

ity time with client.
(13, 15, 25, 26, 37)

15. Decrease the statements of being a victim while increasing statements that reflect personal empowerment.
(11, 29, 33, 43)

16. Terminate verbalizations of excuses for the perpetrator.
(10, 18, 19, 29, 42)

17. Perpetrator takes responsibility for the abuse.
(28, 29, 30, 31)

18. Perpetrator agrees to seek treatment. (5, 30, 47)

19. Verbalize a desire to begin the process of forgiveness of the perpetrator and others connected with the abuse.
(27, 29, 32, 34)

20. Perpetrator asks for the client's forgiveness and pledges respect for boundaries. (29, 32)

21. Verbally identify self as a survivor of sexual abuse.
(32, 34, 35)

22. Increase the frequency of positive self-statements.
(1, 12, 25, 35)

23. Identify and express feelings about sexual abuse in play therapy and mutual storytelling. (20, 33, 34, 35, 37)

24. Identify and express feelings through artwork and therapeutic games.
(16, 22, 36, 38, 46)

25. Increase the level of trust of others as shown by increased socialization and a

12. Counsel the client's family members about appropriate boundaries.

13. Assess the family dynamics and identify the stress factors or precipitating events that contributed to the emergence of the abuse.

14. Assign the client to draw a diagram of the house where the abuse occurred, indicating where everyone slept, and share the diagram with the therapist.

15. Instruct client to produce family kinetic drawing to assess family dynamics that contributed to emergence of sexual abuse.

16. Ask client to draw a picture of a house; then instruct him/her to pretend that he/she lives in that house and describe what it is like to live there; process client's responses to assess family dynamics and allow for expression of feelings related to abuse.

17. Construct a multigenerational family genogram that identifies sexual abuse within the extended family to help the client realize that he/she is not the only one abused and to help the perpetrator recognize the cycle of boundary violation.

18. Instruct older child to write a letter to the perpetrator that describes his/her feelings about the abuse; process the letter.

greater number of friendships. (39, 40, 41)

26. Increase outside family contacts and social networks. (39, 40, 41)

27. Attend and actively participate in group therapy with other sexual abuse survivors. (40, 41)

28. Decrease frequency of sexualized or seductive behaviors in interactions with others. (25, 43)

29. Complete psychological testing. (15, 16, 47)

30. Parents comply with recommendations regarding psychiatric/substance abuse treatment. (30, 47, 48)

31. Take medication as prescribed by the physician. (47, 48, 49)

__. _____

_____

__. _____

_____

__. _____

_____

19. Employ art therapy (e.g., drawing, painting, sculpting) to help client identify and express feelings he/she has toward perpetrator.

20. Use Angry Tower technique (Saxe) to help client express feelings of anger about sexual abuse: Build tower out of plastic containers; place small doll on top of tower (doll represents object of anger); instruct client to throw small fabric ball at tower while verbalizing feelings of anger connected to the abuse.

21. Instruct client to create drawing or sculpture that reflects how sexual abuse impacted his/her life and feelings about himself/herself.

22. Use Talking, Feeling, Doing game, available from Creative Therapeutics, to first establish rapport with client and then lead into discussion about effects of sexual abuse.

23. Assign "You Are Not Alone" exercise in *Brief Child Therapy Homework Planner* (Jongsma, Peterson, and McInnis) to help client express feelings connected to the sexual abuse and decrease feelings of guilt and shame.

24. Use guided fantasy and imagery techniques to help client express suppressed thoughts, feelings, and

unmet needs associated with sexual abuse.

25. Elicit and reinforce support and nurturance for the client from other key family members.

26. Give directive to disengaged, nonabusive parent to spend more time with the client in leisure, school, or household activities.

27. Assign the client's parents and significant others to read *Allies in Healing* (Davis) to assist them in understanding how they can help the client recover from abuse.

28. Hold a therapy session in which the client and/or the therapist confronts the perpetrator with the abuse.

29. Hold a session in which the perpetrator apologizes to the client and/or other family members.

30. Require the perpetrator to participate in a sexual offenders' group.

31. Assign the client's family to read *Out of the Shadows* (Carnes) to expand their knowledge of sexually addictive behaviors.

32. Assign the client to write a forgiveness letter and/or complete a forgiveness exercise in which he/she verbalizes forgiveness to the perpetrator and/or significant family members. Process the letter.

33. Use child-centered play-therapy principles (e.g., provide unconditional positive regard, offer nonjudgmental reflection of feelings, display trust in child's capacity for growth) to help client identify and express feelings surrounding sexual abuse.

34. Employ psychoanalytic play-therapy approaches (e.g., allow child to take lead; explore etiology of unconscious conflicts, fixations, or developmental arrests; interpret resistance, transference, and core anxieties) to help client express and work through feelings surrounding sexual abuse.

35. Use mutual storytelling technique: Client and therapist alternate telling stories through the use of puppets, dolls, or stuffed animals; therapist first models constructive steps to take to protect self and feel empowered; then client follows by creating a story with similar characters or themes.

36. Use "Feelings and Faces" exercise in *Brief Child Therapy Homework Planner* (Jongsma, Peterson, and McInnis), in which client draws pictures of different emotions. Instruct client to identify times when he/she experienced the different emotions surrounding the sexual abuse.

37. Direct client and disengaged, nonabusive parent to create mutual story through the use of puppets, dolls, or stuffed animals, first in filial play-therapy sessions and later at home, to facilitate a closer parent-child relationship.

38. Employ Color-Your-Life technique (O'Connor) to improve client's ability to identify and verbalize feelings related to sexual abuse: Ask client to match colors to different emotions (e.g., red—anger, blue—sad, black—very sad, yellow—happy) and then fill up blank page with colors that reflect his/her feelings about sexual abuse.

39. Encourage the client to participate in positive peer groups or extracurricular activities.

40. Develop a list of resource people outside of the family to whom client can turn for support and nurturance.

41. Refer the client to a survivor group with other children to assist him/her in realizing that he/she is not alone in having experienced sexual abuse.

42. Assign the client to read *A Very Touching Book* (Hindman), *I Can't Talk About It* (Sanford), or *It's Not Your Fault* (Jance); process the concepts learned.

43. Read *My Body Is Mine, My Feelings Are Mine* (Hoke) in session to identify appropriate and inappropriate forms of touching and to educate client about body safety.

44. Assist the client in making a connection between underlying, painful emotions (e.g., fear, hurt, sadness, anxiety) and sexualized or seductive behaviors.

45. Using anatomically detailed dolls or puppets, have the client tell and show how he/she was abused. Take great caution not to lead the client's description of abuse.

46. In session, play Kids in Court game to help alleviate anxiety about testifying in court.

47. Assess parents for the possibility of having a psychiatric disorder and/or substance abuse problem. Refer parents for psychiatric or substance abuse evaluation and/or therapy if such is found to exist.

48. Arrange for a medication evaluation.

49. Monitor medication compliance, effectiveness, and side effects.

__. _____

_____

__. _____

_____

__. _____

_____

DIAGNOSTIC SUGGESTIONS

Axis I:	309.81	Posttraumatic Stress Disorder
	308.3	Acute Stress Disorder
	296.xx	Major Depressive Disorder
	309.21	Separation Anxiety Disorder
	995.53	Sexual Abuse of Child (Victim)
	307.47	Nightmare Disorder
	300.15	Dissociative Disorder, NOS
	_____	_____
	_____	_____
Axis II:	799.9	Diagnosis Deferred
	V71.09	No Diagnosis on Axis II
	_____	_____
	_____	_____

SLEEP DISTURBANCE

BEHAVIORAL DEFINITIONS

1. Emotional distress (e.g., crying, leaving bed to awaken parents, demanding to sleep with parents) that accompanies difficulty falling asleep or remaining asleep.
2. Difficulty falling asleep or remaining asleep without significant demands made on the parents.
3. Distress (e.g., crying, calling for parents, racing heart, or fear of returning to sleep) resulting from repeated awakening, with detailed recall of extremely frightening dreams involving threats to himself/herself or significant others.
4. Repeated incidents of leaving bed and walking about in an apparent sleep state but with eyes open, face blank, lack of response to communication efforts, and amnesia for the incident upon awakening.
5. Abrupt awakening with a panicky scream followed by intense anxiety and autonomic arousal, no detailed dream recall, and unresponsiveness to the efforts of others to give comfort during the episode.
6. Prolonged sleep and/or excessive daytime napping without feeling adequately rested or refreshed but instead continually tired.

__. _____

_____

__. _____

_____

__. _____

_____

LONG-TERM GOALS

1. Fall asleep calmly and stay asleep without any undue, reassuring parental presence required.
2. Feel refreshed and energetic during waking hours.
3. Cease anxiety-producing dreams that cause awakening.
4. End abrupt awakening in terror and return to a peaceful, restful sleep pattern.
5. Restore restful sleep with a reduction of sleepwalking incidents.

—. _____

_____

—. _____

_____

—. _____

_____

SHORT-TERM OBJECTIVES	THERAPEUTIC INTERVENTIONS
1. Describe current sleep pattern. (1, 2, 3)	1. Explore and assess client's presleep and actual sleep patterns.
2. Identify daily stressors and the associated sleep patterns. (3, 4, 5)	2. Ask client and/or parents to keep a written record of presleep activity, sleep time, awakening occurrences, and caregiver responses to child; provide a form to chart data.
3. Verbalize depressive feelings and share the possible causes. (5, 6)	
4. Describe experiences of emotional trauma that continue to disturb sleep. (7, 9)	3. Review record of client's presleep and sleep activity to assess for overstimulation, caregiver reinforcement, and contributing stressors.
5. Describe disturbing dreams. (1, 2, 8)	
6. Reveal sexual abuse incidents that continue to be disturbing. (9)	4. Assess the role of daily stressors in the interruption of the client's sleep.
7. Cooperate in a physical exam. (10)	5. Meet with the family to assess the level of tension and
8. Parents develop a practice of setting firm limits on the	

client's manipulatory behavior. (11, 12)

9. Parents identify sources of conflict or stress within the family. (5, 13)

10. Parents verbalize the resolution of conflict within the family. (5, 13, 14)

11. Parents consistently adhere to a bedtime routine as developed in a family therapy session. (12, 15)

12. Follow a sleep-induction schedule of events. (11, 12, 15, 16)

13. Report resolution of traumas or fears that have interfered with sleep. (17, 18, 19, 20)

14. Remain alone in the bedroom without expressions of fear. (19, 20, 21)

15. Practice deep-muscle relaxation exercises. (22, 23)

16. Utilize biofeedback training to deepen relaxation skills. (24)

17. Cooperate in a physical exam for medication evaluation. (6, 25)

18. Take psychotropic medication as prescribed to assess its effect on sleep. (25, 26)

—. _____

_____

—. _____

_____

—. _____

_____

conflict and its effect on the client's sleep.

6. Assess the role of depression as a cause of the client's sleep disturbances. (See Depression in this *Planner*.)

7. Explore recent traumatic events that interfere with the client's sleep.

8. Probe the nature of the client's disturbing dreams and their relationship to life stress.

9. Explore the possibility of sexual abuse to the client that has not been revealed. (See Sexual Abuse Victim in this *Planner*.)

10. Refer the client to a physician to rule out any physical and pharmacological causes for the sleep disturbance.

11. Meet with the parents to help them set firm limits on the client's manipulative behavior.

12. Meet with the client and his/her parents to establish a bedtime routine that is calming and attentive but consistent and firm. Involve the client in the development process.

13. Meet with parents alone to assess the degree of stress in their relationship and its possible impact on the child's sleep behavior; refer for conjoint sessions if necessary.

14. Hold family therapy sessions to resolve conflicts and reduce the tension level in the home.

15. Assign parents to keep a written record of adherence to client's bedtime routine; review record at future sessions and reinforce successful implementation while redirecting failures.

16. Reinforce client's consistent adherence to a calming sleep-induction routine.

17. Use play-therapy techniques to assess and resolve emotional conflicts.

18. Interpret the client's play behavior as reflective of his/her feelings toward family members.

19. Assess the client's fears associated with being alone in the bedroom in terms of their nature, severity, and origin.

20. Explore client's general level of anxiety and treat if necessary. (See Anxiety in this *Planner.*)

21. Confront the client's irrational fears and teach cognitive strategies (e.g., positive, realistic self-talk) to reduce them.

22. Train the client in deep-muscle relaxation exercises with and/or without audiotape instruction.

23. Use relaxation tapes to train client in calming self as preparation for sleep

(e.g., *Relaxation Imagery for Children* by Weinstock, available from Childswork/Childsplay, LLC, or *Magic Island: Relaxation for Kids* by Mehling, Highstein, and Delamarter, available from Courage to Change).

24. Administer electromyographic (EMG) biofeedback to monitor, train, and reinforce the successful relaxation response.

25. Arrange for an evaluation regarding the need for antidepressant medication for the client to enhance restful sleep.

26. Monitor the client for medication compliance, effectiveness, and side effects.

—. _____
_____

—. _____
_____

—. _____
_____

DIAGNOSTIC SUGGESTIONS

Axis I:	309.21	Separation Anxiety Disorder, Early Onset
	312.9	Disruptive Behavior Disorder NOS
	307.42	Primary Insomnia
	307.44	Primary Hypersomnia
	307.45	Circadian Rhythm Sleep Disorder
	307.47	Nightmare Disorder
	307.46	Sleep Terror Disorder
	307.46	Sleepwalking Disorder
	309.81	Posttraumatic Stress Disorder

	296.xx	Major Depressive Disorder
	300.4	Dysthymic Disorder
	296.0x	Bipolar I Disorder
	296.89	Bipolar II Disorder
	296.80	Bipolar Disorder NOS
	301.13	Cyclothymic Disorder
	_____	_____
	_____	_____
Axis II:	799.9	Diagnosis Deferred
	V71.09	No Diagnosis on Axis II
	_____	_____
	_____	_____

SOCIAL PHOBIA/SHYNESS

BEHAVIORAL DEFINITIONS

1. Hiding, limited or no eye contact, a refusal or reticence to respond verbally to overtures from others, and isolation in most social situations.
2. Excessive shrinking or avoidance of eye contact with unfamiliar people for an extended period of time (i.e., six months or longer).
3. Social isolation and/or excessive involvement in isolated activities (e.g., reading, listening to music in his/her room, playing video games).
4. Extremely limited or no close friendships outside the immediate family members.
5. Hypersensitivity to criticism, disapproval, or perceived signs of rejection from others.
6. Excessive need for reassurance of being liked by others before demonstrating a willingness to get involved with them.
7. Marked reluctance to engage in new activities or take personal risks because of the potential for embarrassment or humiliation.
8. Negative self-image as evidenced by frequent self-disparaging remarks, unfavorable comparisons to others, and a perception of self as being socially unattractive.
9. Lack of assertiveness because of a fear of being met with criticism, disapproval, or rejection.
10. Heightened physiological distress in social settings manifested by increased heart rate, profuse sweating, dry mouth, muscular tension, and trembling.

—. _____

_____

—. _____

_____

—. _____

_____

LONG-TERM GOALS

1. Eliminate anxiety, shyness, and timidity in most social settings.
2. Establish and maintain long-term (i.e., six months) interpersonal or peer friendships outside of the immediate family.
3. Initiate social contacts regularly with unfamiliar people or when placed in new social settings.
4. Interact socially with peers or friends on a regular, consistent basis without excessive fear or anxiety.
5. Achieve a healthy balance between time spent in solitary activity and social interaction with others.
6. Develop the essential social skills that will enhance the quality of interpersonal relationships.
7. Resolve the core conflicts contributing to the emergence of social anxiety and shyness.
8. Elevate self-esteem and feelings of security in interpersonal peer and adult relationships.

—. _____

_____

—. _____

_____

—. _____

_____

SHORT-TERM OBJECTIVES	THERAPEUTIC INTERVENTIONS
1. Complete psychological testing. (1, 4)	1. Arrange for psychological testing to assess the severity of the client's anxiety and gain greater insight into the dynamics contributing to the symptoms.
2. Complete psychoeducational testing. (2, 4)	
3. Complete a speech/language evaluation. (3, 4)	2. Arrange for psychoeducational testing of the client to rule out the presence of a
4. Comply with the behavioral and cognitive strategies and	

gradually increase the frequency and duration of social contacts. (5, 6, 7, 8, 9)

5. Agree to initiate one social contact per day. (6, 7, 9, 11)

6. Increase positive self-statements in social interactions. (9, 11, 12, 13)

7. Verbally acknowledge compliments without excessive timidity or withdrawal. (11, 13)

8. Increase positive statements about peer interactions and social experiences. (9, 13, 14, 15)

9. Increase participation in interpersonal or peer group activities. (7, 10, 12, 15, 16)

10. Identify strengths and interests that can be used to initiate social contacts and develop peer friendships. (12, 17, 18, 19)

11. Increase participation in school-related activities. (15, 20)

12. Decrease the frequency of self-disparaging remarks in the presence of peers. (21, 22, 23)

13. Increase assertive behaviors to deal more effectively and directly with stress, conflict, or intimidating peers. (22, 23, 24, 25)

14. Verbalize how current social anxiety and insecurities are associated with past rejection experiences and criticism from significant others. (26, 27, 28, 35)

learning disability that may contribute to social withdrawal in school setting.

3. Refer the client for a comprehensive speech/language evaluation to rule out possible impairment that may contribute to social withdrawal.

4. Give feedback to the client and his/her family regarding psychological, psychoeducational, and speech/language testing.

5. Actively build the level of trust with the client through consistent eye contact, active listening, unconditional positive regard, and warm acceptance to help increase his/her ability to identify and express feelings.

6. Design and implement a systematic desensitization program in which the client gradually increases the frequency and duration of social contacts to help decrease his/her social anxiety.

7. Develop reward system or contingency contract to reinforce client for initiating social contacts and/or engaging in play or recreational activities with peers.

8. Train the client to reduce anxiety by using guided imagery in a relaxed state, with the client visualizing himself/herself dealing with various social situations in a confident manner.

15. Enmeshed or overly protective parents identify how they reinforce social anxiety and overly dependent behaviors. (29, 30, 31, 32)

16. Parents reinforce the client's positive social behaviors and set limits on overly dependent behaviors. (7, 30, 31)

17. Verbally recognize the secondary gain that results from social anxiety, self-disparaging remarks, and overdependence on parents. (28, 29, 32)

18. Overly critical parents verbally recognize how their negative remarks contribute to the client's social anxiety, timidity, and low self-esteem. (31, 34)

19. Parents set realistic and age-appropriate goals for the client. (30, 31, 34, 35)

20. Parents comply with recommendations regarding therapy and/or medication evaluations. (33, 34, 35)

21. Express fears and anxiety in individual play-therapy sessions or through mutual storytelling. (36, 37, 38, 39)

22. Identify and express feelings in art. (40, 41, 42)

23. Express feelings and actively participate in group therapy. (43, 44)

24. Take medication as directed by the prescribing physician. (1, 45, 46)

9. Assist the client in developing positive self-talk as a means of managing his/her social anxiety or fears.

10. Assign the task of initiating one social contact per day.

11. Use behavioral rehearsal, modeling, and role play to reduce anxiety, develop social skills, and learn to initiate conversation.

12. Use "Greeting Peers" exercise in *Brief Child Therapy Homework Planner* (Jongsma, Peterson, and McInnis) to reduce social isolation and help client begin to take steps toward establishing peer friendships.

13. Praise and reinforce any emerging positive social behaviors.

14. Ask the client to list how he/she is like his/her peers.

15. Encourage participation in extracurricular or positive peer group activities.

16. Instruct client to invite a friend for an overnight visit and/or set up an overnight visit at a friend's home; process any fears and anxiety that arise.

17. Ask the client to make a list or keep a journal of both positive and negative social experiences; process this with the therapist.

18. Assign "Show Your Strengths" exercise in *Brief Child Therapy Homework*

—. _____
_____
—. _____
_____
—. _____
_____

Planner (Jongsma, Peterson, and McInnis). Have client first identify 5 to 10 strengths or interests. Review list in next therapy session and instruct client to utilize three strengths or interests in upcoming week to initiate social contacts or develop peer friendships.

19. Explore social situations in which client interacts with others without excessive fear or anxiety. Process these successful experiences and reinforce any strengths or positive social skills that client uses to decrease fear or anxiety.

20. Consult with school officials about ways to increase the client's socialization (e.g., raising flag with group of peers, tutoring a more popular peer, pairing the client with another popular peer on classroom assignments).

21. Provide feedback on any negative social behaviors that interfere with the ability to establish and maintain friendships.

22. Teach assertiveness skills to help communicate thoughts, feelings, and needs more openly and directly.

23. Use Draw Me Out (Shapiro) game in therapy sessions to help overcome shyness and communicate more effectively with peers.

24. Assign reading of *Why Is Everybody Always Picking*

On Me? A Guide to Understanding Bullies for Young People (Webster-Doyle) to teach client effective ways to deal with aggressive or intimidating peers.

25. Play Stand Up for Yourself (Shapiro) game in therapy sessions to help teach client assertive behaviors.

26. Explore for a history of rejection experiences, harsh criticism, abandonment, or trauma that fostered the client's low self-esteem and social anxiety.

27. Encourage and support the client in verbally expressing and clarifying feelings associated with past rejection experiences, harsh criticism, abandonment, or trauma.

28. Conduct a family therapy session to assess the dynamics contributing to the client's social anxiety and withdrawal.

29. Assess how overly protective parents reinforce the client's dependency and social anxiety.

30. Encourage the parents to reinforce or reward the client's positive social behaviors (e.g., calling a friend, playing with peers outside the home) and to set limits on overly dependent behaviors (e.g., pleading, clinging to the parents in social settings).

31. Instruct the parents to ignore occasional and mild antisocial or aggressive behaviors by the client (unless they become too intense or frequent) during the initial stages of treatment so as not to extinguish emerging assertive behaviors.

32. Assist the client and parents in developing insight into the secondary gain received from social anxiety and withdrawal.

33. Assess parents for presence of an anxiety or affective disorder that may contribute to client's shyness. Refer parents for medication evaluation and/or individual therapy if appropriate.

34. Assess the parent-child dyad to determine whether the parents place unrealistically high standards on the client that contribute to the anxiety and feelings of insecurity.

35. Teach parents reasonable expectations for the developmental level of the child.

36. Use child-centered play-therapy principles (e.g., provide unconditional positive regard, display genuine interest, reflect feelings and fears, demonstrate trust in child's capacity for self-growth) to help client overcome his/her social anxieties and feel more confident in social situations.

37. Use psychoanalytic play-
therapy approaches (e.g.,
explore and help client understand etiology of unconscious conflicts, fixations, or
arrests; interpret resis-
tance, transference, or core
anxieties) to help client
work through and resolve
issues contributing to the
social phobia or shyness.

38. Employ Ericksonian play-
therapy technique whereby
therapist speaks through
"wise doll" (or puppet) to audience of other dolls (or puppets) to teach client positive
social skills that can be used
to overcome shyness.

39. Use puppets, dolls, or
stuffed animals to model
positive social skills (e.g.,
greeting others, introducing
self, verbalizing positive
statements about self and
others) that help client feel
more confident in social interactions.

40. Employ art therapy (drawing, painting, sculpting,
etc.) in early stages of therapy to help establish rapport and develop trusting
relationship with client.

41. Instruct client to draw picture or create sculpture
that reflects how he/she
feels around unfamiliar people or when placed in new
social settings.

42. Instruct client to draw objects or symbols on a large
piece of paper or poster

board that symbolize his/her positive attributes; then discuss how client can use strengths to establish peer friendships.

43. Arrange for client to attend group therapy to improve his/her social skills.

44. Give the client a directive to self-disclose two times in each group therapy session.

45. Arrange for a medication evaluation of the client.

46. Monitor the client for compliance, side effects, and overall effectiveness of the medication. Consult with the prescribing physician at regular intervals.

__. _____
    _____

__. _____
    _____

__. _____
    _____

DIAGNOSTIC SUGGESTIONS

Axis I:	300.23	Social Phobia
	300.02	Generalized Anxiety Disorder
	300.00	Anxiety Disorder NOS
	309.21	Separation Anxiety
	300.4	Dysthymic Disorder
	296.xx	Major Depressive Disorder
	311	Depressive Disorder NOS
	309.81	Posttraumatic Stress Disorder
	_____	_____
	_____	_____

Axis II: 799.9   Diagnosis Deferred
                 V71.09   No Diagnosis on Axis II

                 _____   _____

                 _____   _____

SPECIFIC PHOBIA

BEHAVIORAL DEFINITIONS

1. Persistent and unreasonable fear of a specific object or situation because an encounter with the phobic stimulus provokes an immediate anxiety response.
2. Avoidance or endurance of the phobic stimulus with intense anxiety resulting in interference of normal routines or marked distress.
3. Sleep disturbed by dreams of the feared stimulus.
4. Mention of the phobic stimulus produces a dramatic fear reaction.
5. Parents have catered to client's fear and thereby reinforced it.

—. _____
   _____
—. _____
   _____
—. _____

LONG-TERM GOALS

1. Reduce the fear of the specific stimulus object or situation that previously provoked immediate anxiety.
2. Eliminate the interference from normal routines and remove the distress over the feared object or situation.
3. Live phobia-free while responding appropriately to life's fears.
4. Resolve the conflict underlying the phobia.
5. Learn to overcome fears of noise, darkness, people, wild animals, and crowds.

—. _____
   _____
   _____
—. _____
   _____
   _____
—. _____
   _____

SHORT-TERM OBJECTIVES

1. Verbalize the fear and focus on describing the specific stimulus for it. (1, 2)

2. Construct a hierarchy of situations that evoke increasing anxiety. (3)

3. Become proficient in progressive deep-muscle relaxation. (4, 5)

4. Identify a nonthreatening, pleasant scene to promote relaxation through guided imagery. (6)

5. Cooperate with systematic desensitization to the anxiety-provoking stimulus object or situation. (7)

6. Engage in *in vivo* desensitization to the stimulus object or situation. (8)

7. Draw pictures of feared stimulus objects or situations. (9)

8. Attend and freely participate in play-therapy sessions. (10, 11, 12)

9. Collect pleasant pictures or stories regarding the phobic

THERAPEUTIC INTERVENTIONS

1. Actively build a level of trust with the client that will promote the open showing of thoughts and feelings, especially the fearful ones.

2. Discuss and assess the client's fear, its depth, its history of development, and the stimulus for it.

3. Direct and assist the client in the construction of a hierarchy of anxiety-producing situations.

4. Train the client in progressive relaxation methods.

5. Use biofeedback techniques to facilitate the client's relaxation skills.

6. Train the client in the use of relaxing guided imagery for anxiety relief.

7. Direct systematic desensitization (i.e., imagery-based graduated exposure to phobic stimulus while deeply relaxed) procedures to reduce the client's phobic response.

8. Assign and/or accompany the client in *in vivo* desensi-

stimulus and share them in therapy sessions. (13, 14, 15)

10. Write out or read a real or imagined story that describes an encounter with the feared object or situation. (16)

11. Create a pleasant ending to disturbing dreams of feared stimuli or situations. (17)

12. Identify self-devised strategies to cope with the fear. (18, 19)

13. Clarify and verbalize fears. (20, 21)

14. Engage in the feared behavior or encounter the feared situation and freely experience the nondevastating anxiety. (8, 22, 23, 24)

15. Family demonstrate support for the client as he/she tolerates more exposure to the phobic stimulus. (24, 25, 26)

16. Identify the symbolic significance of the phobic stimulus as a basis for fear. (2, 27)

17. Verbalize the separate realities of the irrationally feared object or situation and the emotionally painful experience from the past that is evoked by the phobic stimulus. (2, 28, 29, 30)

18. Share the feelings associated with a past emotionally painful situation that is connected to the phobia. (29, 30)

19. Differentiate real situations that can produce rational

tization (graduated live exposure) contact with the phobic stimulus object or situation.

9. Assign client to draw three things or situations that cause him/her to be fearful. Process completed drawings with therapist.

10. Use child-centered play-therapy approaches (e.g., provide unconditional positive regard, reflect feelings in nonjudgmental manner, display trust in child's capacity to act positively in his/her best interest) to increase abilities to handle fearful encounters.

11. Interpret the feelings expressed in play-therapy sessions and relate them to fear client experiences in specific situations.

12. Employ psychoanalytic play-therapy approach, in which issues are explored in order to gain understanding of the unconscious conflicts or fixations or core anxieties and to assist the client in resolving the issues that feed his/her fear.

13. In sessions with the client, use pleasant pictures, readings, or storytelling about the feared object or situation as a means of desensitizing him/her to the fear-producing stimulus.

14. Read and process "Maurice Faces His Fear" from *Brief*

fear from distorted, imagined situations that can produce irrational fear. (31)

20. Implement specific cognitive and behavioral coping strategies to effectively reduce fear in phobic situations. (32, 33, 34)

21. Verbalize the cognitive beliefs and messages that mediate the anxiety response. (35)

22. Implement positive self-talk to terminate fearful response to phobic situations. (35, 36)

23. Encounter the phobic stimulus object or situation while feeling in control, calm, and comfortable. (8, 24, 25, 37, 38)

—. _____
   _____

—. _____
   _____

—. _____
   _____

Child Therapy Homework Planner (Jongsma, Peterson, and McInnis) to help the client identify fears and their origins.

15. Use humor, jokes, riddles, and stories to enable the client to see his/her situation/fears as not possibly as serious as believed and to help instill hope without disrespecting or minimizing his/her fears.

16. Use a narrative approach (Epston and White) in which the client writes out the story of his/her fear and then acts out the story with the therapist to externalize the issue. Then assist the client in writing an effective coping resolution to the story that can also be acted out.

17. Utilize a neurolinguistic programming (NLP) approach to bad dreams regarding feared stimuli: Ask the client to describe his/her dream. Then have the client talk about and draw a picture of how he/she would like it to end. Next have the client again describe the dream, and when he/she gets to the scary part, have him/her squeeze a hand to act as a remote control that switches to the desired ending. Repeat the process three times. Instruct the client to place the picture under his/her pillow. (See

Agre in *101 Favorite Play Therapy Techniques.*)

18. Work with client using a "stuffed animal collaborative team" (Winnie the Pooh, Barney, Clifford, Curious George, Big Bird, etc.) (see Sleekman in *Solution-Focused Therapy with Children*) or whoever else may be his/her favorite characters. Have child introduce characters and say what he/she likes about each; then proceed to have the client ask how each character would try to resolve the fear.

19. Ask client weekly/biweekly for an update on fearful incidents and how he/she handled each. Give feedback, coach, and positively reinforce as is appropriate or warranted.

20. Assist the client in identifying his/her fears by using "Line Down the Middle of the Page" (see Conyers in *101 Favorite Play Therapy Techniques*), in which a line is placed down the middle of a sheet of paper and the client then lists what is good on one side and what is bad on the other.

21. Construct with client a "worry can" by having him/her draw scary pictures or write scary words on construction paper, which is then cut out and glued to the side of a coffee can. Next, have client write out

all of his/her worries on construction paper, cut them out, fold them, and place them in the worry can. When completed, can's contents can be shared with parents/teacher or other significant adult involved in client's daily life. Contents could be burned as a ceremonial end to fears.

22. Use a strategic intervention (see Fisch, Watzlawick, and Weakland) in which enactment of a symptom is prescribed, allowing the client to make an obvious display of the anxiety (e.g., if the symptom is fear of screaming in a public place, direct the client to go there and do so). Process the client's catastrophizing expectations.

23. Play an enjoyable game with the client in the presence of the feared object or situation as a way of desensitizing him/her. (This may mean leaving the office to conduct a session.)

24. Hold family sessions in which the family is instructed to give support as the client faces the phobic stimulus and to withhold support if the client panics and fails to face the fear (see Pitman); offer encouragement, support, and redirection as required.

25. Assist the family in overcoming the tendency to rein-

force the client's phobia; as the phobia decreases, teach them constructive ways to reward the client's progress.

26. Assess and confront family members when they model phobic fear responses for the client in the presence of the feared object or situation.

27. Probe, discuss, and interpret the possible symbolic meaning of the phobic stimulus object or situation.

28. Clarify and differentiate between the client's current irrational fear and past emotionally painful experiences.

29. Encourage the client to share feelings from the past through active listening, unconditional positive regard, and questioning.

30. Reinforce the client's insight into past emotional pain and its connection to present anxiety.

31. Help client differentiate between real and imagined situations that produce fear. Confront client when he/she responds to imagined situations as if they are real.

32. Teach the client cognitive and behavioral coping strategies (diversion, deep breathing, positive self-talk, muscle relaxation, and so on) to implement when experiencing fear.

33. Use a goal-oriented metaphor to alleviate

the fear by reading with the client *The Blammo-Surprise! Book* (Lankton). As a follow-up, have parents read the story to client at bedtime in between sessions.

34. Teach techniques from "The Therapist on the Inside" (see Grigoryev in *101 Favorite Play Therapy Techniques*) to help client develop the internal structures to handle fears: Client evokes memory of therapist as coach and consultant to facilitate working through the particular fear successfully.

35. Identify the distorted schemas and related automatic thoughts that mediate the client's anxiety response.

36. Use cognitive restructuring techniques to train the client in revising distorted core schemas that trigger negative self-talk; assist the client in replacing negative messages with positive, realistic messages that will counteract a fear response.

37. Monitor and coach client in use of positive self-talk, progressive relaxation, guided imagery, or deep-breathing techniques so that client will use and master these skills.

38. Review and verbally reinforce the client's progress toward overcoming the anxiety.

—. _____
_____
—. _____
_____
—. _____
_____

DIAGNOSTIC SUGGESTIONS

Axis I: 300.00   Anxiety Disorder NOS
300.02   Generalized Anxiety Disorder
300.29   Specific Phobia

_____   _____
_____   _____

Axis II: 799.9   Diagnosis Deferred
V71.09   No Diagnosis on Axis II

_____   _____
_____   _____

SPEECH/LANGUAGE DISORDERS

BEHAVIORAL DEFINITIONS

1. Expressive language abilities, as measured by standardized tests, that are substantially below the expected level.
2. Expressive language deficits, as demonstrated by markedly limited vocabulary, frequent errors in tense, and difficulty recalling words or producing sentences of developmentally appropriate length or complexity.
3. Receptive and expressive language abilities, as measured by standardized tests, that are significantly below the expected level.
4. Receptive language deficits, as manifested by difficulty understanding simple words or sentences, certain types of words such as spatial terms, or longer, complex statements.
5. Deficits in expressive and/or receptive language development that significantly interfere with academic achievement or social communication.
6. Consistent failure to use or produce developmentally expected speech sounds.
7. Repeated stuttering, as demonstrated by impairment in the normal fluency and time patterning of speech.
8. Deficits in speech sound production or fluency that significantly interfere with academic achievement or social communication.
9. Selective mutism, as characterized by a consistent failure to speak in specific social situations (e.g., school) despite speaking in other situations.
10. Social withdrawal and isolation in the peer group, school, or social settings where verbal interaction may be expected.
11. Recurrent pattern of engaging in acting-out, aggressive, or negative attention-seeking behaviors when encountering frustration with speech or language problems.

__. _____

_____

—. _____
_____
—. _____
_____

LONG-TERM GOALS

1. Accept the need for and cooperate actively with speech therapy.
2. Achieve the speech and language goals identified in the Individualized Educational Plan (IEP).
3. Improve the expressive and receptive language abilities to the
   level of capability.
4. Achieve mastery of the expected speech sounds that are appropriate for the age and dialect.
5. Eliminate stuttering; speak fluently and at a normal rate on a regular, consistent basis.
6. Develop an awareness and acceptance of speech/language problems so that there is consistent participation in discussions in the
   peer group, school, or social settings.
7. Parents establish realistic expectations of their child's speech/lan-
   guage abilities.
8. Resolve the core conflict that contributes to the emergence of selective mutism so that the client speaks consistently in all social
   situations.
9. Eliminate the pattern of engaging in acting-out, aggressive, or
   negative attention-seeking behaviors when experiencing the frustration associated with speech/language problems.

—. _____
_____
—. _____
_____
—. _____
_____

SHORT-TERM OBJECTIVES

1. Complete a speech/language evaluation to determine eligibility for special education services. (1, 6, 7)

2. Comply with a psychoeducational evaluation. (2, 6, 7)

3. Complete psychological testing. (3, 6)

4. Complete neuropsychological testing. (4, 6)

5. Cooperate with a hearing or medical examination. (5, 6)

6. Parents cease verbalizations of denial in the family system about the client's speech/language problem. (6, 7, 12)

7. Comply with the recommendations made by a multidisciplinary evaluation team at school regarding speech/language or educational interventions. (6, 7, 8, 13)

8. Parents and client verbalize an acceptance of appropriate special education services to address the speech/language deficits. (6, 7, 8, 12)

9. Comply with speech therapy and cooperate with the recommendations or interventions offered by the speech/language pathologist. (7, 8, 9)

10. Parents, teachers, and speech/language pathologist implement interventions

THERAPEUTIC INTERVENTIONS

1. Refer the client for a speech/language evaluation to assess the presence of a disorder and determine his/her eligibility for special education services.

2. Arrange for a psychoeducational evaluation to assess the client's intellectual abilities and rule out the presence of other possible learning disabilities.

3. Arrange for psychological testing to determine whether emotional factors or ADHD are interfering with the client's speech/language development.

4. Arrange for a neurological examination or neuropsychological evaluation to rule out the presence of organic factors that may contribute to the client's speech/language problem.

5. Refer the client for a hearing and/or medical examination to rule out health problems that may be interfering with his/her speech/language development.

6. Attend an IEP committee meeting with the client's parents, teachers, and the speech/language pathologist to determine client's eligibility for special education services; design educational interventions; establish speech/language goals; and

that maximize the client's strengths and compensate for impairments. (7, 9, 10, 11, 13)

11. Parents maintain regular communication with client's teachers and speech/language pathologist. (7, 8, 9, 10)

12. Parents comply and follow through with reward system to reinforce client for improvements in speech/language development. (11, 13, 14)

13. Increase the time spent with parents in activities that build and facilitate speech/language development. (14, 15, 16)

14. Parents recognize and verbally acknowledge their unrealistic expectations for or excessive pressure on the client to develop speech/language abilities. (17, 18, 19)

15. Parents recognize and terminate their tendency to speak for the client in social settings. (19, 20, 21, 22)

16. Improve the lines of communication in the family system. (19, 22, 23)

17. Increase the frequency of social interactions in which he/she takes the lead in initiating or sustaining conversations. (21, 24, 25, 26, 34)

18. Decrease level of anxiety associated with speech/

outline emotional issues to deal with in counseling.

7. Consult with the client, his/her parents, teachers, and the speech/language pathologist about designing effective intervention strategies that build on the client's strengths and compensate for weaknesses.

8. Refer the client to a private speech/language pathologist for extra assistance in improving speech/language abilities.

9. Encourage the parents to maintain regular communication with the client's teachers and the speech/language pathologist to help facilitate speech/language development.

10. Educate the parents about the signs and symptoms of the client's speech/language disorder.

11. Encourage the parents to give frequent praise and positive reinforcement regarding the client's speech/language development.

12. Challenge the parents' denial surrounding the client's speech/language problem so that the parents cooperate with the recommendations regarding placement and interventions for the client.

13. Consult with speech/language pathologist about designing a reward system to reinforce client for achiev-

language problems.
(25, 27, 35, 37)

19. Increase the frequency of positive statements about peer group activities and school performance.
(25, 26, 27, 29)

20. Decrease the frequency and severity of aggressive acting-out and negative attention-seeking behaviors due to speech/language frustration. (28, 29, 30, 31)

21. Decrease the frequency and severity of dysfluent speech. (32, 33, 35, 36, 37)

22. Comply with systematic desensitization program to decrease the rate of speech and to control stuttering. (32, 36)

23. Express feelings in individual play-therapy sessions. (30, 38, 41)

24. Verbalize an understanding of how selective mutism is associated with past loss, trauma, or victimization. (39, 40, 41, 42)

25. Verbally identify the dynamics or conflicts in the family system that contribute to selective mutism. (39, 40, 42)

26. Express feelings through artwork and mutual story-telling. (29, 31, 42)

27. Take prescribed medication as directed by the physician. (5, 43)

ing goals in speech therapy and mastering new speech behaviors.

14. Use "Home-Based Reading and Language Program" in *Brief Child Therapy Homework Planner* (Jongsma, Peterson, and McInnis), whereby client first reads to parents for 15 minutes four times weekly and then retells the story to build his/her vocabulary. Use reward system to maintain client's interest and motivation.

15. Give a directive for the client and his/her family to go on a weekly outing; afterward, require the client to share his/her feelings about the outing to increase his/her expressive and receptive language abilities (see "Tell All About It" in *Brief Child Therapy Treatment Planner* by Jongsma, Peterson, and McInnis).

16. Instruct parents to sing songs (e.g., nursery rhymes, lullabies, popular songs, songs related to client's interests) with client to help him/her feel more comfortable with his/her verbalizations in home.

17. Confront and challenge the parents about placing excessive or unrealistic pressure on the client to "talk right."

18. Assist the parents in developing realistic expectations

__. _____
   _____

__. _____
   _____

__. _____
   _____

about the client's speech/
language development.

19. Observe parent-child inter-
    actions to assess how family
    communication patterns af-
    fect the client's speech/lan-
    guage development.

20. Explore parent-child in-
    teractions to determine
    whether the parents often
    speak or fill in pauses for
    the client to protect him/her
    from feeling anxious or in-
    secure about speech.

21. Encourage the parents to
    allow the client to take the
    lead more often in initiating
    and sustaining conversa-
    tions.

22. Teach effective communica-
    tion skills (e.g., active lis-
    tening, reflecting feelings,
    "I" statements) to facilitate
    the client's speech/language
    development.

23. Assist the client and his/her
    parents to develop an un-
    derstanding and acceptance
    of the limitations surround-
    ing the speech/language
    disorder.

24. Gently confront the client's
    pattern of withdrawing in
    social settings to avoid ex-
    periencing anxiety about
    speech problems.

25. Assign the client the task of
    contributing one comment
    to classroom discussion
    each day to increase his/her
    confidence in speaking be-
    fore others.

26. Assign the client the task of sharing toys or objects during show-and-tell to increase his/her expressive language abilities.

27. Teach the client positive coping mechanisms (e.g., deep-breathing and muscle relaxation techniques, positive self-talk, cognitive reconstructuring) to use when encountering frustration with speech/language problems.

28. Teach the client self-control strategies (e.g., cognitive restructuring, positive self-talk, "stop, look, listen, and think") to inhibit the impulse to act out when encountering frustration with speech/language problems.

29. Assign reading of "Shauna's Song" in *Brief Child Therapy Homework Planner* (Jongsma, Peterson, and McInnis) to help client verbalize his/her insecurities about speech/language problems. In therapy session, process client's responses to the review questions.

30. Use child-centered play-therapy principles (e.g., demonstrate genuine interest and unconditional positive regard, reflect feelings, express trust in client's capacity for self-growth) to help client face and work through his/her insecurities regarding speech/language problems.

31. Use mutual storytelling technique whereby client and therapist alternate telling stories through use of puppets, dolls, or stuffed animals; therapist first models constructive ways to handle frustrations surrounding speech/language problems; then client follows by telling a story with similar characters or themes.

32. Design and implement a systematic desensitization program in which a metronome is introduced and then gradually removed to slow the client's rate of speech and help control stuttering.

33. Teach the client effective anxiety-reduction techniques (relaxation, positive self-talk, cognitive restructuring) to decrease the anticipatory anxiety in social settings and help control stuttering.

34. Assign client to initiate three social contacts per day with peers to help him/her face and work through anxieties and insecurities related to stuttering in the presence of peers (see "Greeting Peers" in *Brief Child Therapy Treatment Planner* by Jongsma, Peterson, and McInnis).

35. Consult with speech/language pathologist and teachers about designing a program in which client

orally reads passages of gradually increasing length or difficulty in classroom. Praise and reinforce client's effort.

36. Consult with speech/ language pathologist about designing *in vivo* desensitization program (e.g., using deep-muscle relaxation while exposing client to gradually more-anxiety-producing situations) to help client overcome anxiety associated with stuttering.

37. Use role playing and positive coping strategies (e.g., positive self-talk, cognitive restructuring) to extinguish anxiety that triggers stuttering in various social settings (e.g., reading in front of class, talking on phone, introducing self to unfamiliar peer).

38. Employ psychoanalytic play-therapy approaches (e.g., allow child to take lead; explore etiology of unconscious conflicts, fixations, or developmental arrests; interpret resistance, transference, and core anxieties) to help client work through his/her feelings surrounding past loss, trauma, or victimization that contributes to selective mutism.

39. Assess the family dynamics that contribute to the client's refusal to use speech in some situations.

40. Explore the client's background history of loss, trauma, or victimization that contributed to the emergence of selective mutism.

41. Employ Ericksonian play-therapy technique whereby therapist speaks through "wise doll" (or puppet) to audience of other dolls or puppets to teach client effective ways to cope with past loss, trauma, or victimization.

42. Use art therapy (drawing, painting, sculpting, etc.) in early stages of therapy to establish rapport and help client with selective mutism begin to express his/her feelings through artwork.

43. Arrange for a medication evaluation if it is determined that an emotional problem and/or ADHD are interfering with speech/language development.

___. _____

_____

___. _____

_____

___. _____

_____

DIAGNOSTIC SUGGESTIONS

Axis I: 315.31   Expressive Language Disorder
315.31   Mixed Receptive-Expressive Language Disorder
315.39   Phonological Disorder
307.0   Stuttering
307.9   Communication Disorder NOS
313.23   Selective Mutism
309.21   Separation Anxiety Disorder
300.23   Social Phobia

_____   _____

_____   _____

Axis II: 317   Mild Mental Retardation
V62.89   Borderline Intellectual Functioning
799.9   Diagnosis Deferred
V71.09   No Diagnosis on Axis II

_____   _____

_____   _____

Appendix A

BIBLIOTHERAPY SUGGESTIONS

General

Many references are made throughout this book to the following therapeutic homework resource, which was developed by the authors as a corollary to the *Child and Adolescent Psychotherapy Treatment Planner* (Jongsma, Peterson, and McInnis):

Jongsma, A., L. Peterson, and W. McInnis (1999). *Brief Child Therapy Homework Planner.* New York: John Wiley & Sons, Inc.

Academic Underachievement

Bloom, J. (1990). *Help Me to Help My Child.* Boston: Little, Brown.
Martin, M., and C. Greenwood-Waltman, eds. (1995). *Solve Your Child's School-Related Problems.* New York: HarperCollins.
Pennington, B. (1991). *Diagnosing Learning Disorders.* New York: Guilford.
Silverman, S. (1998). *13 Steps to Better Grades.* Plainview, NY: Childswork/ Childsplay, LLC.
Smith, S. (1979). *No Easy Answers.* New York: Bantam Books.

Adoption

Burlingham-Brown, B. (1994). *Why Didn't She Keep Me?* South Bend, IN: Langford.
Covey, S. (1997). *The 7 Habits of Highly Effective Families: Building a Beautiful Family Culture in a Turbulent World.* New York: Golden Books Publishing Co.
Girard, L. W. (1986). *Adoption Is For Always.* Niles, IL: Albert Whitmore & Co.
Jewett, C. (1982). *Helping Children Cope with Separation and Loss.* Harvard, MA: Harvard Common Press.
Kranz, L. (1995). *All About Me and More About Me.* Norland, AZ: Keepsakes.
Krementz, J. (1996). *How It Feels to Be Adopted.* New York: Alfred Knopf.

Medina, L. (1984). *Making Sense of Adoption*. New York: Harper & Row.
Schooler, J. (1993). *The Whole Life Adoption Book*. Colorado Springs, CO: Pinon Press.
Stinson, K. (1998). *I Feel Different*. Los Angeles, CA: Manson Western Co.

Anger Management

Canter, L., and P. Canter (1988). *Assertive Discipline for Parents*. New York: HarperCollins.
Green, R. (1998). *The Explosive Child*. New York: HarperCollins.
Kaye, D. (1991). *Family Rules: Raising Responsible Children*. New York: St. Martins.
Phelan, T. (1995). *1-2-3 Magic: Training Your Preschoolers and Preteens to Do What You Want*. Glen Ellyn, IL: Child Management, Inc.
Shapiro, L. E. (1996). *The Very Angry Day That Amy Didn't Have*. Plainview, NY: Childswork/Childsplay, LLC.
Shapiro, L. E. (1995). *Sometimes I Like to Fight, but I Don't Do It Much Anymore*. Plainview, NY: Childswork/Childsplay, LLC.
Shapiro, L. E. (1995). *How I Learned to Control My Temper*. Plainview, NY: Childswork/Childsplay, LLC.
Shore, H. (1994). *The Angry Monster Workbook*. Plainview, NY: Childswork/Childsplay, LLC.

Anxiety

Block, D. (1993). *Positive Self-Talk for Children*. New York: Bantam Books.
Deaton, W. (1993). *My Own Thoughts: A Growth and Recovery Book for Young Girls*. Alameda, CA: Hunter House.
Elkind, D. (1981). *The Hurried Child: Growing Up Too Fast Too Soon*. New York: Addison-Wesley.
McCauley, C. S., and R. Schachter (1988). *When Your Child Is Afraid*. New York: Simon & Schuster.
Moser, Adolph (1988). *Don't Pop Your Cork on Mondays!* Kansas City, MO: Landmark Editions, Inc.

Attachment Disorder

Gil, E. (1983). *Outgrowing the Pain*. Rockville, MD: Laurel Press.
Greenspan, S. (1995). *The Challenging Child*. Reading, MA: Perseus Books.
Jewett, C. (1982). *Helping Children Cope with Separation and Loss*. Harvard, MA: Harvard Common Press.
Moser, A. (1994). *Don't Rant and Rave on Wednesday*. Kansas City, MO: Landmark Editions, Inc.

Moser, A. (1998). *Don't Despair on Thursday*. Kansas City, MO: Landmark Editions, Inc.

Turecki, S. (1985). *The Difficult Child*. New York: Bantam Books.

Attention-Deficit/Hyperactivity Disorder (ADHD)

Barkley, R. (1995). *Taking Charge of ADHD: The Complete, Authoritative Guide for Parents*. New York: Guilford Press.

Ingersoll, B. (1988). *Your Hyperactive Child*. New York: Doubleday.

Parker, H. (1992). *The ADD Hyperactivity Handbook for Schools*. Plantation, FL: Impact Publications.

Phelan, T. (1995). *1-2-3 Magic: Training Your Preschoolers and Preteens to Do What You Want*. Glen Ellyn, IL: Child Management, Inc.

Quinn, P., and J. Stern (1991). *Putting on the Brakes*. New York: Magination Press.

Saxe, S. (1997). "The Angry Tower." In H. Kaduson and C. Schaefer (eds.), *101 Favorite Play Therapy Techniques* (pp. 246–249). Northvale, NJ: Jason Aronson, Inc.

Shapiro, L. (1993). *Sometimes I Drive My Mom Crazy, but I Know She's Crazy About Me*. King of Prussia, PA: Center for Applied Psychology.

Silverman, S. (1998). *13 Steps to Better Grades*. Plainview, NY: Childswork/Childsplay, LLC.

Shapiro, L. E. (1996). *The Very Angry Day That Amy Didn't Have*. Plainview, NY: Childswork/Childsplay, LLC.

Shapiro, L. E. (1995). *Sometimes I Like to Fight, but I Don't Do It Much Anymore*. Plainview, NY: Childswork/Childsplay, LLC.

Autism/Pervasive Developmental Disorder

Brill, M. (1994). *Keys to Parenting the Child with Autism*. Hauppauge, NY: Barrons.

Marcus, L. M. and E. Schopler (1989). *Parents as Co-Therapists with Autistic Children*. In C. E. Schaeffer and J. M. Briesmeister (eds.), *Handbook of Parent Training: Parents as Co-Therapists for Children's Behavior Problems* (pp. 337–360). New York: John Wiley & Sons, Inc.

Rimland, B. (1964). *Infantile Autism*. New York: Appleton Century Crofts.

Siegel, B. (1996). *The World of the Autistic Child*. New York: Oxford.

Simons, J., and S. Olsihi (1987). *The Hidden Child*. Bethesda, MD: Woodbine House.

Blended Family

Brown, M. (1947). *Stone Soup*. New York: Simon & Schuster.

Covey, S. (1997). *The 7 Habits of Highly Effective Families*. New York: Golden Books.

Fassler, D., M. Lash, and S. Ives (1988). *Changing Families.* Burlington, VT: Waterfront Books.

Newman, M. C. (1992). *Stepfamily Realities.* Oakland, CA: New Harbinger.

Seuss, Dr. (1961). *The Sneetches and Other Stories.* New York: Random House.

Visher, E., and J. Visher (1982). *How to Win as a Stepfamily.* New York: Brunner/Mazel.

Conduct Disorder/Delinquency

Canter, L., and P. Canter (1988). *Assertive Discipline for Parents.* New York: HarperCollins.

Phelan, T. (1995). *1-2-3 Magic: Training Your Preschoolers and Preteens to Do What You Want.* Glen Ellyn, IL: Child Management, Inc.

Redl, F., and D. Wineman (1951). *Children Who Hate.* New York: Free Press.

Saxe, S. (1997). "The Angry Tower." In H. Kaduson and C. Schaefer (eds.), *101 Favorite Play Therapy Techniques* (pp. 246–249). Northvale, NJ: Jason Aronson, Inc.

Shapiro, L. E. (1996). *The Very Angry Day That Amy Didn't Have.* Plainview, NY: Childswork/Childsplay, LLC.

Shapiro, L. E. (1995). *Sometimes I Like to Fight, but I Don't Do It Much Anymore.* Plainview, NY: Childswork/Childsplay, LLC.

Shore, H. (1991). *The Angry Monster.* King of Prussia, PA: Center for Applied Psychology.

Depression

Black, C., (1979). *My Dad Loves Me, My Dad Has a Disease.* Denver: MAC.

Ingersoll, B., and S. Goldstein (1995). *Lonely, Sad and Angry: A Parent's Guide to Depression in Children and Adolescents.* New York: Doubleday.

Kerns, L. (1993). *Helping Your Depressed Child.* Rocklin, CA: Prima.

Moser, A. (1994). *Don't Rant and Rave on Wednesdays!* Kansas City, MO: Landmark Editions, Inc.

Disruptive/Attention Seeking

Canter, L., and P. Canter (1988). *Assertive Discipline for Parents.* New York: HarperCollins.

Kaye, D. (1991). *Family Rules: Raising Responsible Children.* New York: St. Martins.

Phelan, T. (1995). *1-2-3 Magic: Training Your Preschoolers and Preteens to Do What You Want.* Glen Ellyn, IL: Child Management, Inc.

Shapiro, L. E. (1995). *How I Learned to Think Things Through.* Plainview, NY: Childswork/Childsplay, LLC.

Divorce Reaction

Gardner, R. (1971). *The Boys and Girls Book About Divorce*. New York: Bantam.

Grollman, E. (1975). *Talking About Divorce*. Boston: Beacon Press.

Ives S., D. Fassler, and M. Lash (1985). *The Divorce Workbook*. Burlington, VT: Waterfront.

Phelan, T. (1995). *1-2-3 Magic: Training Your Preschoolers and Preteens to Do What You Want*. Glen Ellyn, IL: Child Management, Inc.

Rotes, E., ed. (1981). *The Kid's Book of Divorce*. New York: Vintage.

Tolon, M., and L. Brown (1986). *Dinosaur's Divorce: A Guide for Changing Families*. New York: Atlantic Monthly Press.

Wadeson, H. (1995). *The Dynamics of Art Psychotherapy*. New York: John Wiley & Sons, Inc.

Enuresis/Encopresis

Houts, A. C., and M. W. Mellon (1989). "Home-Based Treatment for Primary Enuresis." In C. E. Schaefer and J. M. Briesmeister (eds.), *Handbook of Parent Training: Parents as Co-Therapists for Children's Behavior Problems* (pp. 60–80). New York: John Wiley & Sons, Inc.

Ilg, F., L. Ames, and S. Baker (1981). *Child Behavior: Specific Advice on Problems of Child Behavior*. New York: Harper & Row.

Whittenhouse, E., and W. Pudney (1996). *A Volcano in My Tummy*. Denver, CO: New Social Publishers.

Fire Setting

Green, R. (1998). *The Explosive Child*. New York: HarperCollins.

Millman, H., and C. Schaefer (1977). *Therapies for Children: A Handbook of Effective Treatments for Problem Behaviors*. San Francisco: Jossey-Bass.

Shore, H. (1994). *The Angry Monster Workbook*. Plainview, NY: Childswork/Childsplay, LLC.

Whittenhouse, E., and W. Pudney (1996). *A Volcano in My Tummy*. Denver, CO: New Social Publishers.

Gender Identity Disorder

Bradley, S., and K. Zucker (1995). *Gender Identity Disorder and Psychosexual Problems in Children and Adolescents*. New York: Guilford.

Grief/Loss Unresolved

Gof, B. (1969). *Where Is Daddy?* Boston: Beacon Press.

Grollman, E. (1967). *Explaining Death to Children*. Boston: Beacon Press.

Mellonie, B., and R. Ingpen (1983). *Lifetimes.* New York: Bantam Books.

Moser, A. (1996). *Don't Despair on Thursday.* Kansas City, MO: Landmark Editions, Inc.

Nystrom, C. (1990). *Emma Says Goodbye.* Batavia, IL: Lion Publishing Co.

O'Toole, D. (1989). *Aarvy Aardvark Finds Hope.* Burnsville, NC: Compassion Books.

Temes, R. (1992). *The Empty Place.* Dallas, TX: New Horizons.

Low Self-Esteem

Block, D. (1993). *Positive Self-Talk for Children.* New York: Bantam Books.

Briggs, D. (1970). *Your Child's Self-Esteem.* Garden City, NY: Doubleday.

Dobson, J. (1974). *Hide or Seek: How to Build Self-Esteem in Your Child.* Old Tappan, NJ: F. Revell Co.

Loomans, D., and J. Loomans (1994). *Full Esteem Ahead.* Fort Collins, CO: Kramer, Inc.

Moser, A. (1991). *Don't Feed the Monster on Tuesday!* Kansas City, MO: Landmark Editions, Inc.

Sanford, D. (1986). *Don't Look at Me.* Portland, OR: Multnomah Press.

Shapiro, L. (1993). *The Building Blocks of Self-Esteem.* King of Prussia, PA: Center for Applied Psychology.

Medical Condition

Bluebond-Langner, M. (1996). *In the Shadow of Illness.* Princeton, NJ: Princeton University Press.

Fromer, M. (1998). *Surviving Childhood Cancer: A Guide for Families.* Oakland, CA: New Harbinger.

Huntley, T. (1991). *Helping Children Grieve.* Minneapolis, MN: Augsburg Fortress.

Krisher, T. (1992). *Kathy's Hats: A Story of Hope.* Morton Grove, IL: Concept Books.

MacLellan, S. (1999). *Amanda's Gift: One Family's Journey through the Maze of Serious Childhood Illness.* Roswell, GA: Health Awareness Communications.

Mental Retardation

Huff, M., and R. Gibby (1958). *The Mentally Retarded Child.* Boston: Allyn and Bacon.

Millman, J., and C. Schaefer. (1977). *Therapies for Children: A Handbook of Effective Treatments for Behaviors.* San Francisco: Jossey-Bass.

Sanford, D. (1986). *Don't Look At Me.* Portland, OR: Multnomah Press.

Trainer, M. (1991). *Differences in Common.* Rockville, MD: Woodbine House.

Watson, G. S., and A. M. Gross (1997). "Mental Retardation and Developmental Disorders." In R. T. Ammerman and M. H. Herson (eds.), *Handbook of Prevention and Treatment with Children and Adolescents* (pp. 495–520). New York: John Wiley & Sons, Inc.

Oppositional Defiant

Abern, A. (1994). *Everything I Do You Blame on Me*. Plainview, NY: Childswork/Childsplay, LLC.

Barkley, R., and C. Benton (1998). *Your Defiant Child: Eight Steps to Better Behavior*. New York: Guilford.

Dobson, J. (1978). *The Strong-Willed Child*. Wheaton, IL: Tyndale House.

Gardner, R. (1990). *The Girls and Boys Book About Good and Bad Behavior*. Cresskill, NJ: Creative Therapeutics.

Greenspan, S. (1995). *The Challenging Child*. Reading, MA: Perseus Books.

Kaye, K. (1991). *Family Rules: Raising Responsible Children*. New York: St. Martins.

Riley, D. (1997). *The Defiant Child: A Parent's Guide to Oppositional Defiant Disorder*. Dallas: Taylor Publishing.

Wenning, K. (1996). *Winning Cooperation from Your Child*. New York: Aronson.

Peer/Sibling Conflict

Baruch, D. (1949). *New Ways in Discipline*. New York: MacMillan.

Bieniek, D. (1996). *How to End the Sibling Wars*. King of Prussia, PA: Childswork/Childsplay, LLC.

Faber, A., and E. Mazlish (1982). *How to Talk So Kids Will Listen and Listen So Kids Will Talk*. New York: Avon.

Faber, A., and E. Mazlish (1987). *Siblings Without Rivalry*. New York: Norton.

Ginott, H. (1965). *Between Parent and Child*. New York: MacMillan.

Nevick, R. (1996). *Helping Your Child Make Friends*. King of Prussia, PA: Childswork/Childsplay, LLC.

Physical/Emotional Abuse Victim

Miller, Alice. (1984). *For Your Own Good*. New York: Farrar Straus & Giroux.

Monahon, Cynthia. (1983). *Children and Trauma: A Parent's Guide to Helping Children Heal*. New York: Lexington Press.

Posttraumatic Stress Disorder

Flannery, Raymond Jr. (1995). *Post-Traumatic Stress Disorder: The Victim's Guide to Healing and Recovery*. New York: Crossroad Publishing.

Matsakis, Aphrodite (1996). *I Can't Get Over It: A Handbook for Trauma Survivors.* Oakland, CA.: New Harbinger.

School Refusal

Martin, M., and C. Greenwood-Waltman, eds. (1995). *Solve Your Child's School-Related Problems.* New York: HarperCollins.

Millman, H., and C. Schaefer (1977). *Therapies for Children: A Handbook of Effective Treatments for Problem Behaviors.* San Francisco: Jossey-Bass.

Millman, M., C. Schaefer, and J. Cohen (1980). *Therapies for School Behavioral Problems.* San Francisco: Jossey-Bass.

Webster-Doyle, T. (1999). *Why Is Everybody Always Picking on Me? A Guide to Understanding Bullies for Young People.* Middlebury, VT: Peace Publications.

Yule, W. (1989). "Parent Involvement in the Treatment of the School Phobic Child." In C. E. Schaefer and J. M. Briesmeister (eds.), *Handbook of Parent Training: Parents as Co-Therapists for Children's Behavior Problems* (pp. 223–244). New York: John Wiley & Sons, Inc.

Separation Anxiety

Fraiberg, S., (1959). *The Magic Years.* New York: Scribners.

Ginott, H. (1965). *Between Parent and Child.* New York: MacMillan.

Ingersoll, B., and S. Goldstein (1995). *Lonely, Sad and Angry: A Parent's Guide to Depression in Children and Adolescents.* New York: Doubleday.

Kerns, L. (1993). *Helping Your Depressed Child.* Rocklin, CA: Prima.

Kliman, G., and A. Rosenfeld (1980). *Responsible Parenthood.* New York: Holt, Rinehart, and Winston.

Mikulas, W. L., and M. F. Coffman (1989). "Home-Based Treatment of Children's Fear of the Dark." In C. E. Schaefer and J. M. Briesmeister (eds.), *Handbook of Parent Training: Parents as Co-Therapists for Children's Behavior Problems* (pp. 179–202). New York: John Wiley & Sons, Inc.

Sexual Abuse Victim

Colao, F., and T. Hosansky (1987). *Your Children Should Know.* New York: Harper & Row.

Davis, L. (1991). *Allies in Healing.* New York: HarperCollins.

Hagan, K., and J. Case (1988). *When Your Child Has Been Molested.* Lexington, MA: Lexington Books.

Hindman, J. (1983). *A Very Touching Book . . . For Little People and for Big People.* Durkee, OR: McClure-Hindman Associates.

Jance, J. (1985). *It's Not Your Fault.* Charlotte, NC: Kidsrights.

Sanford, D. (1986). *I Can't Talk About It.* Portland, OR: Multnomah Press.

Specific Phobia

Block, D. (1993). *Positive Self-Talk for Children.* New York: Bantam Books.

Brown, J. (1995). *No More Monsters in the Closet.* New York: Prince Paperbacks.

Garber, S., M. Garber, and R. Spitzman (1993). *Monsters Under the Bed and Other Childhood Fears.* New York: Villard.

Sleep Disturbance

Ferber, R. (1985). *Solve Your Child's Sleep Problems.* New York: Simon & Schuster.

Ilg, F., L. Ames, and S. Baker (1981). *Child Behavior: Specific Advice on Problems of Child Behavior.* New York: Harper & Row.

Social Phobia/Shyness

Martin, M., and C. Greenwood-Waltman, eds. (1995). *Solve Your Child's School-Related Problems.* New York: HarperCollins.

Millman, M., C. Schaefer, and J. Cohen (1980). *Therapies for School Behavioral Problems.* San Francisco: Jossey-Bass.

Webster-Doyle, T. (1998). *Why Is Everybody Always Picking on Me? A Guide to Understanding Bullies for Young People.* Middlebury, VT: Peace Publications.

Zimbardo, P. (1987). *Shyness: What It Is and What to Do About It.* New York: Addison-Wesley.

Speech/Language Disorders

Ainsworth, S., and J. Fraser (1998). *If Your Child Stutters: A Guide for Parents.* Memphis, TN: Stuttering Foundation of America.

Heinze, B. A., and K. L. Johnson (1987). *Easy Does It: Fluency Activities for School-Aged Stutterers.* East Moline, IL: Linguisystems.

Millman, M., C. Schaefer, and J. Cohen (1980). *Therapies for School Behavioral Problems.* San Francisco: Jossey-Bass.

Appendix B

INDEX OF DSM-IV CODES ASSOCIATED WITH PRESENTING PROBLEMS

Academic Problem   V62.3
  Academic Underachievement

Acute Stress Disorder   308.3
  Physical/Emotional Abuse Victim
  Posttraumatic Stress Disorder
  Sexual Abuse Victim

Adjustment Disorder   309.xx
  Posttraumatic Stress Disorder

**Adjustment Disorder
With Anxiety**   309.24
  Blended Family
  Divorce Reaction
  Medical Condition

**Adjustment Disorder With
Depressed Mood**   309.0
  Adoption
  Blended Family
  Depression
  Divorce Reaction
  Grief/Loss Unresolved
  Medical Condition

**Adjustment Disorder With
Disturbance of Conduct**   309.3
  Blended Family
  Disruptive/Attention Seeking
  Divorce Reaction
  Fire Setting
  Medical Condition

**Adjustment Disorder
With Mixed Anxiety
and Depressed Mood**   309.28
  Divorce Reaction
  Medical Condition

**Adjustment Disorder
With Mixed Disturbance
of Emotions and Conduct**   309.4
  Adoption
  Attachment Disorder
  Disruptive/Attention Seeking
  Divorce Reaction
  Fire Setting
  Grief/Loss Unresolved
  Medical Condition

Alcohol Dependence   303.90
  Low Self-Esteem

Anorexia Nervosa   307.1
  Low Self-Esteem

Anxiety Disorder NOS   300.00
  Anxiety
  Social Phobia/Shyness
  Specific Phobia

Asperger's Disorder   299.80
  Autism/Pervasive Developmental
    Disorder
  Mental Retardation

Attention-Deficit/Hyperactivity Disorder, Combined Type   314.01
Academic Underachievement
Adoption
Anxiety
Attention-Deficit/Hyperactivity
  Disorder (ADHD)
Disruptive/Attention Seeking
Enuresis/Encopresis

Attention-Deficit/Hyperactivity Disorder, Predominantly Hyperactive-Impulsive Type   314.01
Attention-Deficit/Hyperactivity
  Disorder (ADHD)
Conduct Disorder/Delinquency
Disruptive/Attention Seeking
Low Self-Esteem
Oppositional Defiant
Peer/Sibling Conflict

Attention-Deficit/Hyperactivity Disorder, Predominantly Inattentive Type   314.00
Academic Underachievement
Attention-Deficit/Hyperactivity
  Disorder (ADHD)

Attention-Deficit/Hyperactivity Disorder NOS   314.9
Anger Management
Attachment Disorder
Attention-Deficit/Hyperactivity
  Disorder (ADHD)
Conduct Disorder/Delinquency
Fire Setting
Oppositional Defiant
Peer/Sibling Conflict

Autistic Disorder   299.00
Autism/Pervasive Developmental
  Disorder
Mental Retardation

Bereavement   V62.82
Depression
Grief/Loss Unresolved

Bipolar Disorder NOS   296.80
Sleep Disturbance

Bipolar I Disorder   296.0x
Attention-Deficit/Hyperactivity
  Disorder (ADHD)
Depression
Sleep Disturbance

Bipolar II Disorder   296.89
Depression
Sleep Disturbance

Borderline Intellectual Functioning   V62.89
Academic Underachievement
Low Self-Esteem
Mental Retardation
Speech/Language Disorders

Cannabis Dependence   304.30
Low Self-Esteem

Child Antisocial Behavior   V71.02
Anger Management
Conduct Disorder/Delinquency
Disruptive/Attention Seeking
Peer/Sibling Conflict

Childhood Disintegrative Disorder   299.10
Autism/Pervasive Developmental
  Disorder
Mental Retardation

Circadian Rhythm Sleep Disorder   307.45
Sleep Disturbance

Communication Disorder NOS   307.9
Speech/Language Disorders

Conduct Disorder/ Adolescent-Onset Type   312.8
Physical/Emotional Abuse Victim

Conduct Disorder/ Childhood-Onset Type   312.8
Anger Management
Attention-Deficit/Hyperactivity
  Disorder (ADHD)
Conduct Disorder/Delinquency
Disruptive/Attention Seeking
Fire Setting

Gender Identity
Disorder NOS   302.6
  Gender Identity Disorder

Generalized Anxiety
Disorder   300.02
  Anxiety
  Divorce Reaction
  Low Self-Esteem
  Medical Condition
  Physical/Emotional Abuse Victim
  School Refusal
  Separation Anxiety
  Social Phobia/Shyness
  Specific Phobia

Impulse-Control
Disorder NOS   312.30
  Anger Management
  Fire Setting

Intermittent Explosive
Disorder   312.34
  Anger Management
  Conduct Disorder/Delinquency

Learning Disorder NOS   315.9
  Peer/Sibling Conflict

Major Depressive Disorder   296.xx
  Enuresis/Encopresis
  Low Self-Esteem
  Medical Condition
  Physical/Emotional Abuse Victim
  Posttraumatic Stress Disorder
  School Refusal
  Separation Anxiety
  Sexual Abuse Victim
  Sleep Disturbance
  Social Phobia/Shyness

Major Depressive Disorder,
Recurrent   296.3x
  Attachment Disorder
  Depression
  Grief/Loss Unresolved

Major Depressive Disorder,
Single Episode   296.2x
  Depression
  Grief/Loss Unresolved

Mathematics Disorder   315.1
  Academic Underachievement

Mental Retardation, Mild   317
  Academic Underachievement
  Autism/Pervasive Developmental
    Disorder
  Low Self-Esteem
  Mental Retardation
  Speech/Language Disorders

Mental Retardation,
Moderate   318.0
  Mental Retardation

Mental Retardation,
Profound   318.2
  Mental Retardation

Mental Retardation, Severe   318.1
  Mental Retardation

Mental Retardation, Severity
Unspecified   319
  Autism/Pervasive Developmental
    Disorder
  Mental Retardation

Mixed Receptive-Expressive
Language Disorder   315.31
  Speech/Language Disorders

Neglect of Child (Victim)   995.5
  Low Self-Esteem

Nightmare Disorder   307.47
  Physical/Emotional Abuse Victim
  Separation Anxiety
  Sexual Abuse Victim
  Sleep Disturbance

No Diagnosis or Condition
on Axis I or II   V71.09
  Adoption
  Anger Management
  Anxiety
  Attachment Disorder
  Attention-Deficit/Hyperactivity
    Disorder (ADHD)
  Autism/Pervasive Developmental
    Disorder

Relational Problem NOS   **V62.81**
  Blended Family
  Oppositional Defiant
  Peer/Sibling Conflict

Rett's Disorder   **299.80**
  Autism/Pervasive Developmental
    Disorder
  Mental Retardation

Schizophrenia   **295.xx**
  Autism/Pervasive Developmental
    Disorder

Selective Mutism   **313.23**
  Speech/Language Disorders

Separation Anxiety Disorder   **309.21**
  Anxiety
  Divorce Reaction
  Low Self-Esteem
  School Refusal
  Separation Anxiety
  Sleep Disturbance
  Social Phobia/Shyness
  Speech/Language Disorders

**Sexual Abuse of Child
(Victim)**   **995.5**
  Low Self-Esteem
  Posttraumatic Stress Disorder
  Sexual Abuse Victim

Sleep Terror Disorder   **307.46**
  Separation Anxiety
  Sleep Disturbance

Sleepwalking Disorder   **307.46**
  Sleep Disturbance

Social Phobia   **300.23**
  Low Self-Esteem
  School Refusal
  Separation Anxiety
  Social Phobia/Shyness
  Speech/Language Disorders

Somatization Disorder   **300.81**
  School Refusal
  Separation Anxiety

Specific Phobia   **300.29**
  Specific Phobia

**Stereotypic Movement
Disorder**   **307.3**
  Autism/Pervasive Developmental
    Disorder

Stuttering   **307.0**
  Speech/Language Disorders

**Undifferentiated
Somatoform Disorder**   **300.81**
  Divorce Reaction

Appendix C

INDEX OF THERAPEUTIC GAMES, WORKBOOKS, TOOL KITS, VIDEOTAPES, AND AUDIOTAPES

Product	Author
Anger Control Toolkit	Shapiro, et al.
Don't Be Difficult	Shapiro
Coping with Anger Target Game	Shapiro
Draw Me Out!	Shapiro
Feelings Poster	Bureau for At Risk Youth
Heartbeat Audiotapes	Lamb
How I Learned to Control My Temper	Shapiro
Kids in Court	Unknown
Let's Work It Out: A Conflict Resolution Tool Kit	Shapiro
Magic Island: Relaxation for Kids	Mehling, Highstein, and Delamarter
My Two Homes	Shapiro
Once Upon a Time Potty Book and Doll Set	Unknown
Relaxation Imagery For Children	Weinstock
Stand Up for Yourself	Shapiro
Stop, Relax, and Think	Bridges
The Anger Control Game	Berg
The Angry Monster Workbook	Shore
The Angry Monster Machine	Shapiro
The Good Mourning Game	Bisenius and Norris
The Helping, Sharing, and Caring Game	Gardner
The Self-Control Patrol Game	Trower
The Talking, Feeling, and Doing Game	Gardner
The Ungame	Zakich
You and Me: A Game of Social Skills	Shapiro

The products listed above can be purchased by contacting the following companies:

A.D.D. Warehouse
300 Northwest 70th Avenue, Suite 102
Plantation, FL 33317
Phone: 1-800-233-9273
www.addwarehouse.com

Childswork/Childsplay, LLC
P.O. Box 1604
Secaucus, NJ 07096-1604
Phone: 1-800-962-1141
www.childswork.com

Courage to Change
P.O. Box 1268
Newburgh, NY 12551
Phone: 1-800-440-4003

Creative Therapeutics
P.O. Box 522
Cresskill, NJ 67626-0522
Phone: 1-800-544-6162
www.rgardner.com

Western Psychological Services
Division of Manson Western Corporation
12031 Wilshire Boulevard
Los Angeles, CA 90025-1251
Phone: 1-800-648-8857
www.wpspublish.com

BIBLIOGRAPHY

Breiner, J. (1989). "Training Parents as Change Agents for Their Developmentally Disabled Children." In C. E. Schaefer and J. M. Briesmeister (eds.), *Handbook of Parent Training: Parents as Co-Therapists for Children's Behavior Problems* (pp. 269–304). New York: John Wiley & Sons, Inc.

James, B. (1989). *Treating Traumatized Children.* New York: Lexington Books.

Landreth, G. (1991). *Play Therapy: The Art of the Relationship.* Muncie, IN: Accelerated Development, Inc.

Leland, H. (1983). "Play Therapy for Mentally Retarded and Developmentally Disabled Children. In C. E. Schaefer and K. J. O'Connor (eds.), *Handbook of Play Therapy* (pp. 436–454). New York: John Wiley & Sons, Inc.

Martin, M., and C. Greenwood-Waltman, ed. (1995). *Solve Your Child's School-Related Problems.* New York: HarperCollins.

Mendell, A. E. (1983). "Play Therapy with Children of Divorced Parents." In Schaeffer and K. J. O'Connor (eds.), *Handbook of Play Therapy* (pp. 320–354). New York: John Wiley & Sons, Inc.

Millman, H., and C. Schaefer (1977). *Therapies for Children: A Handbook of Effective Treatments for Problem Behaviors.* San Francisco: Jossey-Bass.

Millman, H., C. Schaefer, and J. Cohen (1980). *Therapies for School Behavioral Problems.* San Francisco: Jossey-Bass.

O'Connor, K. J. (1983). "The Color-Your-Life Technique." In C. E. Schaeffer and K. J. O'Connor (eds.), *Handbook of Play Therapy* (pp. 251–258) New York: John Wiley & Sons, Inc.

O'Connor, K. J. (1991). *The Play Therapy Primer: An Integration of Theories and Techniques.* New York: John Wiley & Sons, Inc.

Saxe, S. (1997). "The Angry Tower." In H. Kaduson and C. Schaefer (eds.), *101 Favorite Play Therapy Techniques* (pp. 246–249). Northvale, NJ: Jason Aronson, Inc.

Wadeson, H. (1980). *Art Psychotherapy.* New York: John Wiley & Sons.

Watson, G. S., and A. M. Gross (1997). "Mental Retardation and Developmental Disorders." In R. T. Ammerman and M. H. Herson (eds.), *Handbook of Prevention and Treatment with Children and Adolescents* (pp. 495–520). New York: John Wiley & Sons, Inc.

ABOUT THE DISK*

TheraScribe® 3.0 and 3.5 Library Module Installation

The enclosed disk contains files to upgrade your TheraScribe® 3.0 or 3.5 program to include the behavioral definitions, goals, objectives, and interventions from *The Child Psychotherapy Treatment Planner.*

Note: You must have TheraScribe® 3.0 or 3.5 for Windows installed on your computer in order to use *The Child Psychotherapy Treatment Planner* library module.

To install the library module, please follow these steps:

1. Place the library module disk in your floppy drive.
2. Log in to TheraScribe® 3.0 or 3.5 as the Administrator using the name "Admin" and your administrator password.
3. On the Main Menu, press the "GoTo" button, and choose the Options menu item.
4. Press the "Import Library" button.
5. On the Import Library Module screen, choose your floppy disk drive a:\ from the list and press "Go." Note: It may take a few minutes to import the data from the floppy disk to your computer's hard disk.
6. When the installation is complete, the library module data will be available in your TheraScribe® 3.0 or 3.5 program.

Note: If you have a network version of TheraScribe® 3.0 or 3.5 installed, you should import the library module one time only. After importing the data, the library module data will be available to all network users.

User Assistance

If you need assistance using this TheraScribe® 3.0 or 3.5 add-on module, contact Wiley Technical Support at:

Phone: 212-850-6753
Fax: 212-850-6800 (Attention: Wiley Technical Support)
E-mail: techhelp@wiley.com

---

*Note: This section applies only to the book with disk edition, ISBN 0-471-34765-5.

Practice*Planners*™

Treatment Planners cover all the necessary elements for developing formal treatment plans, including detailed problem definitions, long-term goals, short-term objectives, therapeutic interventions, and DSM-IV diagnoses.

- ❏ **The Complete Adult Psychotherapy Treatment Planner, Second Edition**
  277pp / 0-471-31924-4 / $39.95
- ❏ **The Child and Adolescent Psychotherapy Treatment Planner**
  240pp / 0-471-15647-7 / $39.95
- ❏ **The Chemical Dependence Treatment Planner**
  256pp / 0-471-23795-7 / $39.95
- ❏ **The Continuum of Care Treatment Planner**
  170pp / 0-471-19568-5 / $39.95
- ❏ **The Couples Therapy Treatment Planner**
  272pp / 0-471-24711-1 / $39.95
- ❏ **The Employee Assistance (EAP) Treatment Planner**
  176pp / 0-471-24709-X / $39.95
- ❏ **The Pastoral Counseling Treatment Planner**
  176pp / 0-471-25416-9 / $39.95
- ❏ **The Older Adult Psychotherapy Treatment Planner**
  274pp / 0-471-29574-4 / $39.95
- ❏ **The Behavioral Medicine Treatment Planner**
  226pp / 0-471-31923-6 / $39.95

Homework Planners feature dozens of behaviorally-based, ready-to-use assignments which are designed for use between sessions... as well as a disk (Microsoft Word) containing all of the assignments, allowing you to customize them to suit your unique style and your clients' needs.

- ❏ **Brief Therapy Homework Planner**
  236pp / 0-471-24611-5 / $49.95
- ❏ **Brief Couples Therapy Homework Planner**
  208pp / 0-471-29511-6 / $49.95
- ❏ **Brief Child Therapy Homework Planner**
  304pp / 0-471-32366-7 / $49.95
- ❏ **Brief Adolescent Therapy Homework Planner**
  304pp / 0-471-34465-6 / $49.95

Documentation Sourcebooks provide all the forms and records that therapists need to meet the documentation requirements of the managed care era. All of the documents are also provided on disk so they can be easily customized.

- ❏ **The Clinical Documentation Sourcebook, Second Edition**
  304pp / 0-471-32692-5 / $49.95
- ❏ **The Psychotherapy Documentation Primer**
  203pp / 0-471-28990-6 / $39.95
- ❏ **The Couple & Family Clinical Documentation Sourcebook**
  176pp / 0-471-25234-4 / $49.95
- ❏ **The Child Clinical Documentation Sourcebook**
  256pp / 0-471-29111-0 / $49.95
- ❏ **The Chemical Dependence Treatment Documentation Sourcebook**
  320pp / 0-471-31285-1 / $49.95
- ❏ **The Forensic Documentation Sourcebook**
  224pp / 0-471-25459-2 / $75.00

Name _____

Affiliation _____

Address _____

City/State/Zip _____

Phone/Fax _____

Email _____

www.wiley.com/practiceplanners

To order, call 800-225-5945
(Please refer to promo #063 0-4052 A when ordering.)

or, send this page, with payment, to:
John Wiley & Sons, Inc, Attn: M. Fellin,
605 Third Ave., New York, NY 10157-0228

❏ Check enclosed ❏ Visa ❏ Mastercard ❏ American Express

Card # _____

Expiration Date _____

Signature _____

* Please add your local sales tax to all orders.

TheraScribe® 3.5 for Windows®

The Computerized Assistant to Psychotherapy Treatment Planning

→ Used in thousands of behavioral health practices and treatment facilities, *TheraScribe® 3.5* is a state-of-the-art Windows®-based treatment planning program which rapidly generates comprehensive treatment plans meeting the requirements of all major accrediting agencies and most third-party payers.

→ In just minutes, this user-friendly program enables you to create customized treatment plans by choosing from thousands of prewritten built-in short-term goals, long-term objectives, therapeutic interventions, automated progress notes, and much more.

→ This networkable software also tracks treatment outcome, stores clinical pathways, and provides ample room for narrative patient histories, treatment summaries, and discharge notes.

→ And best of all, this flexible system can be expanded to include the data in this *Child Psychotherapy Treatment Planner.*

✎CHILD PSYCHOTHERAPY Upgrade to THERASCRIBE 3.5✎

The behavioral definitions, goals, objectives, and interventions from this *Child Psychotherapy Treatment Planner* can be imported into *TheraScribe® 3.5: The Computerized Assistant to Treatment Planning.* For purchase and pricing information, please send in the coupon below.

- -

For more information about ***TheraScribe® 3.5*** or the ***Child Psychotherapy Upgrade,*** fill in this coupon, and mail it to: M. Fellin, John Wiley & Sons, Inc., 605 Third Avenue, New York, NY 10158

❑ Please send me information on *TheraScribe® 3.5*
❑ Please send me information on the *Child Psychotherapy Upgrade to TheraScribe® 3.5*

Name _____

Affiliation _____

Address _____

City/State/Zip _____

Phone _____

(W) **WILEY**
Publishers Since 1807

For information on how to install disk, refer to the **About the Disk** section on page 318.

WILEY

Publishers Since 1807

*Note: This section applies only to the book with disk edition, ISBN 0-471-34765-5.